Words of the Uprooted

Documents in American Social History

A series edited by
Nick Salvatore

A complete list of titles
in the series appears at
the end of the book.

Words of
the Uprooted

JEWISH IMMIGRANTS
IN EARLY TWENTIETH-
CENTURY AMERICA

Robert A. Rockaway

Cornell University Press

ITHACA AND LONDON

First published 1998 by Cornell University Press.

First printing, Cornell Paperbacks, 1998.

Printed in the United States of America.

Library of Congress Cataloging-in-Publication Data

Words of the uprooted : Jewish immigrants in early twentieth-century
   America / [compiled by] Robert A. Rockaway.
      p.   cm.—(Documents in American social history)
   ISBN 0-8014-3455-6 (cloth: alk. paper)
   ISBN 0-8014-8550-9 (pbk.: alk. paper)
      1. Jews, East European—United States—Correspondence.   2. United
   States—Emigration and immigration.   3. Immigrants—United States—
   Correspondence.   4. Industrial Removal Office (U.S.)   I. Rockaway,
   Robert A., 1939– .   II. Series.
   E184.J5W885   1998
   362.84'924073—dc21   97-52123

Cornell University Press strives to use environmentally responsible suppliers
and materials to the fullest extent possible in the publishing of its books. Such
materials include vegetable-based, low-VOC inks and acid-free papers that are
also either recycled, totally chlorine-free, or partly composed of nonwood fibers.

Cloth printing   10 9 8 7 6 5 4 3 2 1
Paperback printing   10 9 8 7 6 5 4 3 2 1

To the Memory of My Father,
Jack Rockaway

Contents

Acknowledgments   xi

Introduction: The IRO and Eastern European Immigration   1

Part One   The IRO as an Institution

  1. *Letters from Traveling Agents*   39

    David Bressler (1905)
    Morris Waldman (1907)
    Elias Margolis (1908)
    Abraham Solomon (1912–1913)

  2. *Letters from Communities*   70

    Atlanta, Georgia (1913)
    Lafayette, Indiana (1907)
    Los Angeles, California (1910)

  3. *Letters from Local Agents*   81

    Samuel Levy (Bloomington, Illinois)
    Jacob Furth (Cleveland, Ohio)
    Isaac Kuhn (Champaign, Illinois)

Part Two   The Immigrants

4. *Interactions with the IRO*   117

   Letters of Gratitude   117

   Chaim Zadik Lubin (Wichita, Kansas)
   Charles Zwirn (La Crosse, Wisconsin)
   Louis Friedman (Detroit, Michigan)
   M. Goldstein (Columbus, Ohio)
   Jacob Finkelstein (Cincinnati, Ohio)

   Letters of Request   128

   Jacob Schiffman (Detroit, Michigan)
   Joseph Lipetz (Oklahoma City, Oklahoma)
   Benny Finkelkraut (Minneapolis, Minnesota)
   H. Schreiber (Chicago, Illinois)

   Letters of Complaint   141

   Mrs. Samuel Friedman (Minneapolis, Minnesota)
   Moses Goldstein (Chattanooga, Tennessee)
   Mary Rubin (New Orleans, Louisiana)
   Israel Ginsberg (Chicago, Illinois)
   Joseph Davidowitz and Froim Kravitz (Memphis, Tennessee)
   Harry Liss et al. (Spokane, Washington)
   Jake Liboff et al. (Gary, Indiana)

5. *Economic Adjustment*   165

   Nathan Toplitzky and Miriam Hart (Detroit, Michigan)
   Morris Weinkrantz (Des Moines, Iowa)
   Alex Grubman (Portland, Oregon)
   Barnet Marlin (Atlanta, Georgia)
   Max Fruchtman (Pensacola, Florida)

6. *Social/Cultural Adjustment*   183

   Raphael Gershoni (Atlanta, Georgia)
   David Selechanok (Columbus, Ohio)
   Sarah Goldenberg (St. Louis, Missouri)
   Monroe Goldstein (New York City)
   Leta Chlanin and Nachum Geishin
     (New York City and Cleveland, Ohio)

7. *Immigrant Perceptions of America*   198

    Abraham Cohen (St. Louis, Missouri)
    Leo Stamm (Meridian, Mississippi)
    Simon Sachs (Dubuque, Iowa)

    Epilogue: Motivations and Misconceptions   205

Notes   211

Index   225

Acknowledgments

While doing research for a book on the Jews of Detroit more than twenty-five years ago, I learned about the Industrial Removal Office (IRO) archives, located at the American Jewish Historical Society. At the time, the material reposed in large wooden crates labeled "Seltzer." IRO staffers had placed the records in these containers when the agency closed its doors in 1922. The items remained unindexed and were covered with the accumulated dust of almost fifty years. As I pried open the cases, I felt like an archaeologist uncovering a long-lost treasure. As a favor to the historical society's librarian, Nathan Kaganoff, I roughly collated the IRO correspondence into broad categories and placed them in manila folders. I remember thinking that someday I would like to return to the Industrial Removal Office and its immigrant correspondence. This book fulfills that ambition.

In writing this volume, I received unending consideration and assistance from the staff of the American Jewish Historical Society, who responded to every request. My sincere thanks goes to them for their help and unfailing patience through the years. I also offer thanks to friends and colleagues Zvi Gitelman, Arnon Gutfeld, Lloyd Gartner, Barry Rubin, and Nick Salvatore, who read portions of this manuscript and made valuable suggestions. A special thanks goes to Cornell University Press editor Roger Haydon for his interest and encouragement. Finally, my appreciation goes to the Memorial Foundation for Jewish Culture, whose grant many years ago subsidized the initial photocopying of the letters in this book.

ROBERT A. ROCKAWAY

Tel-Aviv, Israel

Words of the Uprooted

Introduction
The IRO and Eastern
European Immigration

"On the 1st of May 1905 I was sent out of New York by the Removal Office and I don't regret it. . . . In New York, being a man of no trade, I was forced to peddle in order to make a living. Every time I tapped at different doors it was like receiving wounds in my heart. Even then there were no chances of making a living. Hunger drove me to shovel snow in the streets; and my future was like darkness. Such was my distressful condition in New York. On the other hand, from the very first day I arrived in Columbus, I felt much better and more comfortable. . . . During the season, I earn $20.00 a week, and it is a steady position. Last year I have put into the bank $450.00 besides the money I sent to my wife and children. . . . I again thank you and also everybody of the Removal Office."

This letter, written in Yiddish by David Selechanok, is one of the thousands that eastern European Jewish immigrants sent to the Industrial Removal Office (IRO) in New York City. American Jewish leaders created this organization in 1901 to remove unemployed Jewish immigrants from New York City and relocate them to smaller Jewish communities, where jobs existed, throughout the United States. Between 1901 and its closure in 1922, the IRO dispatched more than 75,000 Jewish immigrants from the New York area to 1,500 communities in every state of the Union.

A variety of motives had spurred these leaders to establish the IRO. The unending flow of Jewish immigrants swarming into New York's Lower East Side generated enormous problems for both the immigrants and the city's Jewish establishment. Packed together in the Jewish quarter, the newcomers endured filth, poor sanitation, disease, and soaring rates of

delinquency and crime. By distributing the immigrants to other locations, the IRO hoped to alleviate some of these problems. In addition, dispersing the immigrants would ease the immense burden placed upon New York's Jewish charities by hundreds of indigent and sick newcomers.

American Jews also believed, rightly or wrongly, that New York's huge eastern European Jewish enclave offered a prime breeding ground for radical movements such as socialism and anarchism. Detaching the immigrants from this environment and shipping them to smaller Jewish communities in the midwest, south, and west would forestall their subversion and facilitate their Americanization. This, the IRO founders imagined, would enhance the image of the Jew in the eyes of the general public and reduce antisemitism.

The story of the people whom the IRO "removed" began in an oppressive and inhospitable Russia and culminated in American towns with names such as Chino, Logansport, Des Moines, and Pensacola. These places—and hundreds of others like them—may not have been Eden, but they did offer the immigrants a new start and a chance for a better life.

Like David Selechanok, thousands of these individuals wrote to the IRO. In their correspondence, they depicted their living conditions, their success or failure, their anxiety and despair, and their hopes and aspirations. Their letters also reveal stages in the process of Americanization as well as their view of the American dream. These are unique documents in that they give voice to individual men and women who formed part of the "great immigration" to the United States and who participated, as well, in a singular experiment in American history. This book illuminates the story of these people and that of the organization that dispersed them.

From the beginning of the nineteenth century, almost all of Russia's Jews lived in a geographic area called the Pale of Settlement. Extending from the Baltic Sea to the Black Sea, this region encompassed the fifteen westernmost provinces of the Russian Empire in what is today, roughly, Lithuania, Latvia, Belarus, and Ukraine. Until the Revolution of 1917, Jews endured persistent government efforts to convert them to Christianity and suffered all manner of oppressive taxes and anti-Jewish legislation.[1]

Under Tsar Alexander II (1855–81), the Jewish community experienced some alleviation in conditions, and Jews began to achieve prominence in the country's economic and cultural life. Increasing numbers also became involved in Russian revolutionary parties. Although Jews consti-

---

Left: Lower East Side, New York City, circa 1920. Courtesy, American Jewish Archives, Hebrew Union College, Jewish Institute of Religion, Cincinnati, Ohio

tuted a minority among the revolutionaries, Russian intellectuals and government officials contended that they played a leading role.[2]

On 1 March 1881, terrorists assassinated Alexander. The incident proved disastrous for Russia's Jews and a turning point in modern Jewish history. Capitalizing on the ensuing confusion, antisemites incited shop-keepers, tradesmen, workers, and peasants to vent their grief and anger on the Jews. Within two months of the tsar's murder, a series of bloody pogroms swept Ukraine. In more than two hundred separate localities, bands of rioters—many fortified by liquor—rampaged through Jewish quarters in an orgy of looting, burning, rape, and murder. Almost every-where the police and army reacted slowly and reluctantly to thwart the rioters. In several cases, soldiers joined the attackers.[3]

Although Russian Jewry suffered extensive physical and material dam-age, the psychological impact of the pogroms devastated them even more. Large-scale massacres had occurred and might well occur again. This realization produced a gnawing insecurity that pervaded the Jewish community.

Pogroms may have been the immediate catalyst for Jews to leave Rus-sia, but economic deprivation remained a crucial determinant in their de-cision to depart. In May 1882, the Russian government issued a series of "temporary rules" that remained in force until 1917. Designed to keep the Jews under control, these May Laws further restricted them within the confines of the Pale and led to a worsening of their economic condition.[4]

Surveying events in the Pale in 1882, a contemporary writer observed that Jewish life "has assumed a monotonously gloomy, oppressively dull aspect. . . . Maltreated, plundered, reduced to beggary, put to shame, slan-dered, and dispirited, the Jews have been cast out of the community of human beings." Another witness noted that the May Laws degraded and humiliated the Jews and made them so desperate that they were ready to emigrate anywhere. "Let it be America, Palestine, even beyond the moun-tains of darkness, as long as it is as far away as possible from Russia."[5]

Flee they did. From April 1881 through 1882, thousands of Jews streamed across Russia's western frontier into the Austro-Hungarian province of Galicia. Just across the border, the Galician city of Brody be-came a temporary asylum and transit point for most of the refugees. From Brody, the immigrants traveled by train to Vienna or Berlin and then moved on to one of the major European ports—Hamburg, Bremen, Rot-terdam, Amsterdam, or Antwerp.[6]

Realizing that something must be done for their suffering brethren in the east, European Jewish leaders formed relief committees in Paris, Ber-lin, Vienna, London, and other major cities. Yet despite their desire to help, no European Jewish leader or community displayed any great enthusiasm at the thought of masses of destitute Jews coming to their countries. By 1880, German, French, and British Jews had achieved emancipation and acculturation and could be found among their country's economic, political, and cultural leaders. They feared that their hard-won status would be jeopardized by an influx of alien, backward, lower-class, Yiddish-speaking Jews. They worried that their gentile neighbors would fail to differentiate between them and these "unenlightened" newcomers. The rise of racial antisemitism and the establishment of antisemitic organizations in Germany and Austria fueled their concern. The optimal solution for them was to direct the Russian Jewish refugees to the United States, "that vast, free and rich country, where all who want to work can and will find refuge." [7]

Fortunately for the Europeans, this idea coincided with the refugees' own predilections. Although some immigrants remained in western Europe, the great majority emigrated to America. During the next three decades, economic deterioration, educational and professional isolation, and physical harassment in Russia and eastern Europe caused more than 2 million Jews to come to the United States. This constituted the greatest mass movement of Jews since the Exodus from Egypt. [8]

At the time of the pogroms, the American Jewish community numbered approximately 250,000 persons, most of whom had come—or were descendants of men and women who had come—from German-speaking lands. Over a period of fifty years, these German Jews had acculturated socially and religiously and were comfortably adjusted, politically and economically, to America. [9]

Horrified by events in Russia, American Jewish leaders responded quickly. Led by the editors of the *Jewish Messenger* and the United Jewish Charities of New York, a coalition of Jewish groups established a Russian Relief Committee in May 1881. Jewish communities in Philadelphia, New Orleans, Houston, Milwaukee, and other American cities did the same. [10] Although these committees recognized their obligation to help their brethren, they vehemently opposed any sizable immigration to the United States. Citing economics as their primary justification, they contended that a large influx of impoverished Jews would place an impossible burden on their charities. [11]

Notwithstanding very real fiscal considerations, the American Jews' apprehension resulted from a deeper anxiety than the monetary one. As they saw it, hordes of Orthodox, impoverished, unkempt, and anarchistic coreligionists were arriving at the very time when ideological and social antisemitism was making its initial headway in the United States. They worried that these Russian Jews would have a deleterious effect on American opinions of Jews and posed a genuine danger to the good name and status of Jewish Americans. They supposed that Americans would equate the Americanized German Jewish community, "the better class of Jews," and the newly arrived eastern Europeans, the "vulgar Jews." If this happened, feared the Germans Jews, everything they had worked for would be destroyed. The *American Hebrew* fretted that the entrance of large numbers of poverty-stricken European Jews might generate a prejudice "potentially not less dangerous to the Jews of refinement and culture in this country than the horrors of Russian persecution."[12]

Objective members of the American Jewish establishment recognized that the arrival of the new breed of Jews from eastern Europe did not cause the antisemitism. Nevertheless, many believed, with some reason, that the immigrant presence would intensify it. If the newcomers remained unacculturated or spawned radical movements, they would feed the currents of antisemitism. To lessen the risk, many American Jewish leaders favored limiting the immigration to a small number of single, healthy, skilled workers or farmers. "Let those who do not posses a useful trade stay in Europe," pleaded Isaac Mayer Wise, America's leading Reform rabbi. "We have enough beggars and humbug-seeking vagabonds here."[13]

Officials of some Jewish charities went even further and advocated governmental restriction of immigration and the return of paupers. A few leaders, such as Rabbi Jacob Voorsanger of San Francisco, favored shutting off Jewish immigration to the United States altogether. Since all of these suggestions proved difficult to implement, the *Jewish Messenger* proposed that the American Jewish community protect itself by sending American Jewish missionaries to Russia "to civilize them there rather than give them an opportunity to Russianize us."[14]

Although the enormous tide of eastern European Jews coming to the United States unnerved American Jewish leaders, they nonetheless acknowledged their obligation to help. "Where else can they go?" asked Henry S. Henry, president of New York's Emigrant's Aid Society. "It belongs to us, it is a part of our duty to arrange for their settlement."[15]

Persuaded by France's Alliance Israélite Universelle, the most influential European Jewish philanthropy, to help shoulder the burden, New York's Russian Relief Committee endorsed a European proposal to send some of the Russian immigrants to the United States. The first official boatload of these refugees arrived in New York on 9 September 1881. This marked the beginning of an unstoppable wave of eastern European Jews to the United States.

About 15,000 Russian Jews had come to the United States between 1871 and 1880. More than 18,000 came during the two years from 1881 through 1882. This group proved to be the vanguard of the more than

240,000 eastern European Jews who arrived in the United States between 1881 and 1890.[16] Most of the immigrants landed in the northeast, the vast majority in New York City. New York's Russian Relief Committee quickly realized that it was incapable of coping with the demands made upon it. Its leaders proposed the creation of a permanent society to deal solely with Jewish immigrants. As a result, in November 1881, New York's Jewish establishment created the Hebrew Emigrant Aid Society (HEAS). The charity strove to assist Jewish immigrants "in obtaining homes and employment, and otherwise providing means to prevent them from becoming burdens on the charity of the community." By June 1882, local HEAS committees had been established in twenty-four North American cities.[17]

During its three-year existence, HEAS cared for and dispersed some 14,000 Russian Jewish refugees. Most important, as the *American Hebrew* noted in 1883, "an immense amount of experience has been gathered, which will stand us in good stead when as will doubtless happen, another phase of the same question is presented."[18] This editorial proved to be perceptive and prophetic.

Even before 1881, American Jewish leaders had discussed plans for settling the immigrants in agricultural colonies and in the small towns of the hinterland away from the overcrowded immigrant quarters of New York and other large cities on the East Coast. The reasons for this approach varied. American Jewish leaders sought to disprove the stereotype of the Jew as a petty trader and middleman by preventing the eastern Europeans from resorting to peddling once they came to America. Colonization of the immigrants in the west and south would also alleviate the ill-effects of congestion in the cities, where Yiddish-speaking, gesticulating tenement dwellers were a source of embarrassment and potential anti-semitism. And acculturation and Americanization would also ensue more rapidly once the immigrants left their Yiddish-speaking milieu.

The colonization program would not only clean out the cities but dispel an old myth that Jews would not make successful farmers. "It has been said that Jews can not be farmers," scoffed Judge Myer S. Isaacs. "As if a Jew were other than a man! No more adaptable individual than the Jews—no race more readily affected by environment than the Jewish. The patriarchs were farmers."[19]

At that time, these discussions had few tangible results. By the 1880s, however, circumstances had changed. Rising immigration and the fears it generated made dispersal and colonization increasingly attractive. Hence, throughout the decade, New York and other Jewish communities assisted Jewish immigrants to establish farming settlements in Louisiana, Oregon, Tennessee, Missouri, Arkansas, New Jersey, Colorado, the Dakotas, and

Kansas. Within ten years, however, practically all of them had disbanded. They failed because American Jews declined to give the program their wholehearted support, few of the Russian Jews knew anything about farming, conditions in many of the colonies proved horrendous, and most of the immigrants preferred life in the city.[20]

It is easy to understand why. During the 1880s, the cities of America's northeast experienced unparalleled industrial and metropolitan growth. Offering diversified employment and services, these urban centers became the new frontier, attracting not only the immigrants but native farmers. The cliché "Once they've seen the lights of the city, how are you going to keep them down on the farm?" applied to European newcomers and native-born citizens alike. Jewish leaders knew this. Nonetheless, strategies of colonization and dispersal remained a favorite panacea of Jewish communal leaders and organizations in New York and other cities on the East Coast.[21]

In 1890–91, after six pogrom-free years, Russian Jews suddenly faced a new deterioration in their circumstances. Openings for Jews in schools and universities were severely curtailed. In March 1891, the tsarist government expelled 20,000 Jews from Moscow. Two years later the regime evacuated 70,000 "privileged" Jewish families from the Russian interior. With the accession to the throne of Tsar Nicholas II in 1894, the Jews of Russia entered an era of oppression that only ended with the Tsar's overthrow in March 1917. The regime's campaign of terror and repression destroyed hundreds of Jewish lives and thousands of Jewish homes and shops, and it impoverished Jewish life in the Pale.[22]

The calamitous situation in Russia, coupled with grinding poverty in Galicia and anti-Jewish restrictions and violence in Romania, caused 391,050 Jews to emigrate to the United States from 1891 to 1900 and another 1,387,455 between 1901 and 1914. More than 75 percent of these immigrants came from tsarist Russia. In the thirty-three years before World War I, eastern European Jews constituted one-tenth of all immigrants who entered the United States. This great immigration increased America's Jewish population to 3.5 million by 1914.[23]

Once again, American Jewish leaders expressed ambivalent and wavering attitudes toward the newcomers. On the one hand, they felt a responsibility to assist them. Julius Goldman, who worked with the new immigrants, claimed that "the American Jews have thus far shown more willingness to receive their brethren than any other people." They did so because "we look upon the reception of these people as the first and highest duty, a duty that one human being owes to another, and by that law that one Jew owes to another." In Detroit, Rabbi Leo Franklin of the city's Reform Jewish congregation, Beth El, reminded his parishioners that if the Russian Jew was not all he should be it was "because oppression has temporarily taken the manhood out of him. Yet he is our brother and as Jews we must regard and receive him as such."[24]

On the other hand, the intensification of antisemitism in the United States heightened the established Jewish community's sense of insecurity. For more than twenty years, Rabbi Isaac Mayer Wise had predicted disaster if large numbers of Russian Jews filled the cities on the East Coast. They would create all manner of problems, he said, which would ruin "the good reputation of Judaism" in the eyes of American Christians and "without fail lower our social status."[25]

After 1891, however, the desperate straits of Russia's Jews transcended American Jewry's concerns about their status and overcame their worries about antisemitism. "These refugees from Russia are our brethren. Their virtues and vices are ours," conceded the *American Hebrew*. "We are responsible for them to God, to our adopted country and to humanity."[26]

Accordingly, at the very time that the American public and Congress began moving in the direction of restricting immigration, leaders of the German Jewish community fought for a liberal immigration policy. Any lingering ambivalence they may have felt about this stance evaporated in the face of the pogroms in Russia between 1903 and 1906.[27]

From the 1890s to the First World War, the German Jewish community poured time and money into helping the immigrants. By 1910 American Jews were spending $10 million annually on philanthropy. Despite the enormous financial burden placed on it, the American Jewish community created all manner of agencies to help the immigrant adjust to and settle in America. In every large American city, the German Jews created bureaus to cope with problems of poverty, unemployment, illness, family desertion, juvenile crime, mechanical training for the newcomers, and Americanization. Cyrus Sulzberger, director of New York's United Hebrew Charities, once described the manifold activities of his agency on a typical day in 1901:

> We make 145 investigations. . . . We record 35 applications for employment, and find employment for 17 people. We grant transportation to three people and give half a ton of coal to seven. We distribute 150 articles of clothing and furniture. We give two nights' lodging and seven meals. We have fifteen visits made by our doctors, and sixteen calls made upon our doctors in their offices. We have 45 cases for our nurses. Our doctors write 38 prescriptions, and there is one surgical operation. Thirty-six garments are made or repaired in our work room; 125 immigrants are registered at the Barge Office, making a total of 678 different kind of things done in an ordinary working day.[28]

The development and expansion of American Jewish philanthropy paralleled similar movements within the broader American community. With the growth of scientific charity after the Civil War, philanthropy assumed a professional air as paid workers replaced volunteers.[29] Like their non-Jewish counterparts, the German Jewish professionals who administered the communal relief funds employed procedures, such as investigating the applicant, which they considered to be efficient, practical, modern, and scientific methods of dispensing aid. The eastern Europeans came from a milieu where these practices did not exist. They applied traditional Jewish standards to Jewish charitable agencies in America. The principle of investigation was alien to their philosophy and repugnant to their sensibilities. The record- and account-keeping system of American agencies impressed them as being a cold and thoroughly un-Jewish principle in action. While the immigrants appreciated the assistance they received, their gratefulness was often tinged with resentment at the manner in which the charity was dispensed.

In Detroit, the weekly *Jewish American* newspaper investigated why so many eastern Europeans boycotted the facilities of the United Jewish Charities. The editor discovered that what the German Jewish managers of the relief fund considered to be efficient procedures, the immigrants found to be "hard-hearted, lacking in sympathy, and without the spirit of true charity." They complained that these practices humiliated them and made them feel like beggars. As a result, they refused to apply to the charity for help. In New York, an article in a Yiddish daily noted the cold, professional approach employed by the "aristocratic German Jews in their beautiful offices, desks all decorated, but strict and angry faces. Every poor man is questioned like a criminal, is looked down upon; every unfortunate suffers self-degradation and shivers like a leaf, just as if he were standing before a Russian official."[30]

Charity applicants in Rochester, Indianapolis, Atlanta, Columbus, and Milwaukee—like those in Detroit and New York—felt demeaned by the impersonal approach of the Germans and by the restrictions and stipulations attached to their benevolence. These differing attitudes and perceptions created misunderstandings and tension between the newcomers and their German Jewish benefactors and led the immigrants to set up their own charitable organizations.[31]

Although the conflict between Germans and eastern Europeans was occasionally bitter, it was sometimes softened by the sensitivity and commitment of extraordinary Jewish leaders. Attorney Louis Marshall and philanthropist Jacob Schiff, both eminent national figures, defended the eastern Europeans to their detractors and labored to unite the two groups into one community. And almost all the leaders of the German community participated in undertakings and expenditures to ease the hardships of eastern European immigrants.[32]

Since the established Jewish community opposed immigration restriction and the immigrants appeared determined to congregate in the larger cities, the problem of urban congestion, especially in New York, became acute. In 1881, at the outset of the great immigration, New York contained about 80,000 Jews. Twenty years later, the city that Henry Adams dubbed "the sink of races" boasted a Jewish population of 510,000. The Jewish district on the Lower East Side alone equaled the entire population of Detroit. Leo Levi, president of B'nai B'rith, the national Jewish fraternal organization, called New York's Jewish quarter a "worse hell than was ever invented by the imagination of the most vindictive Jew-hater of Europe."[33]

The avalanche of newcomers into New York almost bankrupted its Jewish charitable organizations, especially the city-wide United Hebrew Charities. New York's Jewish leaders believed that unless a far-reaching solution were found, the UHC and the community faced a disaster. Consequently, the idea of removing the immigrants from New York and dispersing them throughout the United States again received serious consideration.[34]

This time, however, New York and the American Jewish community received help in the form of financial assistance from the Baron de Hirsch Fund. Born in Munich, Germany, to a Jewish banking family, Baron Maurice de Hirsch (1831–96) went on to amass his own fortune—estimated at $100 million—primarily in railroad construction. After the death of his only son in 1888, Hirsch devoted more and more of his time and resources to philanthropy. He early advocated removing the Jews from Russia and settling them on land in the New World. In 1891, Hirsch established the Jewish Colonization Association (JCA) to settle Russian Jews on farming colonies in North and South America. He also set up the Baron de Hirsch Fund to provide a wide variety of aid to eastern European Jewish immigrants in the United States.[35]

In an effort to reduce New York's problem, the trustees of the de Hirsch Fund tried every possible solution, including agricultural colonization, removal of industries to outlying districts, and the transportation of families to smaller towns and industrial centers.[36] Nothing worked. Thousands of newcomers continued to enter New York City and stay. A large influx of needy Romanian Jewish immigrants, who were fleeing anti-Jewish measures in that country, generated additional pressures. Unable to cope, the United Jewish Charities faced insolvency. It became obvious that a more systematic approach was needed.

In June 1900, at the first National Conference of Jewish Charities, the

Baron Maurice de Hirsch. Courtesy, American Jewish Historical Society, Waltham, Mass.

UHC urged representatives of communities in the interior of the United States to relieve the burden on New York.[37] By July a Romanian Relief Committee had been created, and proposals had been drafted to distribute the Romanian immigrants to communities other than New York. Because it had branch lodges throughout the country, the B'nai B'rith agreed to be the agency through which this removal would be administered. Leo Levi, president of the organization, instructed all local lodges to find suitable employment for the Romanian immigrants. The local groups responded to his request.

Twelve German Jews founded the B'nai B'rith (Sons of the Covenant) in 1843 to serve as a fraternal order and benevolent society. In its early years, the organization's goals centered around social service projects such as orphanages, hospitals, and homes for the aged and on helping new immigrants adjust to America. By the 1880s, Jewish communities in almost every major and midsized American city supported at least one B'nai B'rith chapter, sometimes more. Because of its philanthropic tradition and extensive network of lodges, Jewish leaders concluded that the B'nai B'rith was the ideal organization to oversee the distribution of newcomers.[38]

Despite its enthusiasm, the B'nai B'rith could not provide the assistance necessary to meet the demands of increasing numbers of immigrants. Particularly in Jewish communities in the nation's interior, members had little experience in handling eastern European immigrants. Within a short time, the American Jewish leadership realized that removal work demanded a more permanent type of administration, which the B'nai B'rith could not provide.

At the 1901 meeting of the National Conference of Jewish Charities, civic leader Cyrus Sulzberger described tens of thousands of eastern European Jews packed "like raisins" into Manhattan's Lower East Side. "Open up that ghetto," he pleaded. "Go back to your communities and tell them . . . to take these thousands of newcomers off New York's hands." Nathan Bijur, a New York attorney and vice president of the conference, concurred: "Are you going to let them rot there, or are you going to help us get them out?" Leo Levi warned that the government might close off immigration from eastern Europe altogether if the congestion in New York persisted. Distribution could thus prove the best and perhaps only way of undercutting those who strove to restrict immigration.[39]

The appeals and warnings proved effective. In the ensuing months the United Hebrew Charities of New York, the B'nai B'rith, the Baron de Hirsch Fund, and several other agencies jointly established the Industrial Removal Office (IRO). Its central purpose was the systematic diversion of Jewish immigrants, on an individual basis, to smaller Jewish communities throughout the United States.

David Bressler. Courtesy, American Jewish Archives, Hebrew Union College, Jewish Institute of Religion, Cincinnati, Ohio

Despite a preference for agricultural settlements, few Jewish leaders harbored any illusions about their success. They admitted that agriculture was not the answer for those drawn to the cities by economic skills or tastes. It made more sense to send immigrants accustomed to urban life to medium-sized cities that could absorb them. Consequently, a greater realism pervaded the IRO's operation.

Advertising itself as "the society which settles unemployed Jews of New York in other cities in this country," the IRO began operating in a rented store on Stanton Street in New York City. Later it relocated to 174 Second Avenue, which remained the organization's address until it ceased operation.[40]

After a series of temporary directors, representatives of the United Hebrew Charities and the de Hirsch Fund hired David Bressler, a young lawyer who had supervised removal for the Romanian Aid Society, to be general manager of the IRO. The German-born Bressler (1879–1942) came to the United States with his family in 1884. He attended the City College of New York and the Jewish Theological Seminary of America and received a law degree from the New York Law School in 1900. Bressler spent most of his adult life working with Jewish immigrants. He directed the IRO from 1903 to 1916. After leaving the IRO, he opened an insurance agency but remained active in Jewish communal life. He joined the American Jewish Joint Distribution Committee, which was created to assist Jews who suffered through war or persecution. Bressler played a leading role in this and other Jewish and non-Jewish relief agencies until his death.

Bressler was fortunate to have a number of able individuals assisting him in his work. Morris D. Waldman (1879–1945), a Hungarian-born Reform rabbi turned social worker, served as Bressler's first assistant from 1903 to 1907. Waldman and Bressler came from similar backgrounds and maintained a close personal relationship.

Philip Seman (1881–1957), a young social worker, replaced Waldman. Born in Warsaw, Seman came to the United States in 1892. He earned a B.S. degree from Adelphi College in 1902 and a law degree from the Washington University Law School in 1908. Seman served as Bressler's assistant from 1908 to 1916. After his IRO work, he became director of the Jewish People's Institute of Chicago and was a co-founder of the B'nai B'rith Hillel Foundation, the international Jewish college student organization.[41]

As a professional social worker, Bressler incorporated the ideology and aims of his vocation in running the IRO. In the New York office, he stressed efficiency and businesslike practices. This meant keeping detailed statistics and extensive files on every aspect of the IRO's work, publishing

Morris D. Waldman. Courtesy, American Jewish Archives, Hebrew
Union College, Jewish Institute of Religion, Cincinnati, Ohio

Philip Seman. Courtesy, American Jewish Archives, Hebrew Union College, Jewish Institute of Religion, Cincinnati, Ohio

annual reports, accounting for all money received and disbursed, hiring and paying trained and competent office workers, and personally supervising the New York staff and field operatives.[42]

From the outset, the IRO encountered difficulty in convincing the immigrants to leave New York City. "Once an immigrant breathes the atmosphere of the East Side strange as it may seem," conceded the *American Hebrew*, "it is difficult to get him to change his place of residence, to where the air and the surroundings are healthier and purer."[43]

Many immigrants were also too frightened and bewildered to face the trauma of a second uprooting. In an attempt to capture immigrant interest before they settled in New York, the IRO published articles in the European Jewish press lauding the attractiveness and opportunities available in other American localities. Similar literature was distributed on the steamers bound for New York. The IRO also posted two Yiddish-speaking representatives at Ellis Island, one of them a rabbi, to meet the disembarking Russian Jews and induce them to travel on to inland towns and cities. In addition, the agency propagandized at meetings of immigrant associations, in the New York Yiddish press, and at settlement houses. The main office also mailed circulars to newly arrived Jewish immigrants whose names had been provided by communal workers, and it sent agents into immigrant homes to sell the idea of relocation.[44]

Another major obstacle was the continued opposition of communities to receive large numbers of immigrants. These communities still regarded their cooperation as a favor to New York. Southern Jews in particular felt that northern Jewish leaders unfairly sought to exploit their region. To forestall this, they argued that their climate would be uncomfortable for eastern Europeans, that few factories or economic opportunities existed in their section, and that Jews could not work alongside black labor. Why should the south be asked to take more immigrants than, say, upstate New York or New England? asked the *Jewish Spectator* of Tennessee.[45]

Sometimes a community's negative experience with the immigrants spoiled future cooperation with the IRO. "Let me tell you that all the people sent here, from the first to the last, were all a burden to the community," charged Sam Rostoff, a Lafayette, Indiana, businessman. "To inform you of all the scandals that took place on account of the people you sent here would be enough to fill a book." He requested that the IRO not send any more men to Lafayette. A group of Indianapolis Jewish leaders accused the IRO of sending one man who was "consumptive," another who was a "shrimp, inefficient and would not accept a job," and a large number of men who became "dependent." They accordingly refused to give the IRO "carte blanche to unload inefficient people" on them.[46] At some point, almost every community—north, south, east, and west—complained about receiving immigrants.

To overcome local resistance, David Bressler, Cyrus Sulzberger, Leo Levi, and the IRO's assistant managers traveled throughout the country promoting the program and cajoling communities to help. These visits enhanced relations between the New York office and local Jewish leaders. The trips proved especially valuable because the travelers also gathered intelligence about the local economic situation. "There are a great many things about Atlanta that we do not know anything about and I am determined to find out what the conditions here are," wrote Morris Waldman to Bressler in October 1906. "From all appearances this is the finest town in the south and one would imagine from a first impression that it is a city in the first class. I shall venture no further opinion, however, until I have made a thorough study of the manufacturing industries." Waldman's caution resulted from a concern that "we have had an entirely erroneous idea concerning that very important feature of Atlanta's life." [47] The more exact the economic information, the more realistic the IRO could be in its expectations from the local community.

Starting in 1904, the IRO engaged a number of college-educated young men to serve as its traveling agents. The IRO dispatched these men to various sections of the country. Their tasks entailed promoting the IRO program in cities and towns that had a Jewish population, establishing local IRO committees, and investigating employment opportunities for Jewish immigrants. Since traveling agents had to work with Jewish leaders who espoused different versions of Judaism (Orthodoxy or Reform) or ideologies (Zionism or socialism), and who often exhibited strong egos, David Bressler preferred emissaries who were personable, enthusiastic, and, above all, diplomatic.

Concerned that dissension within a community could seriously hamper the IRO's work, Bressler cautioned his agents not to take sides in any local disputes. In order to get the feuding sides to collaborate, he suggested that the agents not hurry their stay in town. "Remain a day or two longer, and propitiate and gratiate, pat on the back, and create a spirit of good feeling; let them understand what we are after, and let them feel, if necessary, that upon them rests the responsibility, and the consequences if this responsibility is not properly accepted." [48]

Immediately upon entering a community, the traveling agent arranged meetings with the president of the local B'nai B'rith chapter (if one existed), Jewish business leaders, and the heads of the various local Jewish charities and organizations. In every instance, the agents sought to enroll the Jewish leadership in the IRO's program. In most cases, local leaders agreed to accept and find jobs for a specified number of immigrants each month. The traveling agents also canvassed the local industrial scene to gather information about job opportunities and, whenever possible, obtain orders for employment. The agents then sent the IRO the offers of employment, stating the name of the employing firm, the nature of the work, and the person who would be willing to receive and care for the immigrant after arrival.

To secure the active cooperation of Jewish charities and organizations in as many cities as possible, the IRO had to assure them that they would be virtually free from any financial responsibilities. In practice, this led the office to grant each community an allocation of $25 for every family and $10 for each individual sent.[49]

Although not large, the sums allotted for removals generally proved satisfactory. Sometimes, however, smaller, less wealthy communities found this insufficient and asked for more. After visiting Louisville in March 1912, an IRO representative reported that the local "committee absolutely refused to accept families, except on conditions that we reimburse them in whatever sum they may be called upon to expend for the family during the first six months of their residence in Louisville." Bressler wrote to the community saying that he wished he could oblige them. "But unfortunately this was impossible, because of the limited funds at our disposal." If the IRO accommodated Louisville and other communities who had comparable requests, "we would be at the end of our financial rope before the year ended."[50]

During the first few years of the IRO's operation, local Jewish communities set up committees, usually organized by B'nai B'rith lodges, to receive and care for the men sent. The committees kept the main office informed about the availability of jobs in their cities and towns and committed themselves to accepting a monthly quota of immigrants. In 1906, for example, the Nashville Jewish community agreed to accept "three to four persons per week and two families per month." The community preferred the IRO to send them "shoemakers, carpenters, cabinetmakers, wood-turners, wood-polishers, upholsterers, tinsmiths, locksmiths, and ironworkers of all kinds." The Jewish community of Texarkana, Texas, promised to "receive two men monthly, and a family every three months. They must be men in trades."[51]

Bressler selected the host communities carefully and put off sending immigrants to places where he questioned the community's ability to care for them. "I very much doubt the wisdom of sending our people to any place where the community is not prepared to handle them," he said. "It may be all right to send a dozen or 20 to cities like St. Louis, New Orleans, San Francisco and other cities of that size where there is an organization to take care of them; but it would be an entirely different matter if they were sent to small communities where there is no good organization to handle them." To do so, said Bressler, "would only serve to create a big howl," create bad publicity, and jeopardize the program.[52]

To avert such a consequence, Bressler, his assistants, and the IRO's traveling agents made periodic forays to assess the capabilities of communities to absorb immigrants. "It was impossible to do anything in Champaign, Illinois," wrote Elias Margolis after one such trip. "There are only half a dozen Jewish families there of the particularly selfish sort and not one of them could be interested in cooperating with us." Bloomington, Illinois, was different. The community held "a Jewish population of forty families, of which about fifteen belong to the Russian-Roumanian class, and possesses a Jewish temple with rabbi." Margolis happily reported that Bloomington's community agreed to cooperate with the IRO.[53]

In many communities, the committee system proved unsatisfactory. This prompted the IRO to replace committees with paid agents. Depending on the work load, agents received a salary ranging from $40 to $75 per month. Female agents sometimes started at $25 per month. Wherever possible, Bressler preferred to pay his agents rather than to rely on volunteers. This reflected his desire to upgrade and professionalize the IRO's operation. "If we want to maintain an efficient organization and good spirit," he said, "we must continue salary, in good times and bad times—and furthermore, the best interests of our work demand higher salaries." Higher salaries, he felt, would attract "a higher grade of men" to work for the IRO.[54]

Most of the time, the agents hired were professionals employed by a local Jewish charity or settlement house or were persons who had been recommended to the IRO by local Jewish leaders. In some cases, local business or civic leaders volunteered for the task. Bressler always sought agents who demonstrated character, competence, and an ability to deal with immigrants in a sympathetic but professional manner. Not every agent hired proved suitable to the job. During one of his trips to the midwest in 1905, Bressler determined that the agent in Cleveland was "not the right man. He is a young fellow—about 25—with very little sympathy for the people he must handle, and to him the entire movement is in the nature of a business proposition." Worse, the agent's poor attitude made him persona non grata with practically every Jewish leader in the city. After meeting with officers of the local relief committee, Bressler removed the man from his post. The Milwaukee agent, on the other hand, proved "to be a fairly decent fellow, although I am not overly much impressed with him." Nevertheless, reflected Bressler, so long as an agent was properly supervised and did his work, he "need not be an intellectual colossus." The agent in Kansas City had the intellect but not the integrity. He sent the IRO bogus reports, failed to keep his commitments, and did little for the immigrants. Morris Waldman ruefully admitted that the agent turned out to be "a slick customer" who "hood-winked us all for a long time." The antics of the Kansas City agent convinced the central office "that an occasional tour of inspection is necessary." [55] From then on, inspection tours by IRO officials became a regular component of the operation.

Like many other early-twentieth-century social reformers, Bressler emphasized the constructive benefits that could be gotten from a change in environment. He believed that providing the Russian Jews with the "proper environment" would allow them to develop their "inherent virtues" and lead to their becoming "a welcome addition to the Jewish communities of our land" and an "important factor" in the industrial life of the country. [56]

To guide the communities in working toward this goal, Bressler issued them a set of "general rules." These included an injunction never to regard the arriving immigrant as a charity case. "His primary motive for leaving New York was to secure employment. . . . He should, therefore, be treated as a newcomer who has come to fill a definite place in the life of the community." Since the change of environment was supposed to benefit the removal, the community was asked "to provide the arriving mechanic as far as possible with work which will demand and make use of his fullest ability and skill." This was to obviate the problem many skilled workers encountered in New York, where they were "forced to accept employment in one of the needle trades, because they cannot secure work at their respective trades." Duplicating this state of affairs in the new home, warned Bressler, "would be fatal." Finally, each community was urged "to make the stranger feel at home." This meant not regarding him "with a patronizing air" and not injuring his self-respect. In short, admonished Bressler, "each community must bring to the work of handling this problem of distribution, common sense, system and sympathy." [57]

The IRO relied primarily on its local representatives, supplemented by reports from its traveling officers, to gain a picture of local conditions. Using scientific procedures, and to keep their files current, the IRO regularly sent its representatives questionnaires that they filled out and returned. Part of the survey included queries about the size of the general and Jewish population; the number of educational facilities, libraries, and universities; whether any instruction in English was given to immigrants; the number of Jewish congregations and fraternal, social, and benevolent organizations; the "predominating nationality of Jews" who lived in the town; and the occupation of the Jews. The questionnaire also asked about the seasonal temperatures, cost of living, industrial and business conditions, wages for various occupations, the occupations most in demand, the railroads that entered the city, the number and kind of banks, and whether the town had a chamber of commerce or a businessmen's association.

The IRO expected its agents—or the community—to locate jobs and arrange lodging, board, transportation, and other necessities of daily living for the men sent. Generally, the local representatives canvassed their city's economy and job market and reported their findings to the New York office. "The city is on a building boom at the present time and indications point that some day labor of all classes will be in great demand," reported E. D. Freund from Birmingham, Alabama, in 1912. "At the present time, however, situations are hard to locate due to the fact that a number of the furnaces have closed down for the summer and that naturally puts a number of men out of employment." The agent in Fresno, California, reported that as of January 1913 carpenters earned $23 per week, butchers $18 per week, ironworkers $5 per day, and plumbers $3.50 per day. The artisans and mechanics that could most easily find employment, however, were those who could work on the railroad.[58]

Whenever possible, the New York office tried to accommodate the participating community's requests—but only up to a point. "If the wishes of some of the cooperating cities were taken into account," noted Bressler, "the applicants would have to be drafted from among the successful immigrants. This would not solve the immediate problem of the man who looks to distribution as his economic salvation." Therefore, "while it is possible to comply with the expressed preferences of the cooperating cities in respect to trades, size of families, married men or single men, to a certain extent," he said, "the IRO reserves for itself the right of final selection."[59]

Upon receipt of information from the community, New York forwarded the résumés of men with pertinent occupations and awaited approval for the men to be sent. "Ignatz Binstock, wood worker and machine operator. Binstock does not yet speak English, having been in the country but three months, but brings splendid references showing he was a good worker in Austria," read one such résumé sent to Detroit. "If you can find him work in one of the factories of your city, he will undoubtedly make fine progress. He is 25 years old and unmarried."[60]

Frequently, the IRO advertised its wares without waiting for requests from the local agent. "Morris Wold, tinsmith, is a first class workman and in good health, and Meyer Burde, machinest, about 12 years at his trade, a very worthy case, and in good health. Have we your permission to send them?"[61]

A community's acceptance or rejection depended on whether the applicant had a trade and could be placed. Of primary concern was that the removal not end up on the city's Jewish or non-Jewish charity rolls. If an applicant's occupation was unsuitable or he was in poor health, the community refused to accept him. "In regard to the Max Marks application, would say that we have spoken with the Employer's Association, who tell

us that work of the kind he desires is very, very hard to secure in this city,"
read one agent's letter from Detroit. "Under these circumstances we do
not feel that we can give our permission to have him sent here." The Detroit agent also rejected Yechiel Moshkowitz because "he is a cripple and
only able to peddle." [62]

Sometimes local companies, learning of the IRO, sent requests for help
directly to the New York office. Mr. J. Schwartz of the Progressive Couch
Company needed a "first class couch maker, one who thoroughly understands putting leather tufted pads and can make nice side ruffles." The
firm of R. L. Alder needed "a highly skilled paper hanger, who is sufficiently conversant with the English language to understand orders and to
make himself understood." Harry B. Clark asked for "a nice young mens
costum tailor." The man sent could "be one who is not able to speack
anglish [sic]." [63] All these employers promised steady employment to the
men hired. In most cases of this nature, the IRO referred the employer to
the local agent. The IRO maintained a policy of not sending anyone to a
community without the consent of the local agent or local committee.
Where there was no local agent, the New York office handled the request.

Unemployed immigrants who knew about the IRO applied at the main
office. With the help of an investigator—a trained communal worker
employed by the IRO—each applicant filled out an application form. The
questionnaire included the applicant's name, address, occupation in the
United States, occupation abroad, length of time in the United States, last
employer, length of time employed, nature of employment, employer references, and whether the applicant had ever received aid from New York's
United Hebrew Charities. The report also included the following declara-
tion and release to be signed by the applicant's wife: "I herewith consent
that my husband be sent out of town by the Industrial Removal Office and
I promise not to become a charge upon any institution during his absence." If the investigator felt that the applicant satisfied the IRO's crite-
ria and that his family would not become public charges in his absence,
he was placed on a list of prospective removals.

In one unusual case, an applicant who described himself as "a professional burglar anxious to reform and lead an honest life" asked the IRO
to send him to Hutchinson, Kansas, where he had found employment. The
applicant received a warm endorsement from Abraham Cahan, the fa-
mous editor of the *Jewish Daily Forward*. Cahan asked David Bressler to
interview the applicant personally. "I hope that by speaking to him you
will obtain correct impressions as to the reliability of his 'penitence' and
that you will see your way clear to helping him." [64]

The IRO's bureaucratic procedures, which the German Jewish Bressler
and his employees perceived as being efficient, modern, and scientific, up-

set some of the applicants. They saw the filling out of forms and the interrogation as insensitive, impersonal, and heartless. Bressler viewed the questions concerning the applicant's financial status as a necessary formality before granting a loan for transportation or other costs. Some applicants, however, regarded the experience as demeaning. After politely thanking him for his help, the wife of one applicant upbraided Bressler for quizzing her about the family's ability to repay the loan. "You humiliated me by asking why I do not pawn my jewelry . . . why I did not sell my furniture . . . why I do not borrow from friends," wrote Mrs. Samuel Friedman. "You should not think that everyone that comes into the office to ask for aid must be cheat, a liar or ignorant. . . . Some may be such I admit, but there are exceptions and a man like you should know the difference." Despite his professional approach to the IRO, Bressler remained cognizant of the immigrant's sensibilities. He acknowledged the woman's letter and thanked her for her suggestions.[65] This exchange reflected some of the discord that existed between the immigrants and the German Jews who assisted them.

Immigrants who applied to the IRO were divided into three broad divisions: direct or original removals, request removals, and reunion removals. Direct or original removal applicants left the selection of their destination entirely to the judgment of the IRO officials. Request removals comprised men who asked to be sent to some city where they had relatives or friends with whom they had been in correspondence. The IRO sent request removals to their destination only after notifying the community so that it could expresss an opinion on the matter. IRO officials followed this course because they wanted to ascertain whether the relatives or friends were themselves economically independent and able to assist the newcomer. Reunion removals were men who asked to be sent to join families or friends who had been previously sent out by the IRO.[66]

As a rule, the IRO first sent heads of families to their new destination. This gave the immigrants an opportunity to adjust and establish themselves in their new environment without the complication and burden of their families. Once the removal settled in, the IRO sent his family to him.

Despite the screening process, not every immigrant proved absorbable. This could create problems, especially if the local community refused to receive any more removals. "Fort Wayne has had a sad experince with our three men," wrote a concerned Elias Margolis in May 1908. "Constantinoff sent to Goldstein as a bushelman, turned out to be a wife-beater and generally undesirable and disappeared. Rubinstein got discouraged and left for New York after costing the community quite a sum of money. Solinger sent as a paper hanger to Treep, gets an occasional job and is still a problem, his wife being sick in the bargain." As a result, said Margolis,

"our committee here wouldn't even entertain the idea of cooperation."
To repair the damage, "we will have to go slowly with Fort Wayne and
come back next spring when they will have forgotten somewhat their sad
experiences."[67]

The IRO never promised the applicant that it would find him a particular job at a certain salary in the community to which he was being sent.
The agents did their best to find him work in his trade or something close
to it, but frequently the removal had to take the job that was available. In
practice, the Industrial Removal Office had became a humanized labor
exchange situated in New York, with subsidiary branches in other parts
of the country.

Bressler received many appreciative letters from immigrants praising
the IRO and its work. "I thank you for myself and my family from the
bottom of our hearts," wrote one removal from Wichita, Kansas. "You
are the real doctors, bringing people back to life again. . . . I now make a
respectable living. . . . I only wish other Jews can be helped the way you
helped me." Another from Denver begged "to extend my thanks to you
for sending me out of New York. I earn $10 a week, and do not have to
work on *shabos* [Saturday]." "You are men who help men," asserted an
immigrant in Birmingham, Alabama. "I came to you while I was in N.Y.
to send me wherever you want. I couldn't make a living for my wife and
child. I thank you because I make a fine living and I'll never forget you."[68]

Notwithstanding the praise, the results of the IRO were mixed. The
organization's correspondence reveals innumerable problems accompa-
nying relocation. A large number of immigrants struggled with lost or
delayed baggage, furniture, or tools; troubles over unpaid bills; and misunderstandings about transportation costs. Whenever possible, the IRO
expected the immigrants to pay at least part of this cost. One newcomer,
upset at being made to contribute $7 toward his brother's transportation,
retorted that the IRO "acted like a robber" in taking the money from
him.[69] And local communities complained incessantly about their difficulties with the immigrants.

For their part, relocated immigrants complained about poor conditions
and lack of opportunity. "You have sent us to make a living and we are
suffering here," wrote a group of unhappy immigrants in St. Louis. "Please
investigate and you'll find that men are falling from hunger and nobody
pays any attention to them. . . . Please have pity on us and command
Mr. Beinstock [the local agent] that he may treat us as human beings and
get work for us." The IRO investigated the complaint "in order to be
able to face the public (the press) with absolute facts." They found the immigrants' grievances to be exaggerated.[70] Another immigrant protested
that "by sending me to Seattle, you have really killed me, as I am out of
work over four weeks, destitute, lonely, naked, and in a position of star-

vation." He appealed to Bressler to "help me to go back east."[71] Bressler refused the man's request, citing the IRO's policy of not advancing removals money to return to New York.

In an address before the National Conference of Jewish Charities in May 1910, Bressler formulated the broader aspects of the distribution program. "The aim of the Removal Office is to act as an invisible force to direct the stream of Jewish workingmen to our Western country," he said. The IRO "sets before itself the ideal that the time may come that of the Jews who land at Ellis Island in any one year, a majority of them will voluntarily and instantly depart for the interior of their own initiative and without outside assistance." Another goal was to match the unemployed immigrant, who had a particular trade, with the sparsely settled community that needed people with just such skills.[72]

Bressler never achieved all his objectives. Despite the IRO's efforts, it soon became clear that the vast majority of Jews who came to New York City would never leave. Between 1901 and 1917, the IRO relocated 75,000 immigrants, only 6 percent of the Jewish newcomers to America. The ethnic enclaves or voluntary ghettos of the large cities provided havens for the newly uprooted. Urban Jewish neighborhoods supplied familiarity, friends, relatives, synagogues, kosher meat, and Hebrew teachers. The ghetto meant Yiddish culture. "If I were [still] in New York," said a recent removal earning a decent living in the south, "I could go to the Yiddish theater in the evenings, hear a lecture, visit people whose conversation I enjoy, join a club or take active part in some movement. In short, after working hours, be a man."[73]

One person who viewed the slow pace of removal with alarm was noted banker and philanthropist Jacob Henry Schiff (1847–1920), the greatest American Jewish philanthropist of his generation. Born in Frankfurt am Main, Germany, into a family of bankers, scholars, and rabbis, he emigrated to New York in 1865. In 1885, he became head of the banking firm of Kuhn, Loeb, and Company. Schiff contributed millions of dollars to Jewish and non-Jewish causes, believing that a man's giving should be done in his lifetime under his own supervision. He used his personal wealth and influence on behalf of Jews everywhere, and his widespread philanthropic and communal activities made him the foremost figure of American Jewry.[74]

Schiff had long believed that the United States had the capacity to absorb millions of Russian Jewish immigrants, provided their geographical distribution was assured. He feared that, unless this were done, those who favored immigration restriction would win the day. After the bloody pogroms of 1903 and 1905, Schiff became concerned about more than just dispersing the newcomers to the hinterland; he wanted to "take every one of our persecuted people out of Russia and bring them to the United

States." There seemed only one way to fulfill his goal and halt the further crowding of the immigrant ghettos: to prevent the immigrants from reaching Ellis Island by rerouting them to immigration stations in other areas of the country.[75]

In 1906, Congress debated a bill to establish an entry station for immigrants in Galveston, Texas. Schiff and others—including his friend Oscar Straus, secretary of commerce and labor, under whose jurisdiction immigration lay—used their influence to secure passage of the bill. The Galveston plan, which Schiff called "my project," envisioned bringing the Jewish immigrants to Galveston and distributing them in areas west of the Mississippi. By avoiding the eastern seaboard entirely, this scheme guaranteed all the benefits of removal and resolved the pain of a second uprooting.

The idea was for the Jewish Terrritorial Organization (ITO) in London and the German Hilfsverein to gather Jewish emigrants in Russia, finance their journey to America, and direct them to Galveston.[76] In Galveston, the IRO would take over and guide the immigrants to towns and cities west of the Mississippi. Schiff pleged $500,000 to initiate the project. He believed this would be sufficient to settle from 20,000 to 25,000 immigrants in the American hinterland. Schiff felt that a properly handled operation could move up to 4 million Jews into the interior of the United States. Morris Waldman, who served as David Bressler's assistant, went to Galveston to manage the IRO office there.[77]

Waldman worked hard to make the IRO's western operation succeed. He visited cities throughout the west and, wherever possible, got each community to set up a committee to find jobs for the immigrants. Most Jewish communities agreed to help. Waldman attributed their positive response to the shock they felt after the Russian pogroms of 1905.

The reception of the immigrants and their degree of success varied from place to place. In 1907, for example, the immigrants sent to Kansas City, Missouri, received a warm welcome, got jobs, saved money, and within a few months were able to send for their families. Those sent to St. Paul, Minnesota, found work the first day and claimed to be pleased with the Jewish community and their situation. The group sent to New Orleans fared far less well. New Orleans took twelve men, more than any other city. The local committee, however, experienced difficulty in finding work for them. A week after they arrived, four of the immigrants wrote a letter to the *Yiddishe Tageblatt,* a New York Yiddish daily, bemoaning their plight. They complained that they found no work in their trades (carpenters), that the city contained few Jews, "and those that are here do not interest themselves in us and do not want to help us." They could not find work among the Christians, they said, "because we don't understand the language. We are therefore in great distress." [78]

By 1914, after seven years of operation, the Galveston movement deflected no more than 10,000 immigrants from the ports of the northeast. A number of reasons account for its lack of success. The length of the voyage and the poor travel conditions on the Bremen-to-Galveston route discouraged many immigrants. Periodic slumps in the economies of various western states, beginning with the nationwide depression of 1907–09, made placement of the immigrants difficult. Most important, the movement never captured the imagination of the Jewish people as a solution to their problems. Galveston and the American west could never compete with the attraction New York held for hundreds of thousands of Jewish immigrants from eastern Europe. For them, New York remained the "real" America, and no amount of propaganda about the Galveston movement could change their view.[79]

The story of Nathan Kaluzny was typical. Kaluzny came from the village of Davidgorodok in the region of Minsk, where he had worked as a blacksmith. In 1910, at the age of twenty-nine, Kaluzny left his wife and three children in Russia to try his luck in America. He promised to send for them once he had permanently settled. The Jewish Emigration Society's agent in Davidgorodok, a druggist named Betzel Judowitz, offered a convincing argument to dissuade emigrants from entering America through New York or other eastern ports. "We will save you money if you are sent by the Jewish committee via Galveston." Kaluzny decided to go through Galveston because the trip cost less.[80]

Kaluzny arrived in Galveston with 168 other immigrants on 30 May 1910. His final destination was listed as St. Joseph, Missouri, but Kaluzny never made it. He liked Galveston and decided to stay. Although he went to work in the railroad yard and earned a decent wage, something was missing. As he later recalled, "Galveston was a nice, clean city and the people were good to me. But there were not many Jews." Kaluzny was an Orthodox Jew, and although he attended Galveston's Orthodox congregation, the Young Men's Hebrew Association, he wanted more. He had a cousin in New York who sent him a letter inviting him to join him. "New York City," the cousin wrote, "has Jews as well as jobs." Kaluzny could not resist the allure of that great Jewish metropolis. A year after he arrived in Galveston, he left for New York.[81]

Despite relatively small numbers of immigrants, the IRO's Galveston operation did manage to distribute its charges to more than a hundred cities in some twenty-five states. Thus, the Galveston movement contributed to a continuing Jewish presence in various American cities of the west.

In terms of large-scale dispersion, the Industrial Removal Office never reached the proportions that the Jewish leadership had envisioned. From its inception to its liquidation in 1922, the IRO dispatched 79,000 Jews to more than 1,700 communities. California, Illinois, Michigan, Missouri, Ohio, and Wisconsin received the bulk of those sent.[82] Nonetheless, in some localities, the immigrants substantially augmented the Jewish population. Between 1901 and 1917, the IRO sent 2,437 individuals to Colorado. They accounted for 15 percent of the Jewish population of the state. In Los Angeles, it placed 2,300 men, who in turn sent for their families. Later arriving relatives may have swelled the total number of IRO transplants nationwide to 100,000.[83]

In other locales the immigrants helped energize Jewish communal life. In Sioux City, Iowa, the new arrivals joined the existing Orthodox congregation and established their own fraternal and benevolent associations. Their Jewish activism, commented one local historian, helped to keep that city's Jewish community from fading away. In Denver, they established Orthodox synagogues, a variety of social and cultural organizations, and a Hebrew day school.[84]

Contrary to the IRO's optimistic public pronouncements, many removals did not stay in the communities to which they were originally sent. Reports sent back to the main office by traveling agents acknowledge that a large number of removals left after a short time. For example, in his tour of June 1908, Elias Margolis "found in very many of the towns I have visited that quite a number of our men have drifted away from the towns to which we have sent them."[85]

A number of communal studies support Margolis's observation. A sampling of eighty-one men sent to Detroit in 1905 shows that ten left within a year; another sixty left within three years. Of a sample of 101 men sent in 1907, only thirteen remained in the city in 1909. Of the twenty-nine men sent to Columbus, Ohio, in 1905, no more than five remained in the city by 1910. And only 59 percent of the IRO men sent to Indianapolis from 1905 to 1907 still remained in the city a year after they had been sent.[86]

Most of those who left New York appear to have gone back there. Loneliness and the fact that they had more relatives and friends in New York seem to be the chief motives for their return. Others returned to New York because of an absence of Jewish life in their new surroundings. Based on his visits, Elias Margolis concluded that IRO immigrants defected far more often from cities with little or no Jewish communal life than they did from places with a large, well-organized Jewish community.[87] Sometimes the urge to try their luck somewhere else prompted others to leave.

Whatever the reason, a sizable number of removals left the places they had been sent. Nevertheless, David Bressler and the IRO's sponsors continued to promote removal as the best remedy to eliminate poverty

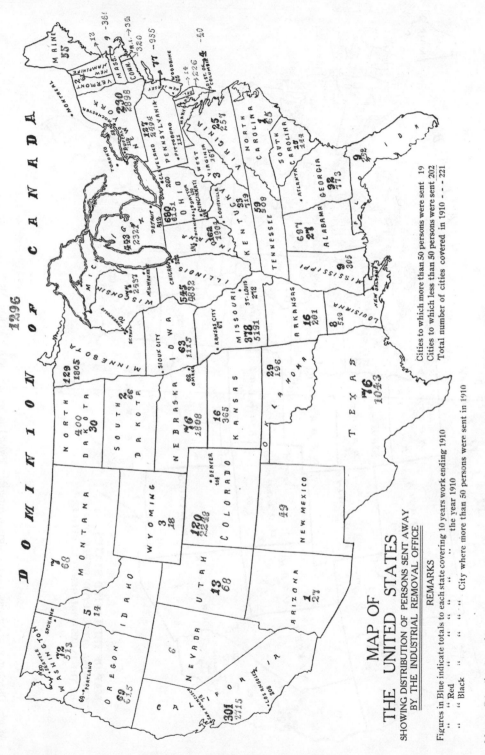

Map 1. Distribution of Persons, 1910. Courtesy, American Jewish Historical Society, Waltham, Mass.

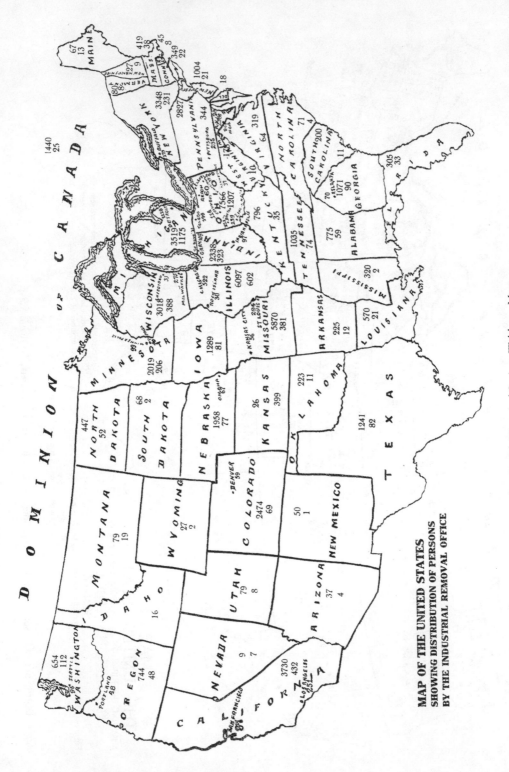

Map 2. Distribution of Persons, 1912. Courtesy, American Jewish Historical Society, Waltham, Mass.

among the immigrants, to hasten their Americanization, and to reduce anti-Jewish prejudice.

Not everyone in the Jewish community regarded distribution as a solution to the immigrants' problems. One outspoken opponent was Isaac Max Rubinow (1875–1936), a Russian-born physician, statistician, and economist. Rubinow insisted that the future of American Jewry lay in the large metropolitan centers, not in the southern and western sections of the country. He based most of his criticism on economic grounds. It was absurd to move Jews to the agricultural and least developed regions of the country, he said. The economic opportunities offered by the larger cities of the northeast could not be matched by the smaller cities or villages. He noted that the large cities attracted not only Jews but other ethnic groups as well as natives and former farmers. To leave the site of modern economic activity spelled regression, especially when Jews were best suited physically to city life and light industry. Jews will continue to populate the cities, he predicted, "because history has made them an industrial and commercial people." He argued that ghetto life did not preclude mobility. In economic terms, the Jewish immigrants were better off than they had been in Europe and, he believed, "better off economically than the other immigrants." [88]

Notwithstanding critics such as Rubinow, IRO partisans believed that the organization's importance transcended the tangible results it achieved. The *American Hebrew* claimed that the IRO influenced large numbers of Jews beyond those it actually relocated. By making *removal* a word of power, the paper said, "the IRO . . . may take credit for the present mobility of the Jewish mass. It has, by direct and indirect methods, filled many a timid Jew, living in a crowded tenement, with courage to pull up stakes and try his luck in the smaller cities." [89]

Although the IRO did not live up to the expectations of its proponents, it gave thousands of immigrants hope and the chance for a better life and remains a unique experiment in American Jewish history.

THE IRO LETTERS

The IRO archive is located at the American Jewish Historical Society on the campus of Brandeis University in Waltham, Massachusetts. This collection includes records of every aspect of the removal work as well as thousands of letters from IRO officials, agents, Jewish communal leaders, local businessmen, national figures, and immigrants.

I divide the documents portion of this study into two parts. The first deals with the IRO as an institution. It contains letters written by David Bressler, his traveling agents, the local communities, and the local agents.

The communications between Bressler and two of his traveling agents—Elias Margolis and Abraham Solomon—yield valuable information about the various Jewish communities of that day and illustrate the biases of the traveling agents and Bressler. The exchanges among Bressler, the local community, and the local agents illuminate the problems and misunderstandings that arose between the central office and its constituents.

Part 2 features the letters of the immigrants. Wherever they were, removals wrote to the IRO. Their motives varied. Most requested that family, friends, or belongings be forwarded to them. Many wrote to complain about the treatment they received or about conditions in the place they had been sent. Some wrote to express their appreciation and praise for the IRO and its agents, and others wrote to describe their successes or failures and to voice their hopes, dreams, and disappointments.

The immigrant correspondence contains thousands of letters from all over the United States. Most of the letters, however, come from cities and towns in states that received the largest number of removals—in particular, California, Illinois, Michigan, Missouri, and Ohio. Together, the five states hosted more than 34,000 removals between 1901 and 1917, 47 percent of the total for this period.[90] The cities that accommodated the largest number of removals were Cleveland, Detroit, Milwaukee, St. Louis, and Atlanta.

The immigrant letters in the IRO collection are arranged by state, beginning with Alabama and ending with Wisconsin. Within each state, the letters are filed under the names of the cities from where they originated. The vast bulk of the letters were written in Yiddish, but some of them are in English, Russian, or Romanian. Since David Bressler and his assistants did not read Yiddish, Russian, or Romanian, many of these letters were translated into or summarized in English by persons employed for this purpose.

These letters, together with the response they elicited from Bressler or his assistants, serve as an important historical source for a number of reasons. Although the immigrant letters that appear in the "letters to the editor" columns of the Yiddish press express the immigrants' daily problems and concerns, they are somewhat suspect. Because the originals of this correspondence no longer survive, and many are signed with appellations such as "The Troubled Mother," "An Unhappy Father," "The Peculiar Daughter," or "Anonymous," questions persist about their authenticity. In the case of the *Jewish Daily Forward,* historians agree that the newspaper's renowned editor, Abraham Cahan, composed many of the letters himself.[91] Since the IRO letters were not written for publication, include the writers' names and addresses, and survive in their original form, they appear to be genuine.

The immigrant letters offer prime examples of the attitudes, tensions, and misunderstandings that poisoned relations between the established German Jewish community (as represented by David Bressler and the IRO) and the eastern European Jews. The letters also present an intimate glimpse into the lives of ordinary people who did not become heads of governments or large corporations. The letters illustrate their worries and cares, their trials and tribulations, and show how the immigrants adjusted to their new surroundings. In addition, we gain some knowledge of the attitudes and ways in which the eastern European Jews viewed the world, the United States, and the places to which they were sent. The letters are also a source of fascinating—sometimes humorous, sometimes sad—stories of immigrant life in early-twentieth-century America and in some instances depict the living and working conditions that existed in mid-sized American cities at that time.

My method is to present the immigrant letters under broad categories such as interaction with the IRO, economic adjustment, social adjustment, and views of American society. A number of these topics contain subdivisions. "Interaction with the IRO," for example, encompasses letters of appreciation, complaints, and requests.

Several factors influenced my selection of letters. I concentrated primarily on those that were written in Yiddish because these formed the vast majority of immigrant correspondence and I could translate them. I excluded English synopses of letters written in Russian or Romanian because these were generally very brief and I could not verify their accuracy. In addition, I looked for letters that reflected the tensions between the eastern European immigrants and their German Jewish benefactors. I also sought letters that included descriptions of the writer's new surroundings, work conditions, and living situation. Wherever possible, I included letters that contrasted the writer's experience in New York with his new environment. I also searched for letters that displayed the writer's attitude toward the local Jewish and non-Jewish community and, conversely, his perception of how the community viewed and treated him. Wherever possible, I sought to find extended correspondence between an immigrant and the IRO and chose letters from cities where sources of information existed about the Jewish community. Since most of the removals held similar expectations and voiced the same complaints, I tried to diversify my selections by including letters that came from disparate geographical areas. In each instance, I selected the best or most representative letters accessible.

PART ONE

The IRO
as an Institution

CHAPTER I

Letters from Traveling Agents

S tarting in 1904, the IRO engaged a number of college-educated young men to serve as traveling agents. The office dispatched these men to the southern, midwestern, and western regions of the United States to promote the IRO program in cities and towns that had a Jewish population, establish local IRO committees, and investigate employment opportunities for Jewish immigrants. As they moved about, the agents sent the IRO detailed reports about conditions in the towns they visited. In return, they received replies and inquiries from David Bressler. These ongoing exchanges often vividly described the local Jewish situation, personalities, and problems. In some instances, the reports underscore the prejudices and predilections of Bressler and his agents.

This section contains selections from four reports. The first are letters written by David Bressler while he was on one of his periodic inspection tours. The next is a report from Morris Waldman, whose tasks included visiting communities in the midwest and west to establish local IRO committees. The final two collections of letters are from the reports of traveling agents Elias Margolis and Abraham Solomon.

THE LETTERS FROM AND TO DAVID BRESSLER

During his tenure as IRO director, Bressler regularly toured different regions of the country to judge for himself how the IRO operated at the local level. In July and August 1905, he visited Buffalo, Cleveland, Milwaukee, and a few other cities. Once he had investigated the local scene, he dispatched his impressions to New York. In Bressler's absence, his assistant, Morris Waldman, managed the New York office. Bressler's accounts highlight the kinds of problems the IRO encountered locally as well as some of the successes it enjoyed. The reports also depict aspects of the IRO's general operation and offer Bressler's evaluation of the local offices and their agents.[1]

* * *

July 20, 1905

Mr. Morris Waldman, Asst. Mgr.,
174 Second Avenue
New York

My Dear Mr. Waldman:—

I arrived in this city [Cleveland] early this morning and am in the midst of a conference between Messrs. Furth and Richter.[2] From the preliminary talk I have had with these gentlemen, it seems that I will have a pretty warm time in this city. Charges and counter-charges galore are flying about the air. I shall, however, take no snap judgment but will investigate thoroughly.

I received your letter of the 18th inst. with enclosures. I am very much disappointed that the work isn't picking up any better. Of course I realize that we are doing all we can to get into the public favor again, but it is the hardest thing in the world to be patient until this is accomplished.

Keep up the good work of distributing the circulars and do not fail to get a list of the incoming immigrants, so that one may be mailed to each of them.[3] I feel confident that good results must follow, if not immediately, then within a reasonable time.

Now as to Buffalo.[4] My judgment is that Buffalo is doing fairly good work. Unknown to Schwartz [the local agent], I called one evening at the Boarding House to which they [the removals] are directed, and much to my surprise and gratification, I found it is filled with men that we had sent there during the past year. There were about 30 men there, all of whom had been sent by us with the exception of 3, so at least they claimed, and in as much as my visit was entirely unexpected, there is no reason to believe that it was a pre-arranged affair. Mr. Saperston, who seems to be of the salt of the earth, told me positively, that at least 75% of the people we sent there are still in Buffalo.[5] He claims to know that from personal investigation and observation, and being at once the President and Investigator of the Relief Society, he has the opportunity, I suppose, of coming in contact with them. Schwartz claims that 75% is a conservative estimate. Most men are employed at their own trade. Quite a number are working for the steel plant outside of the city, not more, however, than about 14. They get from $1.50 a day upwards.

There was considerable disaffection among some of the members of the Relief Society to continuing the removal work for this work had cost the Relief Society over $1,000 during the past year, and in as much as they had to run an entertainment to raise funds to cover their deficit, they said that they could not afford to make any further appropriation for the coming year for removal. I had no desire to make any speeches on this trip, but Saperston told me that they had a meeting of their Board of Directors on Monday night, and that it was up to me to swing them around in our favor again. Under the circumstances, I had to talk. I was afraid that we would have to make some additional financial concessions, but fortunately that was not necessary. Everything is alright again. Schwartz is waxing fat, on the work he hasn't got to do and I wish we could keep him busier than he is. I was treated royally by all hands, particularly by Mrs. Altman, Mr. Saperston and Mr. Schwartz.[6] They are our best friends and I should add Mr. Hoffeler, Treasurer of the Relief Society.[7] I am glad to report that I am feeling pretty well, much better in fact than I have in some time. I am not rushing things but I am taking things quietly and easily. I expect to leave Cleveland tomorrow night if possible and I may or may not go to Detroit. I do not believe, however, that there is much need to stop at Detroit. I may instead go straight on to Milwaukee. I have determined not to go to Memphis or New Orleans because I do not care to risk the hot weather down there. I have been advised against it. I may return by way of Chicago, take a steamer trip through the Great Lakes to Buffalo, stopping off at Detroit on my return.

With kindest regards to all the office force, and trusting that you will not over-work yourself, I am

> Very truly yours,
> David Bressler

* * *

July 21st, 05.

Mr. David M. Bressler,
Milwaukee, Wis.

Dear Mr. Bressler:

I am just in receipt of your letter of the 20th inst., from Cleveland. The report from Buffalo is very encouraging. I note that in all probability you will not take the trip South. Perhaps this is just as well.

You will be glad to hear that we sent 45 [men] yesterday and 51 to-day. Altogether 164 were sent this week, making a total of 377 for the month.

Of course, most of these were request cases, and strange it is how they bunched themselves together in these last two days. The prospects for next week look a little poor, but at the same time I am hopeful. Our circulars are being distributed and sent by mail to the immigrants. . . .

I have been schlemeil enough to get my right fore finger in the electric fan this morning, and fortunately escaped with nothing worse than a gash in the joint. I have just had it fixed up by the surgeon, and I trust that nothing more serious will result than an incapacitated finger for a week or two. Things are certainly coming my way. I will let you hear from me on Monday again. Otherwise everything is O.K. in the office.

The weather was excessively hot this past week, but we kept pretty good natured. It has turned cooler now.

With kind regards from the office staff, I am

Faithfully yours,

P.S. I cannot write as my finger is in a splint.

* * *

July 22, 1905

Mr. Morris Waldman
New York.

My Dear Mr. Waldman:—

Have just arrived from Cleveland.

I found things in Cleveland not quite to my liking. I made a pretty thorough investigation and my conclusion is that the man in charge is not the right man. He is a young fellow—about 25—with very little sympathy for the people that he must handle and to him the entire movement is in the nature of a business proposition. Not alone is he personna non grata with them but with those higher up. It seems that Mr. Furth has been the only man to champion his cause, and I am quite sure that is so only because R. [Richter] has managed to pull the wool over his eyes. I told Mr. F. [Furth] very plainly that he would have to get rid of him, but at his request I agreed to let R. down easy; that is to say, no immediate change will be made, but it will be effected within the next two months.

From interviews that I have had with the President of the Relief and the Superintendent of Relief—both of whom come more or less in contact with the people that we send—I gather that not less than seventy percent are still there. Just how accurate this estimate may be is hard to determine. Mr. F. is inclined to believe that a larger proportion have remained.

I saw a number of the men that we have sent and they tell me that the majority have left Cleveland. Asked why, they say it is due to the fact that R. treats them very badly.

I would not place too much stock in their complaints ordinarily, but when all join in condemnation I cannot fail to take notice. For the present, send as few individuals to Cleveland as possible. I would prefer you send families only. All of them have remained.

Nothing more today, except that I am feeling pretty well. I trust that you and the rest of the office staff are in good health.

With kindest regards, I am,

Faithfully yours,
David Bressler

Mr. Furth has finally agreed with me that Mr. Richter is not the man for the position. I have enlisted the co-operation of several men in Cleveland who have heretofore been inimical to the movement. They hate Richter.

*   *   *

July 27, 1905

Industrial Removal Office
New York City, N.Y.

Dear Sirs:—

I arrived this morning in St. Louis and found your letter with 33 checks awaiting me at the Planter's Hotel. I have signed all the checks and I return them by registered mail.

Now as to Milwaukee.[8] I made a pretty good investigation of the city there, with the result that I can conscientiously say that the fruits of our work are easily discernible in that city. I made perhaps a more comprehensive study of the situation there than at any time previous. No one can say with any degree of accuracy what proportion of the people have remained. But there are several indications that there is being accomplished what we are aiming at; to wit, independent attraction by reason of pioneering settlement.[9] Mr. Billikopf, the superintendent of charities, tells me that if he ever had the slightest doubts as to the far reaching results of our work, they have been dispelled since his experiences in Milwaukee.[10] I am informed by him that there are constantly coming from Russia, Galicia and Roumania, the families or relatives of the men that we have sent there; and while it is possible that only 60 to 75 per cent of the original pioneers have remained, the number that have been attracted by reason of this pioneer settlement, is much larger than the original settlement. Even discounting his rosy view of the situation, I think we can safely place a great deal of reliance on Mr. Billikopf's estimate, for he is in a position where he can understand both sides of the situation. He tells me that comparatively few drifters come to Milwaukee, and those that do he has no difficulty in placing at work.

Our Mr. Rosenthal [the local IRO agent] seems to be a fairly decent fellow, although I am not overly much impressed with him. But as a matter of fact, the agent need not be an intellectual colossus so long as Mr. Rich is directing the work.[11] Under the circumstances, I did not feel justified in discontinuing the Milwaukee agency even for the time being. I have succeeded, however, in reducing our month's expense there from $105.00 to $65.00. I simply told Mr. R. [Rosenthal] that they would have to do the work with that money. In making out this month's check, make it for the smaller figure.

With kindest regards to all, and trusting that Mr. Waldman is in good health, I am,

Very truly yours,
David Bressler

LETTER OF MORRIS WALDMAN

In 1907, David Bressler sent Morris Waldman to Galveston, Texas, to organize and administer the IRO and Galveston plan operations in that city. Waldman managed the Galveston office for one year. As part of his job, he scouted communities in the midwest and west to gain their support. In each community, he established a committee that accepted responsibility for finding jobs for a certain number of immigrants. Waldman jokingly referred to himself as a traveling salesman in the business of selling Jews. He worked closely with David Bressler and regularly sent him reports about his activities and progress.

In July 1907, Waldman inspected some of the cities to which the Galveston plan's first immigrants had been sent. One was Cedar Rapids, Iowa, where he had shipped three immigrants. His report to Bressler describes conditions in Cedar Rapids and the history of the removals sent to that city.[12] Waldman visited the immigrants' lodgings and spoke with them. He makes some caustic observations about their character and behavior and expresses concern that the Russian-based committees charged with recruiting immigrants for Galveston may be misleading the Russians about what to expect in America.[13] He stresses that the immigrants should be told the truth, which would lessen their disappointment and diminish the IRO's chances of encountering problems with the host communities.

In 1907, Cedar Rapids had a tiny Jewish community of fifty persons out of a general population of 24,000. The Jewish community contained one Orthodox synagogue and no Jewish fraternal organizations or societies. Five years later the Jewish population had only risen to seventy-five persons in a general population of 35,000. Most members of the Jewish community were Russian-born.[14]

July 27, 1907

Dear Mr. Bressler—

The cooperation of Cedar Rapids thus far is highly creditable to the community and especially to the chairman of our committee Mr. L. Koppel, a retired business man, who having lost his wife some time ago is prepared to devote much of his spare time to our work.

The three men, Chajukin, Grynberg and Lottman, arrived here July 4th. He let them rest up until Monday the 8th, found jobs for the "carpenters" at their trade and Chajukin at the Quaker Cereal factory. Neither of the carpenters suited. He discovered that one of them, Grynberg knew nothing of the trade, in fact could not tell the difference between a saw and a plane. (I verified this myself to-day in an interview with the man) Lottman is a very mediocre carpenter. Mr. Koppel found another job for him at his trade, at which he is earning now $12.00 a week and will earn more when he makes good. Union wages average $3.50 a day. He got Grynberg a job at the packing houses at $2.50 a day. The latter worked half a day, said it was too hard and left getting $1.25.

With considerable persuasion Mr. K. succeeded in having the sup't agree to give him the lightest work possible. He will get $1.25 a day to begin with. He starts Monday. Grynberg is a lazy schlemiel. Though he has earned some money he hasn't offered to pay a cent for his food. Lottman seems a little more decent. He has paid $5.00 to his landlady. The committee stands good for the remainder.

Chajukin, as I wrote you, had been in the U.S. before and evidently spoiled the other fellows somewhat. A better job has been found for him in a glove factory in Iowa City, nearby, where he is learning cutting and getting $9 per week, according to the statement of the committee, which of course I have not been able to verify, but which I have no doubt is correct.

These three men acted as if it were the committee's duty here to give them board and lodging free and to give them easy work at $3–$4 per day. Koppel is highly incensed at Chajukin for writing a letter of complaint, because he [Koppel] worked like a beaver to find satisfactory positions for the men.

I was over to the boarding house, a clean, comfortable house, kept by a neat Russian woman, a house that you and I would be comfortable in. The house is very pretty—quite lively—with sufficient numbers of Russian Jews to offer some "gesellschaft" [company] to our immigrants. I did not see Lottman as he is at work, but Mr. Koppel tells me that both he and Chajukin say that the committee in Russia told them that we did not have enough workers here, we were anxious to have them come, that jobs were waiting for them at high wages. Grynberg, who seems an extraordinarily dull fellow, did not make such a statement to me. He simply says he was told to go to Galveston and he went. Mr K. told me that he wrote me a letter yesterday giving an account of the whole affair and stating he would not co-operate any longer. Well I've succeeded in having him change his mind. We need him badly here because he is the only man in town who has both the time and inclination for work of this kind.

Judging from what I have seen thus far, I believe our co-workers abroad give these people to understand that they will have absolutely no difficulty in earning the maximum wages at their trade. And if they are unskilled that they will obtain as much as $3–$4 a day as laborers.

I am just as anxious to place as little restriction upon our co-workers as are you or Mr. Sulzberger, but I must impress upon you that the conditions here should be presented truthfully before the immigrants leave Russia. Otherwise they will be sorely disappointed and our friends up the country will lose patience. They are very willing to help and are not at all seeking excuses to avoid the responsibilities, but as they have the hardest work of all, unnecessary obstacles should not be placed in their way. The people [removals] are treated in a kindly fashion but it seems they expect a paternalism which our co-workers here are unwilling to extend and which if extended, in my opinion, would be pauperization.

I want you to know that in the towns I visited, and from which the various factory reports came to us, the immigrants were handled by Russian Jews and the suspicion of coldness and superciliousness can have no ground.

I leave to-night for Kansas City. I may run over to Leavenworth and stop off at Fort Worth. I have not heard any unsatisfactory news from these towns but as they are conveniently situated it will be advisable to ascertain the results there.

Our "removalities" have done well here. Braverman showed me a letter which he intended last month to send to the Jewish Daily News in answer to the letter of Lieb Polansky. I send it to you as an indication of the attitude of the people here and of their anxiety to co-operate.

With kind regards, I am

Faithfully yours,
Morris D. Waldman

THE LETTERS OF ELIAS MARGOLIS

Elias Margolis (1879–1946) was born in Lithuania and came to the United States in 1885.[15] He earned a B.A. at the University of Cincinnati, ordination as a Reform rabbi from Hebrew Union College, and a Ph.D. from Columbia University. Margolis served as an IRO traveling agent from 1908 to 1909 and again in 1912. After his IRO work, he became a manager of the Baron De Hirsch Fund. In 1916, he accepted the pulpit of Congregation Emanu-El in Mt. Vernon, New York, and continued in this position until his death.[16]

From April through June 1908, Margolis toured Indiana and Illinois, visiting forty-five communities in eighty-four days. The five letters in this section are extracts from this junket. Margolis's reports communicate his method of operation and expenses, the cost of living in various towns he visited, the reception he received, and his impressions of the region and Jewish communities. He also indicates the types of prejudice and stereotypes held by the Jewish and non-Jewish residents and employers he encountered.

Terre Haute, Ind.
April 27, 08

Mr. David Bressler
Industrial Removal Office
174 Second ave., New York, N.Y.

Dear Sir:—

I have canvassed the Terre Haute situation thoroughly, with just a few more places to visit tomorrow morning, before proceeding to Brazil and Indianapolis, with the following results:—

The firm of R. L. Alder & Bro., Ohio St., will take a highly skilled paper hanger, who is sufficiently conversant with the English language to understand orders and to make himself understood. None but a very skilled workman will suit and such a man will be guaranteed steady employment throughout the year, at an average wage of $18.00 per week, if not more. Should you have such a man and should you send him, I would suggest that he be meek and gentle in temperament because in the conversation with Mr. Alder I realized that only this type of man would be able to get along with him. If you can send this man, kindly inform them of this at once. Mr. Alder was impressed by the fact that the Jewish workingman is reliable because of his abstinence from drink, which seems to be not the case with the native working man.

The firm of Thorman & Schloss, Terre Haute, Ind., desire immediately the services of two, first-class coat makers, who have been employed by custom tailors in New York City and not by tailors for the trade or clothing houses. In other words, they must be able to turn out garments intended for the so-called swell trade of this city. They can be guaranteed steady employment throughout the year and their wages will average from $20 to $25 a week.

I obtained no immediate results from the large factories, especially the iron and woodworking industries. Most of these are affected by the financial depression and instead of taking on new hands are discharging the old. Nevertheless in a few cases I interested the managers to the extent that they not only promised to do business with us in the near future, but expressed their sorrow that they did not know of our existence in the past. I expect great results in the future from this missionary work and I am not at all disappointed because of the failure at present.

The F. Prox Co. of this city will be able in the future to use machinists and moulders and other kindred mechanics. Mr. Herman Prox of the above firm promised to communicate with us in the future, and I suggest that a letter from the office be sent to him, recognizing this promise and thanking him for his interest. Likewise, the Central Mfg. Company, 9th & Walnut, Terre Haute, Manufacturers of sash and doors, will be able at some time to use a good cabinet maker and carpenters. They should also be written to at once, in order to keep the interest alive. The firm of Frank & Son, 508 Ohio St., manufacturers of overalls, while employing to a large extent women help might in the future be able to use cutters and pressers.

I called upon Mr. W. H. Duncan, Sec'y of the Commercial Club of this city, and explained to him our work. By virtue of his position, he is in close touch with industrial conditions here and has intimate knowledge of the needs of the various factories for workingmen. He has signified his willingness and his intention to keep us informed in the future and to use his good will and influence in placing our men. In good times, it will not at all be difficult to make of this city one of the most important points for Removal work, because the class of labor prevalent up to this day has disgusted all employers, by reason of the fact that they are not reliable and are shiftless. They recognize the higher intelligence of the Russian Jew as a workingman, and from my observation I do not believe that there is any anti-Semitic prejudice here; at least in industrial circles.

The Jewish population of this city is about 500 souls evenly divided between the Russian and the German. The Russian Jews have their own synagogue and the one Bnei Brith Lodge recruits its membership from both wings. The Reformed Jews are a very good class of people and are willing to do whatever they can to promote the welfare of those whom we remove. They seem to suffer, however, from the scientific charity disease, but I have explained to them and impressed it upon them that they must make up their minds that they are obligated to share the burden and the problems of New York, and that they must temper their scientific charity with a little sentiment.

I have formed a Removal Committee here with Rabbi Emil Leipziger, who has been our correspondent in the past, as Chairman, and the other members being Mr. Milton Herz, Mr. Harry Schloss, Mr. L. J. Goldstine and Mr. Augustus Goodman.

With best regards,

Yours very truly,
Elias Margolis

P.S. I just saw Schloss of Thorman & Schloss & he impressed me again with the idea that if we cannot send him first class custom tailors, who have worked at the same thing in N. Y. he doesn't want them; for men's clothes by the way.

Workingmen can rent little houses for $12–$15 a month. Population 60,000 growing and up to date town. Lots of building improvements projected. Living here is moderate.

* * *

Ellwood, Ind., May 5, 1908

Mr. David M. Bressler
Industrial Removal Office
174 Second ave.,
New York City

Dear Sir:—

The one large plant in Elwood, Indiana is the American Sheet & Tin Plate Company. They employ no foreigners at all, and furthermore the class of work done there would not require the kind of mechanics we can send.

I enclose herewith, two requisitions for men.

(1) Mr. David Kessler, 1416 W. Main St., a Merchant Tailor, desires the services of an all round tailor who is also a cutter. He has in mind one of the old fashioned Jewish tailors who is handy in every department of the tailoring trade. Mr. Kessler is on the point of enlarging his business and

will want a man with enough common sense to take charge of his business, at some future time, when he would be engaged in drumming up trade. Kessler himself, is a Hungarian Jew who has been established in this City for the past eighteen years and bears a good reputation as a responsible business man. He would like to have a married man, with a small family, meek and docile in temperament. He might in the future be able to use more men. The wage of this man would be at the beginning, $12.00 a week with good chances for advancement, depending on his ability and reliability.

(2) The firm of Long & Morgan desire the services of a painter, who can do interior and exterior work but not necessarily artistic decoration. If this man proves satisfactory and is experienced, Mr. Long has signified his willingness to send for more men. Mr. Long is a very fine gentleman, of the old school of good Americans and it seems to me that a decent chap, sent to him, would not find it difficult to get along with him. As you will notice from the requisition, this man's wage will average $12.00 a week. This man could be used almost immediately and if you could arrange to have this man sent within a week, Mr. Long will deem it a favor.

This little town of Elwood is in pretty fair financial and industrial condition, despite the depression visible elsewhere. There are only eight Jewish families in this City and there is no evidence of any anti-Jewish feeling here. Five Jewish young men are members of the Elks Lodge which goes far to prove the existence of no prejudice. I have appointed, as our correspondents here, Messers. Ringold Bros., dealers in iron scrap, two fine American young fellows who themselves, will in time be able to send for one or two Jews.

Please write them a letter recognizing their offer to be our correspondents and reminding them that we can furnish them with workingmen.

Living expenses in this town are low. Mr. Long, for instance, assures me that he can get a seven roomed house for his man when he comes, for eight dollars a month. This house sets on three lots and has fruit trees on them in abundance, which seems a veritable paradise to an Eastside Jew of the tenements. Be careful not to send a very Orthodox Jew because kosher meats can be procured only by sending to Indianapolis for it. Living expenses aside from rent, are correspondingly low. The climate is excellent and the health likewise. All in all this town would be an ideal place to settle some of our Jews.

Yours very truly,
Elias Margolis

*   *   *

South Bend, Ind.,
May 22/08

Mr. David M. Bressler
New York City

Dear Sir:

It was impossible to do anything with the factories here. The men we have sent in the past years, have themselves been laid off, especially those working in the Studebaker factory. Mr. Greenbaum, our erstwhile agent, claims that it was because of the Union Square bomb throwing incident.[17] But Mr. G. is particularly biased against the Russian Jews and uses intemperate language when speaking of them. He doesn't try to understand them. He classifies every Orthodox Jew as an anarchist, and he doesn't seem to know that a real Orthodox Jew cannot be an anarchist.

This city presents a peculiar situation. There are about 2,000 Jews here, and of these about 75 are the German-Americans. The balance are Russians, Galicians etc. The few German Jews are very rich, but not only do they despise the Russians but they do not even attempt to help them in any way. There is enough antisemitism as it is, and the lot of the Russian Jew is doubly hard. At bottom Mr G. is perhaps a benevolent man, but he is very autocratic. He is President of the Temple & secretary of the Relief fund, the treasury of which possesses as much as $24 at present.[18]

I find that the main reason for the lay-off at the Studebaker place is the industrial depression. It has been the custom to place our men in that plant by bribing the foremen, and naturally the Jews are the first to go. Even so, they were always given the most difficult and disagreeable work. This is a very fine city, eastern in appearance and apparently rich. When things are better it will be wise to work this town thoroughly on our new method without the medium of an agent.[19]

Rents are very low ($7 up) and living expenses equally low. The population is about 70,000. The Russian Jews have about 3 shuls & smaller chevras.[20] There are two Rabbis. There are no doubt some anarchists among them, but I have the promise of Mr. Leo Cohen, a fine young Russian Jew who belongs to the Temple, & who is also the leader of the South Bend Gate, Knights of Zion, to use his society (the Zionists) as a means of stamping out any pernicious anarchist propaganda, which might do harm to our work here in the future.[21]

With regards,

Sincerely yours,
Elias Margolis

* * *

Decatur, Ill.
June 23, 1908

Mr. David M. Bressler
Industrial Removal Office
174 Second Ave.,
New York City

Dear Sir:—

In reply to yours of the 19th, in regard to statement of expenses, from May 12 to June 12, I beg to say that my method of keeping account of my expenses is to make entry at the close of each day under the following headings, on a monthly account pad. R.R.; Board; Carriage; Bus; Laundry.

The account I sent you represents the totals. I wish to say that the hotels out here are mostly on a basis of $2.50–3.50 per diem, that some of the hotels are on the European plan, necessitating my eating in restaurants, that the time for train leaving often forces me to eat on Pullman diners, and that with all this, I engage room with bath but once a week. Considering this, it is impossible to keep hotel bills down to less than $3.00 per day.

As to the item for carriage and bus hire, I wish to say that transfer companies charge from 25–50 cents for ride to and from station, and that in almost all of these Indiana & Illinois towns they are the only means of locomotion. Considering the distance of depot from hotel & the fact that I carry a heavy suit case and equally heavy hand grip, I have no trunk with me.

As for getting around the various places in town in a rig, I find that the money is well spent & that it is in fact an economy. It has enabled me to make very many of the towns in one day. As I had originally outlined my trip, I figured to stay out until August at least. And had I resorted to walking around to the factories & other concerns, I would have had to spend at least three days to the town, in view of the fact that some of the Jews must be seen also.

I consider $14.00 too much for laundry also, but that's just what I have spent and I have not been over solicitous of my appearance. Traveling on dirty railroads, especially in the spring & summer, wilting sometimes 2 & 3 collars a day, using an awful number of handkerchiefs on account of perspiration, figures up high, especially when hotel laundries are big sources of graft, some of them charging 4 & 5 cents per handkerchief for instance. Here is a specimen week's laundry bill, and you may figure it out yourself.

4 shirts at 15 cents	60 cents
3 suits underwear at 25 cents	75 cents
4 pairs socks at 5 cents	20 cents
1 pajamas at 25 cents	25 cents
12 collars at 3 cents	36 cents
22 handkerchiefs at 4½	99 cents
Total	$3.15

I have certainly tried to keep expenses down to a minimum and if I have not succeeded, it is not my fault. Traveling is an expensive proposition. Personally, even I could live much cheaper at home. I have to have my clothes pressed very often (which doesn't do the clothes any good). I have worn out two pairs of shoes since I am out. One must tip right and left around hotels, and all these have gone out of my own pocket. From May 12–June 12 is a period of 31 days. At $6.00 a day, it figures up to $186. If you think that I have spent too much, then I am ready to stand the difference of $15 & some odd cents out of my own pocket.

If you can send me my salary check to Moline, Ill., c/o Manufacturer's Hotel, where I will be July 1st, I will appreciate it, for I wish to send my mother a check as soon as possible.

With regards,
Sincerely yours,
Elias Margolis

*   *   *

Bloomington, Ill., 6/25/08

Mr. David M. Bressler
Industrial Removal Office
New York City.

Dear Sir:—

It was impossible to do anything in Champaign, Ill., a town of 10,000 population suffering from industrial set back and local option troubles. There are only a half dozen Jewish families there of the particularly selfish sort and not one of them could be interested in cooperating with us.

Bloomington, Ill. Jewish population 40 families, of which 15 belong to the Russian-Roumanian class. Possesses a Jewish temple, with Rabbi. Our representatives will be Mr. Oscar Mandel and Mr. Sig Livingston. Rents for working men's homes are from $10 up and living expenses moderate.

In reply to the letter of May 19th, I wish to say that I have found in very many of the towns I have visited that quite a number of our men have drifted away from the towns to which we have sent them. I do not think, however, that this fact has influenced the employers to any great extent for, as a rule all working men out here are of a drifting class, or are addicted to the use of liquor. It has been the universal complaint wherever I have gone that just when one of these itinerant working men was becoming valuable to his employer and accustomed to the methods of the shop, he would suddenly disappear for parts unknown. Most of these, of course, were men either unmarried or without families. When I tell the employer that we send married men preferably and that we have local Jewish committees to look after their welfare, they at once assume a more confident expression.

Elias Margolis

*   *   *

Aug. 7, 1908

Mr. David Bressler, Mgr.,
Industrial Removal Office
174—2nd Ave., City.

Dear Sir:—

I beg herewith to submit my report on my trip through the states of Indiana and Illinois, from April 18 to July 10th 1908. During this time I visited twenty-four cities in Indiana, twenty cities in Illinois, and made one side trip to Cedar Rapids, Iowa, for the purpose of investigating a dispute between some of our Removal Cases and their employer.

In each town I called on two classes of employers:— 1—The large factories and plants, which employ a large number of hands. 2—The smaller employers, such as merchant tailors, shoemakers, painters and paperhangers, plumbers, etc. In the case of the first class I would almost always obtain a respectful hearing from the superintendent of the plant. In quite a few cases great interest was manifested in our work so that I was asked to go into detailed explanation. In some cases our advance letters were carefully read and served as an introduction to the interview, while in as many our letters were seemingly consigned to the basket unread. In but two cases did I receive a curt dismissal, and in these I recognized the cause to be a feeling against all foreign laborers if not especially against Jewish workingmen.

The reception I received from the lesser employers depended on their immediate and future needs. The merchant tailors, shoemakers, painters and paperhangers, were almost all of them interested, and if they failed to give an immediate requisition, they at least promised future co-operation. Plumbers, tinsmiths, carpenters, were difficult to approach and their future availability may be discounted unless they be visited at another time when industrial conditions are in better shape. The financial depression hit the building and mechanical trades hardest.[22]

On the whole, as judged by my impressions, derived from my experiences, the prospect for future work in the territory I covered is good, provided we are able to lay hands on skilled men, and if we cover the more important cities again. The method of the traveling salesman who goes after a man again and again until he lands an account, will be one we might adopt with advantage. Everywhere my statement that we could furnish a sober and industrious class of mechanics and workingmen who could be relied upon at all times, met at first with the smile of incredulity, and upon repetition and emphasis attracted instant attention and interest. The manufacturing interests of the west are suffering from a shiftless and drunken class of workingmen who work three days, spend three more days in a bar-room, and then disappear for parts unknown. Another complaint I heard frequently was the onesidedness and specializing tendencies of the younger American workingman, which unfits him to grapple with a job which demands a general knowledge and aptness. Many managers admitted the superiority of the old world mechanic, but frankly expressed their doubts as to the existence of Jewish mechanics, especially in the iron and brass working trades. From their knowledge of the western Jew they imagined that all Jews were either storekeepers or junk dealers. The part of our report which gives a list of the trades represented by our 7500 removals in 1907 made a great impression and drove the argument home. Another point which found general favor was the fact that our method of removal was not the cold-blooded method of business employment agencies which took no interest in the workingman when once removed. Our method of establishing resident Jewish committees not only made a good impression but strengthened confidence in our good intentions. It must be explained that many could not at once grasp the idea that the I.R.O. was an institution which spent money without getting any returns. They suspected some "fake" scheme until reassured.

The territory I covered is the most prosperous in the United States, agriculturally and industrially. The towns and cities are pretty and clean, rents are low with one or two exceptions, and living expenses moderate. The Jewish workingman ought to be far happier there, than in the larger cities of the Eastern seaboard. One of the men we sent to Cedar Rapids came to me to the hotel and took me to the six room cottage he had just rented for $14.00 a month. He expected his family a few days later and in speaking of it wept for joy. Here are his words almost verbatim:

"I have been in New York seventeen years and this will be the first time my wife will be able to look upon something she can call home. Oh, yes,

I made a fair living in New York, that is worked six months and walked around another six, even saved a few hundred and then in the tenement where with the foul air and the germs of all diseases and the crowding and the absence of light, my children would one after the other fall victim to all the slum diseases and my few hundred dollars would go to the doctor. And at the end of the seventeen years what is my "tachlis" [end result]? I live in four rooms in Lewis St. on the fourth floor and pay $13.00 a month. Here, my children will have air, light, etc. etc."

When my work of canvassing the factories and trades was completed, I would call on one or several of the most prominent Jewish residents and set about forming local committees. Upon first broaching the subject I would usually encounter a feeling of distrust. As they expressed it, they had enough of itinerant "schnorrers" [beggars] already, the communal purse was small, etc. etc. Upon assuring them that our work would not entail any monetary sacrifice on their part, that we were not sending "schnorrers" but self-respecting workingmen who were coming, not to look for a job but to fill one, my path would become smoother. Sometimes I would be forced to advance to some of the stubborn or indifferent ones, the argument that they were not fulfilling their obligations to the Jewish People by merely attending to their parochial duties; and that the problem of New York Jewry was and ought to be the concern of the Jews of the entire country. A good talk invariably had the desired effect, and in quite a few cases an invitation was at once extended to deliver the same talk to the lodge or congregational meeting in the form of a lecture.

In centers, where removals had been made in the past, the complaint was sometimes voiced that the men didn't stick to their jobs for no valid reason, and would aggravate matters by disappearing and leaving behind them sundry unpaid bills. But on further investigation it was found that these men had been sent about five or six years ago, and to communities that offered little attraction, on account of the absence of any Jewish communal life. In centers where there is a well organized Jewish community, defections have been few. South Bend, Ind. having a population of 50,000, has a Russian Jewish community of about 1500, and even if some of the men we have sent out lose their original positions, they do not leave for other points, but work out their salvation right in South Bend. For the same reason, Peoria, also with a large Russian Jewish population, ought to be as good a center for distribution as South Bend. Evansville, Ind., Fort Wayne, Ind., the tri-cities of Moline, Ill., Rock Island, Ill., and Davenport, Ia., are also in this class.

As to the Removalities of the past, not very many have been sent to the territory I covered. Of the few cases which I could locate, one had left for Brooklyn, one for Indianapolis, and one for parts unknown. Max Zin of Huntington, Ind., sent there in 1905 is in the junk business and is prosperous. He has since married. A. Covnat of Streator, Ill. sent there in 1905 is working as a tinsmith and has been employed for the past four years in the same shop. He is making a fair living and is satisfied, except that his children cannot get any religious instruction, for there are few Jews in Streator and these few are members of the "Christian Liberal Church". Morris Lapper, of Evansville, Ind., sent there in 1903, worked two and a half years as a presser on overalls, suffered trials and tribulations during that time, opened up a little shop as a presser and cleaner and today is the proprietor of an "Emporium" and as he himself boasted with pride, he can buy $5,000.00 worth of goods on credit. He is willing to help anyone you may send to Evansville in the near future. Alexis Bagusin of Quincy, Ill., sent there twelve months ago by the Galveston Bureau is working in a plumber shop. Despite his residence of but one year in this country he answered my questions in faultless English (had attended Evening High School during the winter) and as an evidence of his rapid Americanization he informed me that he was now a full fledged member of the Illinois naval reserve, and more important still he is a good workingman and gives complete satisfaction to his employer. His brother, Matush Bagusin, whom we sent out to him last year is working as a tailor in St. Louis and is making a living.

Respectfully submitted,

Elias Margolis

LETTERS TO AND FROM ABRAHAM SOLOMON

Abraham Solomon worked as an IRO traveling agent during 1912–13, surveying towns in Alabama, Illinois, Indiana, North and South Carolina, Ohio, Tennessee, and Virginia.[23] The letters in this section concern Solomon's visit to Indianapolis, Indiana, and Danville, Illinois, in October 1912 and Birmingham, Alabama, in February 1913. The reports offer Solomon's impressions of these towns, their Jewish communities, their commitment to the ideals of the IRO, their conflicts, and their leaders. He also reiterates his philosophy of organizing IRO committees. His letters and David Bressler's responses offer insight into Solomon's character and biases. Solomon's report on Birmingham is noteworthy because it displays his attitude toward Birmingham's Jewish women and the Orthodox community.

The first item is a telegraph sent by David Bressler to Solomon, warning him about the agent in Indianapolis and asking him to use tact in dealing with the situation there. The two letters that follow are Solomon's report of what ensued once he got to town.

David Bressler had ongoing problems with the Indianapolis Jewish community. The New York office complained that Indianapolis was too demanding about the kind of applicants they would accept. The Indianapolis Jewish community, on the other hand, feared adding to its relief rolls and creating, as they said, "a New York problem" of their own. The community's German Jewish leaders worried that the growth of a foreign enclave of destitute Jews would make the non-Jewish community more anti-Semitic. Thus, they carefully specified the kinds of men they wanted to be sent. The following interchange reflects this tension.

At the time of Solomon's visit, Indianapolis's Jewish population stood at about 6,000 persons. More than 70 percent of this total were eastern European immigrants.[24]

* * *

New York, Sept. 28th, 1912

Mr. A. Solomon
c/o Claypool Hotel
Indianapolis, Ind.

Kaufman denies us exercise our discretion.[25] Insists our sending only identical applicants mentioned in applications first submitted. If applicant was single and we sent another married, though same trade and general industrial efficiency, he kicks because of family responsibility attached. Furthermore, while his requisitions read for skilled men, he always adds condition, "must be willing to do any other kind of work", which is improper and unfair to applicants who leave New York with idea of bettering themselves. Two excellent men sent back by him in last few months, at his insistence, and for no reason. Both men told us same story. Question Kaufman's sympathy; am persuaded he does as little as possible. Indianapolis Committee splendid gentlemen, fully sympathetic and eminently fair. Handle situation with delicacy and tact. Anderson, New Albany not organized, but follow judgment Indianapolis Committee in matter.

David M. Bressler

* * *

Indianapolis, Tuesday, Oct.1, 1912

Dear Mr. Bressler:

A two hour meeting to day. You know the Federation meets weekly. Present, Mr. Kahn, Mr. Kiser and Mr. Efroymson—also 2 federation men.[26] Two of our committeemen out of town.

They are all strong for Mr. Kaufman (who was present). A strong feeling that you raised a "tempest in a teapot."

Some of the arguments were of this order:

a) One man we sent was a consumptive

b) A large number of men were dependent

c) They determined to give us an example in the Katz case. Katz was a "shrimp", inefficient and would not accept a job Kaufman got for him at $8 per week. I don't believe Kaufman's statement.

d) They will refuse to give us cart blanche to unload "inefficient" people on them.

e) Our system is faulty. Indianapolis is not to blame.

f) When Kaufman adds the restriction that the applicant "must be willing to do any kind of work," his object was merely to quote our application which often states "willing to do any sort of work." (How specious!)

Their whole attitude was quibbling. Equivocating. I do not agree with you that these gentlemen are interested in our work.

Without arousing their antagonism, I forced from them the admissions:

1) that Kaufman was wrong in the Katz case, on the family question

2) That justice is not done to the present industrial opportunities of Indianapolis.

To do this, I had 2 days data, a wage scale, etc. There is an Employers Association here placing large numbers of men weekly. They said to me they are ready & willing to co-operate with us but Kaufman never came near them. I used this point to good advantage. Kaufman claims he requisitioned us for 15 men in August.

3) That Kaufman hedges us around with too many restrictions. Result: The committee agreed that all requisitions will come thro the committee & not thro Kaufman. That in asking for men, they will make *no restrictions* and that based on present conditions, they will absorb 10 a month.

(It would have been bad policy to request this understanding in writing, but Kahn will write you).

They would only think of severing Kaufman from the work, on condition that they wash their hands of the I.R.O.

My impression is that they are not sympathetic.—

Eventually might it not be wise to form a new committee distinct of the federation?[27] There is good soil for it here.

I made a good impression on Mr. Kahn and perhaps things will turn out better. Of one thing I am sure—there will be no more of the Kaufmanian restrictions.

What a wonderful opportunity this tour offers. I have nowhere seen such a wide demand for labor nor such a diversification of industries.

And to think that a set of men should take a narrow, local attitude in upholding Kaufman in general, going so far as to insist that he is one of the most sympathetic men, that he is a "father to the removals"!

It made me sick at heart.

I had the goods on them but was careful not to antagonize any one.

As for Kaufman, I consider him a bloated zero-mark. He accused us of trying to make records and said the vast majority of removals could do better in N.Y. That gave me a weapon and I used it. Throughout he squirmed and sweated—there is something cowardly sleek about him.[28]

From here I go to New Albany. I was advised to pass Anderson by.

Sincerely,
A. Solomon

* * *

Tuesday night

Dear Mr. Bressler:—

Under separate cover I mailed agreement with Indianapolis Committee.

After the meeting I had a long talk with Sol Kiser. A powerful remedy for the trouble he's in a source least expected.

I must repeat past history. The Federation was formed owing to the stimulus given Kiser by Max Senior & Cyrus L. Sulzberger.[29] Kiser was active in the Federation, but gradually made enemies. The Removal Committee was absorbed by the Federation, and Kiser was & is chairman only in name and not in fact.

As you know, the Executive Committee of the Federation handles removal work. They meet every Tuesday. And here is the anomalous situation. Kiser, the chairman of the Removal Committee has never been invited, nor has he attended, because he is not a member of the Executive Committee of the Federation!

He has only kept in touch with removal work when Kaufman comes to him with his troubles. Naturally Kiser never knew the facts, never had the means of testing Kaufman's work.

And Mr. Kiser feels he has been slighted and also feels that at last the wrong is to be redressed.

Firstly, he is absolutely to attend the meetings Tuesday; he agrees to keep tabs on Kaufman.

Secondly, he feels slighted that you never wrote to him, except when he wrote first.

If you will make him feel that he is really our chairman, I think you will work a transformation. I would write him stating that his attendance at the meetings, his weight, his office as chairman, etc., will mean the doing away with misunderstandings, restrictions, etc., and that greater results will be produced.

Kaufman made a bad break at the meeting. He blurted out the truth in saying, "The majority of people you send could do better in N.Y." And I shot back: "If you think *that*, how can you conscientiously remain on the

I.R.O. payroll." The committee felt embarrassed and Kiser was particularly annoyed.

To come back to the meeting. Kahn is docile, gentle and, I think, opinionless. He relies utterly on Efroymson.

Let me give you my impressions, psychologically. E. [Efroymson] is clever and something of a Philadelphia lawyer. When he saw things were going badly for Kaufman and that Kaufman was on trial, he switched and put the I.R.O. on trial. The others took the cue.

My belief as to the inside attitude of E. is this: He wants to utilize the $725 to maintain a Federation secretary and he is making a fool of us. He may talk of being anxious to further our cause, but when it came to "brass tacks" he was unmasked.

The antidote to Efroymson is Kiser, and Kiser must be nursed. I am convinced that wherever I.R.O. is a peg for a Federation secretary to hang his hat on, our work is nullified and, yes, prostituted. Now I realize the narrow escape I had in Columbus, when it came to the question of the Federation there handling our work.

I feel reasonably certain the restrictions here are a thing of the past. If not, give me a whack at them later on & *authority*. I would shut down on them, organize a mass meeting, proclaim how charity muzzled our work. The field here is fine. Many Jews are not aware of our work.

And if things don't improve here, then I shall ask, "How long, oh how long shall we bear the charity yoke."

Sincerely,
A. Solomon

*   *   *

October 7, 1912

Mr. A. Solomon

Dear Mr. Solomon:

I have your Indianapolis report: it does not make pleasant reading. I should hate to believe that your estimate of men in whom I have had the greatest confidence, is correct. I appreciate, of course, as in fact my letter of instructions to you frankly stated, that a $720. per annum contribution toward the salary of the Federation Secretary, is not an unimportant consideration in influencing the attitude of the Federation officers. But, I do not want to believe that this is the sole consideration.

Sol Kiser was chairman of the Removal Committee at one time, but was not appointed by us. He was selected by the Committee which was originally formed to take charge of our work. Since that time, the Federation has absorbed the activities of the Removal office, apparently with the consent of the original permit, for we have never had any protest that the work was taken away from them against their wish and consent. Hence, our dealings can be only with the Federation, the original Removal Committee is practically non-existent. Therefore, it can have no chairman.

Under any circumstances, however, it would be exceedingly rash, not to say dangerous tactics, to adopt your suggestions with regard to the use that should be made of Mr. Kiser; and I consider it a very doubtful method to make use of the man by feeding any grudge he may have, be it real, or fancied. All this, however, I will want to talk over with you upon your return to New York, and in the meantime, that we will endeavor to get the best cooperation possible. I have written Mr. Kahn, flatly rejecting their propositions. I will not be tied down by any specific orders for removals. It must be more general and allow us some discretion. We are not here in the capacity of an employment bureau to cater to the needs of individual employers. If we have to come to that, then we might as well call ourselves frankly an employment bureau and make a charge for our services for supplying workers, instead of paying an allowance with each man and having an employment agent who does not find employment for our men, but wants us to find the men for employers he wishes to favor. So far as the agent is concerned, I think that you have sized him up pretty well. To me he has always appeared smug, complacent and sanctimonious, with a vision that is all but broad and comprehensive. But I do not blame him, but rather the men responsible for it.

Very truly yours,
David Bressler

*　*　*

Oct. 13, 1912

Industrial Removal Office, N.Y.

Gentlemen:

I beg to advise you that there has been organized a Danville Committee of the Industrial Removal Office:

Chairman: N. J. Basch
Secretary: Samuel Levin

This committee agrees to absorb a minimum of 2 removals monthly into their community and to that end will submit monthly a report on industrial conditions to you. So that the removals made will best accord with local conditions.

Respectfully,
A. Solomon

*　*　*

Champaign, Ill., Oct 14,

1912 Gentlemen:

Danville Report

About 50 Jewish families. A Reform Temple being built. Rabbi Leipziger (of Terre Haute) comes to Danville twice a month. Many wealthy prominent Jews—but indifferent and of limited horizon. A B'nai B'rith organization

Contrary to the "prophets of evil," I had a good meeting.[30] Stimulating, because I could clearly see how the men before me are potential for real co-operation, if the start is right. I believe we have not had as much co-operation as we have a right to expect from many communities because the organization effected is indefinite—flabby, based on social visits, etc. Pinning them down to receiving a minimum monthly, is not sufficient by itself. There must be outlined to the committee a definite sample modus operandi and a stimulus to work. For example, I include in my agreement that the committee shall submit to us monthly an industrial report. Immediately the burden is put on them to meet. Then I base all my efforts on this: "A cynical, hard or indifferent man, who handles a removal, can not bring out the <u>potentiality</u> in that removal. Hence an indifferent man makes cooperation a failure. And I find out those who are really hard and of no imagination and do not get them on the committees.

I experienced a stroke of good luck. The secretary of the B'nai B'rith is secretary of the I.R.O. Committee. (The committee is not a B'nai B'rith affair exclusively). This man, Sam Levin, is a young lawyer and a brick. After the meeting, he made an appointment to see me at the hotel so that I could give him co-operation pointers. He spent 2 hours with me of his own accord. He volunteers to be "quasi-agent." I promised him you would write to him <u>how</u> to <u>present</u> the <u>industrial</u> <u>report</u>, <u>how</u> to <u>keep up the enthusiasm</u>, <u>how to instill into the committee the "co-operation habit</u>," etc. Address:

Sam Levin, Baum Bldg., Danville, Ill.

II
Industrial Conditions

a) a coal mining district
b) 2 of the largest brick concerns in the U.S.
c) Machine shops, Hardware—Sheet Metal Works, etc.
Mechanics most in demand:
a) Carpenters
b) Machinists (toolmakers)
c) Tinners

III
Personalities Committee Members

Sam Goldberg—Wholesale Liquor Business. Bluff-hearted. good-natured. Reliable

Sam Sincere—Restaurant—somewhat of a politician. A very fat man, hence very good natured. Strong on B'nai B'rith

Sam Zeppin—Big electrical shoe repairer—cobbling. Will requisition us for 6 men.

Louis Goldman & Joseph Blumberg—dry goods business—amiable— but harmless

Alphonse Mies—Leading merchant. Pillar of community. Suave (from Alsace-Lorraine)—powerful.

I. H. Louis—"Prince" of Danville. Wealthy merchant. Firm name Strauss-Louis. Way up in B'nai B'rith councils. Modest, etc.

James Greenebaum—*Royal Cloak Co.* Young—enthusiastic.

N. J. Basch—Committee Chairman. Owner of *"The Bell"* large dept. store. A hustler—one who is highly thought of and successfully handled previous removals.

Sam Levin—Secy. Already described

Jules Strauss—Mr. I. H. Louis's partner & a splendid man.

Otto Newman—Large clothing store. Self-made man. Came to Danville on a freight train 14 years ago with a button in his pocket. etc. etc. etc. Cum Laude

You may expect good results from Danville.

Respectfully,
A. Solomon

*   *   *

Birmingham, Ala. Feb. 21, 1913

Dear Mr. Bressler:

Attached is the Birmingham report.[31] Agreement under separate cover. With kind regards to all in the office, I remain

Sincerely,
A. Solomon

Report

a) Conditions

The Orthodox, because they have independent relief societies, demand recognition. Between them and the Reform Jews there is a dividing wall. The situation has reached a point where, when the Reformers have hit upon an available agent, the Orthodox have so discouraged the prospective appointee that he withdrew. In addition, I am given to understand that when a renewal comes here, the Orthodox make it unpleasant for him.

Of course, the Orthodox state their side of the case so that discredit should be thrown on the Reformers.

b) Diagnosis

The Orthodox wish to have the final say-so in the appointment of an agent. For them, the matter becomes one of intrigue and bargaining and I would consider it disastrous to our work if one of their "dependents" was made agent.

Procedure

Nevertheless I deemed it of prime consequence to give the Orthodox representation on the committee and to secure their good will. It is clear of question that their co-operation is imperative if the newcomer is to be successfully absorbed into the community. Therefore I have secured an Orthodox representation—comprising their leaders—Mr. Gingold, Mr. Roseman and Mr. Greenman.

On account of the fact that the present committee is moribund, I have thought it advisable to infuse new blood into it. And accordingly have added Mr. A. Leo Oberdorfer and Mr. Isidore Shapiro. The former is a lawyer; the latter is B'nai B'rith orator of District No. 7 and a brilliant young man—a lawyer, too.

Agent

There are many conflicting ideas on this subject. One plan is eventually to merge the secretaryship of the Y.M.H.A. and removal agent, and import a social worker.[32] After careful canvass of the field, I find no man available for the work, and who could be satisfactory to both factions. Again I turned to the women—and I found that only amongst them are social workers to be found. I also find them more aggressive, freer from entangling alliances, more intuitively sympathetic with the work. To these qualities must be added, however, practical sense and initiative—and I, accordingly, analysed the various candidates from these points of view.

I want to disclaim any over-zealousness on my part to draft the services of women, in absolute preference to men. In a community like this, however, I think an efficient woman agent the solution of the problem.

The agent I appointed is:

Miss Anna Shapiro

2109 8th Avenue

Birmingham, Ala

Please write her a stimulating letter and send her literature. She is at present a part-time school teacher and intends to resign her job before June. She always hankered for social work—but this tendency is not accompanied by the usual semi-hysterical idealism. She is practical; somewhat in the type of her brother; (Isidore Shapiro, referred to on page 2 & 3) and has the confidence of the Orthodox faction. Dr. Newfield is very enthusiastic about her; so is Bert Jacobs.[33] That augers well. I have an even higher opinion of her than I have of Miss Finkelstein of Nashville.[34]

The Meeting

Description

Present: Dr. Newfield, Mr. Jacobs, Mr. Leader, I. Gingold, M. Roseman, M. Greenman.

The latter three starkly rigid, expressionless. Dr. Newfield speaks, a conciliator. Bert Jacobs talks rattling good sense. Leader trails along. Then our Orthodox friends commence. They malign and abuse the I.R.O.; accuse us of wasting funds; advise us to use our money for farm propaganda. It is a combination of malice, stupidity and the stunted soul. It tests my last ounce of patience. Out of such as these is the higher man to emerge! To me they are atavistic. . . . I patiently start with the A.B.C. of my catechism. By the time I reach the letter M they feel a bit sheepish; at T they waver and by Z they recant.

The committee is re-organized. Chairman, Dr. B. Newfield; Secretary, Benj. Leader; Treasurer, M. Roseman. It is agreed to receive 6 removals monthly. Agent's salary, $40. It is agreed that the industrial report be adopted—but conjointly with this, the permission system is to continue until Miss Shapiro will give up school work. Everything is can work. Yet I suspect these Orthodox and think these men are unreliable. Time will tell. The only hope I have lies in Miss Shapiro. The permission system she will not insist on—thinking it red tape—and she will try to make her reports so timely that the men we send answer the purpose.

Respectfully submitted,
Abraham Solomon

* * *

Birmingham, Ala. Feb. 21, 1913

Industrial Removal Office
174 Second Avenue
New York City

Gentlemen:

I beg to advise you of the re-organization of the Birmingham Committee of the Industrial Removal Office, as follows:

Chairman—Dr. M. Newfield
Secretary—Benj. Leader
Treasurer—M. Roseman
Members—Bertman Jacobs, I. Gingold, M. Greenman.

This committee agrees to make effort to receive 6 direct removals monthly (one of which is to be a family) for the purpose of absorbing them into the community.

The agent appointed is Miss Anna Shapiro, 2109 8th Ave., Birmingham, and her salary is to be $40.00 monthly, conditioned on her satisfactory placing in work six removals monthly.

This committee agrees that the basic method of the co-operation between them and the Industrial Removal Office is to be the Industrial Report, which means that the agent is bound to bi-monthly send you a detailed industrial report on the basis of which you are to select removals; and that along with this new method, applications are to be submitted to the agent (such applications based on the report) for her action, no removals to be sent only on application. This submitting of applications is to be continued until the committee feels that conditions warrant the use of the industrial report method solely.

Very respectfully yours,
Abraham Solomon

Confirmed by Birmingham Committee,
through Benj. Leader, Secretary

* * *

Feb. 24", 1913

Mr. A. Solomon
c/o The Lanier
Macon, Ga.

Dear Mr. Solomon:

I have the agreement of the Birmingham community, and your very interesting explanatory letter. I feel that you have done very good work in Birmingham, and I hope that the fears expressed by you as to the ultimate outcome of the Birmingham agreement will prove unfounded. Nevertheless, I must say that the written modification contained in the agreement virtually places us at the mercy of the committee's whim. The only fixed thing that I see in the agreement is the agent's salary of $40. a month. Otherwise, the agreement is, 1—"to make effort", and 2—"no removals to be sent only on application". Whenever you find yourself powerless to commit a community to definite fixed cooperation, it would be proper that agent's salary be pro-rated; for instance—if the agreement is to take six per month upon a salary of $40. to the agent, three per month should only call for $20 compensation. Otherwise there is no incentive for the agent to work as our champion, except, of course, when a strong, conscientious person is in charge. Even, on this, I would not care to rely too much, because such a person after all is under the more immediate pressure and influence of the local committee.

I want to say here a word on the subject of agent's salary in Southern agencies. Mr. Seman and I have discussed and considered this question, and we are both of the opinion that the value of cooperation from this section of the country has not, from former experience, indicated that a salary of $40. can be earned—that is, for the entire year. Some months a community may take the full quota, but the chances are that the average for the year will be considerably less than the quota agreed upon. Therefore, I believe that wherever possible, the pro-rate system of compensation should be specified and agreed upon. Furthermore, I think a salary of $25. per month, particularly in the instance of a woman, should be the starting point. There will then be an incentive for the agent to make effort to work up to a higher salary. In stating my opinion here, I am not speaking academically, since I have a fairly good knowledge of the Southern communities.

Dr. Newfield and Mr. Jacobs are two of our old stand-bys in Birmingham, and you did well to make one or the other the Chairman of our Committee. Our Orthodox friends in Birmingham have no reason to complain of their treatment by the I.R.O. since every successive committee that has been in charge of the Removal work has always had Orthodox representation thereon. The committee that I last formed some two years ago, numbering eleven persons, had five Orthodox members, but as a matter of fact, when it came to the real work, it was always left to some two or three men—not the Orthodox members of the committee. Our Orthodox brethren in the South, as is not infrequently the case in other sections of the country, evince a disposition to vent their ire against the Reformed members of the community on the I.R.O. simply because the Reformed element has actually done the Removal work. Therefore, I suggest that you do not hurry your stay in any town. Remain a day or two longer, and propitiate and gratiate, pat on the back, and create a spirit of good feeling; let them understand what we are after, and let them feel, if necessary, that upon them rests the responsibility, and the consequences if this responsibility is not properly accepted. I know how it tries one's patience to have to listen to the silly objections of some would-be leaders, but that's all a part of the day's work. You have properly gotten in that frame of mind where you expect this sort of thing and are disappointed when it fails to materialize. In a way, however, this opposition is a good thing, because it gives the opportunity for a thorough thrashing out of differences, and to set ourselves right before them. Let this then be the value that you attach to opposition; rather that, than indifference.

With kindest regards to you, and with best wishes, believe me,

Very sincerely yours,
David Bressler

CHAPTER 2

Letters from Communities

Despite the fact that most communities agreed to cooperate with the IRO, disputes between them and the New York office periodically arose. In most cases, the disputes centered around a removal or removals that the IRO had sent to the host community. The three items included in this section—from Atlanta, Georgia; Lafayette, Indiana; and Los Angeles, California—epitomize the type of mail the IRO received from Jewish communities around the United States.

The first series of letters—between Isaac Springer, a leading figure in Atlanta's Jewish community, and David Bressler—illustrates how misunderstandings could arise.[1] The exchange begins in acrimony and ends on a note of reconciliation.

At this time, Atlanta's population exceeded 150,000, of whom 3,000 were Jews. Economically, most of the city's Jews occupied white-collar positions. The Jewish community supported three Orthodox and one Reform Jewish congregations as well as a number of philanthropic, social, and fraternal organizations. The Atlanta Jewish community of that day was deeply divided along ethnic lines—Russian and German. Although representatives of both groups worked together on the boards of the local Jewish charities, they rarely mixed socially.[2]

LETTERS TO AND FROM ISAAC SPRINGER,
ATLANTA, GEORGIA

June 12, 1913

Industrial Removal Office
New York.

Gentlemen:

I received your letter of June 10th and I am a little surprised with your answer.[3] You write that I should raise ten dollars (10.00). Ten dollars for what? If I want Mr. Dorf here, it would not take much more than that to send him here by boat. But I do not need him here so badly. From the way it looks to me you have a money making business there. I always understood that this was a charity institution, and you are the one employee to use common judgement. It seems that unless the man has pull with you he has to stay in New York and suffer. With you it is nothing but a little fun. As the old saying goes, "Charity begins at home" and we have all we can attend to here. Besides we give our own charity here and when it is necessary to send anyone away or help that one, which we do every day in the year. If anyone is worthy we help him.

We have a society here of which I have been a director a number of years and I know as much about it as the next man.

I do not care to go in to much discussion about it but I may be in New York the next month and have a chance to explain a little more about it. You may have Mr. Dorf if you need him, I do not. I simply would have assisted the man to make a living, when here. This reminds me of Mrs. Silver, when you asked me to sign notes for her.

I did not know you had a bank with the Removal Office.

Yours respectfully,
I. Springer

* * *

June 17, 1913

I. Springer
95 Whitehall Street
Atlanta, Ga.

Dear Sir:

We are in receipt of your letter of the 12th instant and marvel at its contents. Not only are the statements therein not warranted by the facts, but the manner of expressing yourself is distinctly out of place, not to say offensive. Let us look into the facts. Solomon Dorf, a young man of 34 applies to us for transportation to Atlanta, Ga. to join a brother-in-law, Sam Gershon, the latter in business for himself. We would have been perfectly justified in rejecting this application altogether, for it would appear that a man in business should not desire so close a relative as a brother-in-law to apply to a philanthropic institution for assistance. However, we took into consideration the position of the applicant himself, feeling that he should not be made to suffer for the indifference of his better-to-do relatives, and asked that the latter pay a contribution of $10. toward defraying the expense of transportation. What is unfair about this? Your complaint seems to be that we are making money out of the transaction. Do you really believe that? If you do, we are perfectly willing to let you take advantage of the following proposition: if you will underwrite our business to the extent of paying the transportation of every applicant who desires to go to Atlanta, we will see to it that a $10. contribution is made for every ticket that is needed, and we will then turn over whatever profits remain to your account. Or, still better, we will let you underwrite our entire business to all parts of the country, and turn over such contributions as we may receive plus profits. You ought to accept this offer without hesitation, since you believe that on a contribution of $10. toward a ticket to Atlanta we are making money.

But I do not believe that you meant all you said in your letter. Possibly you were not feeling quite right, and I suppose every man gets out of gear once in a while and says things which he would not say if he felt perfectly well. At any rate, there are men in your community who know us well, even if you do not, and who will tell you, if you will show them your letter to us of the 12th instant, that you have not acted nicely. Ask Mr. Isaac Schoen or Leonard Haas, Leon Eplan, Dr. Wildauer, and a dozen others in your community, about us, and see if they think that we are a money making institution.

I agree with you that "Charity begins at home", but is not a brother-in-law a part of the home? Furthermore, we did not ask your Federation to contribute. We only asked a brother-in-law, who is in business for himself, to do his duty—not charity—by his poorer relative.

You say that unless a man has a "pull" with us he must remain in New York and suffer. Well, we have sent away about 70,000 people since we have been in existence. Do you think that all these 70,000 had a "pull" with us? Come to think of it, I guess they had—the "pull" of merit. But don't you really believe that Mr. Dorf should have even greater "pull" with his own brother-in-law so that it would be unnecessary to exercise "pull" with us?

If you will tell us that Mr. Gershon really cannot afford to pay $10. toward the transportation of his brother-in-law, we will send him on without a contribution, as we have done thousands of times before with other worthy applicants. Please remember that we are trying to do our duty as we see it and that it is absolutely our duty to get a contribution where one can be paid, so that it may be applied for other applicants who cannot contribute anything at all. Surely, you do not believe that our funds are inexhaustible and that all we have to do is to draw a check to cover the demands and requirements of everyone who comes along without regard to the ability of the applicants or their relatives to help themselves to some extent.

You come to New York occasionally, so you ought to know what a ticket costs from Atlanta to New York. The same rate applies from New York to Atlanta and yet you think we are making money when we ask for a contribution of $10. toward purchasing a ticket from New York to Atlanta! It may be that it does not cost much more by boat, but we do not send applicants who desire to go to Atlanta by boat, because they object, as a rule, to the longer trip and possible sea-sickness.

Mr. Dorf belongs less to us than he belongs to Mr. Gershon, and he is not in our way. Nevertheless, we are trying to help, but you feel disposed to make a personal matter of it because you say you did not need Mr. Dorf. We never thought you did, but we were told by Mr. Dorf that his relatives wanted him. So what have you to do with it?

The concluding paragraph of your letter convinces me that you were not quite yourself when you wrote it. When did we ever ask you to sign notes for Mrs. Silver? On April 19th you wrote us enclosing a check for $5. on account of a $20. indebtedness which she incurred at the time we sent her and the children to Atlanta. We acknowledged receipt on the 24th and informed you that we would make similar acknowledgement to Mr. Silver. On June 5th you wrote us as follows: "Write me about Mrs. Silver and I will try and get more money for you."—to which we replied in our letter of the 10th that there is $15. due us on a note made by Mrs. Silver and expressing the hope that you will be able to collect it for us. From where on earth did you get the idea, then, that we asked you to sign notes for her? Your cooperation in this Silver matter was purely voluntary on your part and we were very grateful for it. You took the initiative and not we. You seem to believe that you are branding us something awful when you conclude your letter with the statement that you did not know that we have a bank with the Removal Office. Why bank? If an applicant, in order to maintain her self-respect, desires to make some form of indebtedness for money advanced to her, would you deny that privilege? You are in business—in the cloak and suit business, I believe. Have you never taken notes from customers of yours for money that they owe you? Would you, on that account, say that you are conducting a banking business? Although, to tell you frankly, I think a banking business a fine thing and I only wish that I really had one.

No, my dear Mr. Springer, you have not been fair, and I trust to your good common sense to acknowledge it.

Yours truly,
David Bressler

*   *   *

June 19, 1913

Industrial Removal Office
New York

Gentlemen:

Your long letter, which is hardly necessary, received.

In looking over my copy written to you, I find it is not so bad and I do not see where I have anything to take back. I also assure you that I was myself. It seems that is a typical expression. Besides, you can express your opinion, so can I. As for the reference you gave me to these gentlemen, Dr. Wildauer, Schoen, Eplan, I know them well. Raised up with them here in Atlanta. As for your making money is concerned, I have not said that exactly. And people having a pull with you, I still stick to that, notwithstanding your 70,000 which you have sent away. Why did I say that? I had good reason and you will acknowledge that I am right.

Several months ago, we had a prisoner, of your city, in the Federal Prison. He left a wife and two children in your city. When the time came for the prisoner to go out, with the little acquaintance, he showed me the letters from his wife, in which she had been running to the Removal Office for a long time and the answer she received was that she must give some money before they could send her away. Of course she did not have any one to give anything for her and he came to me to help him out. I told him that I would be in New York soon and see if I can help send his wife to Atlanta. Some gentleman investigated this. I know him well but cannot recall his name. I had a long talk with him and after I explained things to him, he wanted me to endorse notes to the amount of $20.00. Of course, I as a businessman explained that I could not do so but I assured him that, if these people make good he would get the $20.00 back, on which I have sent $5.00 already. I will also attend to the balance. He perhaps joked about endorsing.

Now let us go back to Samuel Dorf and his brother-in-law. I am well acquainted with his brother-in-law and I tried my very best to get him to bring him over. He was also in New York not long ago and met Dorf. He told him, "You cost me enough and you won't get another cent out of me," and he sticks to his word. As for my saying that you make $10.00 off each ticket, I did not say that. That is the only thing I did not say. The balance I stick to. I have not acted for any selfish motive. You might be a bigger man than I am but when it comes down to straightness I will prove to you by the same people to whom you have referred me, also to thousands of people in New York with whom I have been dealing for numbers of years. Ask Judge Sanders, around your neighborhood. He might tell you something about me. As you state in your letter I was not myself, as there are no facts whatever. From now on I will try to attend strictly to my own business and let you attend to yours. I remain,

Respectfully,
I. Springer

* * *

June 23, 1913

Mr. I Springer
95 Whitehall Street
Atlanta, Ga.

Dear Sir:

Your favor of the 19th received. I fear nothing will be gained by further correspondence and since you occasionally come to New York, might I suggest that you pay us the honor of a visit. I am sure a little personal chat will go far to removing any misunderstanding which may exist at the present time.

With much good will,

Yours very truly,
David Bressler

* * *

June 23, 1913

David M. Bressler, Mgr.
Industrial Removal Office
174 2nd Ave.
New York

My Dear Sir:

I noticed your signature under that long letter, so I decided not to deal with the whole company any more but direct with you. You, I do not need to ask anyone about. I know you personally and I talked to you and cannot say anything else of you but that you are a gentleman. I do not want any more long letters, neither do I want any hard feelings, as with me it is no personal matter, whatever. Another thing, for three or four times I tried to help somebody with someone's charity, which no man ought to do. A man ought to do that himself, as I have done in many instances, and it pays better in the long run and thus avoids all hard feelings. I also intend to do that from now on.

As far as my business is concerned, I assure you, business which figures up thousands of dollars a year and hundreds of people interested in it, and still it does not bring me to such an embarrassing position in which both you and I were placed. We will therefore call it all off. When I will be in New York, and see you personally, then we might understand each other better.

Inclosed please find check for five dollars (5.00) for which you will kindly send receipt to Mr. Silver. He certainly has made good, better than anyone of all those whom you have sent already.

As for being myself, I am not myself, this time, as I am with a pretty office girl, to whom I am dictating this letter. Of course you cannot call that being by myself?

From what I can see we have no business to fight around especially at this time, when our Atlanta people are full of trouble with a serious murder case charged to one of our finest young men.[4]

A case which every Jew is interested in and worried by and all are waiting with the greatest patience for the trial which comes off on the 30th of this month and hope that his and his family's name will be cleared.

I remain,

Yours truly,
I. Springer

*   *   *

June 26, 1913

Mr. I. Springer
95 Whitehall St.
Atlanta, Ga.

Dear Sir:

I have your valued favor of the 23rd instant with check for $5. from Mr. Silver on account of his indebtedness, for which I thank you very much. I have acknowledged receipt to him as suggested by you.

By this time you have probably received my letter of the 23rd. Your present letter anticipates the suggestion I made therein, namely, that next time you are in New York you give us the pleasure of calling, when I am sure you and we will understand each other thoroughly.

With kind regards and with real appreciation of your friendly tone, I am,

Yours very truly,
David Bressler

LETTERS TO AND FROM SAM ROSTOFF, LAFAYETTE, INDIANA

In this letter of complaint, Sam Rostoff, a Lafayette businessman and community leader, indicates that the community tried helping the removals but that after accepting the community's largesse all of them left.[5] David Bressler follows Rostoff's suggestion and writes to the local Orthodox congregation to learn about the situation. At the time of the correspondence, the Lafayette Jewish community numbered about 350 persons out of a general population of 25,000. It contained one Orthodox and one Reformed congregation, two fraternal organizations, and one social club.[6]

Lafayette, Ind. March 18, 07

Dear Sirs of the Removal Off.

Accidently, I received a pamphlet, of your office, in which you briefly describe the noble work of your society, and the letters of thanks you received from people sent out. How astonished were we, when reading the letter of Rev. Gershuny in reference to the Klimovitzky family, namely that one of the sisters married a rich junk dealer.[7]

Let me tell you that all the people sent here, from the first to the last, were all a burden to the community. As it happened to Gershuny's brother-in-law Max Ness and his family. They were sent here by your office and then the community here sent them back to N.Y. And now I heard that your office is sending them here again. All sent here by your office have left for some other place.

When the Klimovitzky family arrived here, they received from our community 30 dollars in cash, furnished rooms and a month's free groceries. The mother drove the daughter out of her house because she was out of work. She was fortunate enough to become acquainted with one named Mendel Rabiner, a rags peddler 35 years of age. If he earns a dollar or more he is satisfied. He does not care to become rich. And to all this his physiognomy causes people to lock their houses.

The ceremony was performed by Dr. Morganstern of the German

Temple and Dr. Gershuny was not even admitted to attend them, because we all know him well here.

To inform you of all scandals that took place on account of the people sent here would be enough to fill a journal.

Klimovitzky left for Columbus, Shapiro for Minneapolis and the 4 young men for Chicago. To ascertain all details, kindly apply to the "Congregation Bnei Abraham", 9 & Main Sts—or to Jacob Prellman, Sec'y 15" St.

Respectfully,
Sam Rostoff

* * *

March 26th, 07

Congregation B'nei abraham
9th & Main Streets
Lafayette, Ind.

Dear Sirs:—

We beg to enclose a letter sent to us. Will you please let us know the situation in your City.

Your attention will be appreciated.

Yours very truly,
David Bressler

LETTER FROM THE WORKMAN'S CIRCLE
OF LOS ANGELES, CALIFORNIA

The following letter, written in Yiddish, was sent to the IRO by the Arbeiter Ring of Los Angeles, California.[8] Formed in New York in 1892 as a mutual-aid society, the Arbeiter Ring, or Workman's Circle, sought to foster socialism and Yiddish culture among workers. To achieve this goal, it conducted a program of educational, social, and recreational activities for its members and created a network of Yiddish afternoon schools for their children. By 1910, the Workman's Circle boasted 10,000 members and branches all across the United States.[9] One was in Los Angeles.

The letter writers complain that the IRO sends men without first inquiring whether there are jobs available, thus causing them great suffering. The writers threaten to expose the IRO for the harm it causes the Jewish working man.

Los Angeles in 1910 housed about 10,000 Jews out of a total population of approximately 530,000. The city contained three B'nai B'rith lodges; three Jewish charitable associations; and one Orthodox, one Reform, and one Conservative synagogue.[10]

October, 1910

Report and Resolutions of Branch 248 Arbeiter Ring of Los Angeles, California in regard to Removal Office work in Los Angeles.

At our meetings, four persons appeared accusing the Removal Office for having sent them to Los Angeles and promising to give them work, and also to supply them with everything necessary until work is found for them. Arriving in Los Angeles they have met peculiar difficulties such as going around without work besides not having a cent in their pockets. The promises of the Removal Office have resulted in nothing. The agent not only did not supply them with work, but he saw no chances of finding work for them in the near future. They actually had nothing to live upon.

They have, therefore, applied to us with the request that our branch do something in this regard. We have listened to their serious story and have appointed a committee to make investigations. After a thorough investigation that lasted several weeks, the committee at one of our special meetings for this purpose reported the result of their investigations. It is as follows: that the Removal Office has promised those people steady work and good wages. These promises have not been fulfilled. Not one of those sent here found work. The promise to supply them with all the necessaries until they find work has also not been fulfilled. If it were not for the charities which assisted them, they would have died of hunger. When the agent was asked to give these people work, his answer was that the local Removal Office no longer exists and that he can do nothing for them. Our branch therefore requested the agent to appear at our special meeting, and through a series of questions we found the following: that the N.Y. Removal Office has not even once inquired whether there is work in Los Angeles for the people sent here. That the local office had never written to the N.Y. office that there is no work to be found. That the Los Angeles committee, consisting of the most prominent people, took no interest in these men and had not held a single meeting throughout its existence.[11] And that the agent had no prospect of finding work for anybody.

Our committee applied to the Chairman and Secretary requesting that the men who are here should be supplied with work. They promised us to call a meeting of their entire committee, but we have heard nothing of it. Neither have any of the men been supplied with work. Their secretary stated that people are being sent from N.Y. despite their protest. This contradicts the statements of your agent at our meeting. Besides, the secretary had expressed himself very badly calling those men professional schnorrers [beggars]. It was clearly seen that in his heart there was not a spark of sympathy for the sufferers. The chairman also had shown indifference to the entire matter. The entire thing seems to be a toy to those prominent people.

Briefly speaking, we have seen that we cannot expect gratitude from the committee and we have therefore decided to publish all the facts. We admit the usefulness in bringing together members of families by assisting them with money. Such people have good friends or relatives in places to which they desire to be sent. However, in regard to their activity in sending Jewish workingmen to the far west, they [the IRO] are not only incompetent but they also commit an injustice through misleading advertisememts.

The Removal Office separates hundreds of friends and sends them to the far west where they actually starve and where they are compelled to apply to the charities for assistance. When this takes place, they are classified as professional schnorrers. Those tragic incidents that begin in N.Y. and end in the far west will only continue until public opinion is strong enough to put a stop to them.

We, as a progressive workingmen's association, protest against such terrible events and we request that every organization who has the workingmen's interests at heart to arouse a terrific protest and compel the gentlemen of the Removal Office no longer to play with the lives of hundreds of workingmen. We also apply as a branch of the Arbeiter Ring to all the branches and to the general executive to bring this most important question at their meeting. This question should be nearer to the Arbeiter Ring than any other organization.

Copies of these explanatory resolutions have been sent to the Forwarts, Frei Arbeiter Shtimme, Arbeiter, Chicago Jewish Workingmen's World, to the General Executive of the Arbeiter Ring, and also to the General Removal Office, N.Y.[12]

CHAPTER 3

Letters from Local Agents

Although the IRO subsidized most local agents, they resided in the town and had been recommended—and frequently chosen—for the post by the local Jewish leadership. Sometimes the local representative was a communal leader or prominent businessman who served on a voluntary basis. Consequently, the agent's primary loyalty was to his city and its Jewish community. This resulted in perceptions and objectives different from those of the New York office and sometimes led to clashes. The selections here portray the local method of operation, typifying the problems representatives encountered and the rancor that could erupt between them and the New York office.

LETTERS TO AND FROM SAMUEL LEVY, BLOOMINGTON, ILLINOIS

During the first year of the IRO's operation, the Jewish community of Bloomington, Illinois, agreed to received one or two removals every month.[1] To this end, the local B'nai B'rith chapter established a board to oversee the operation. Samuel Levy, a businessman, civic leader, and vice president of the Bloomington Bureau of Associated Charities, chaired this committee. In August 1901, the IRO sent Joe Mellinkopff, a laborer, to Bloomington. Two months later it shipped another laborer, John Weinberg. Neither man proved satisfactory. Levy's correspondence with the IRO describes the difficulties with the men and illustrates the problems that local communities could encounter.

David Bressler had not yet been hired to manage the IRO, and George David, a social worker, was engaged as temporary superintendent. David worked out of the IRO's first office, a rented store at 34 Stanton Street in New York. At this early phase, the IRO had not made any surveys of Jewish communities.

August 21, 1901

Supt. Industrial Removal Office
34 Stanton Street
New York

Dear Sir:

I beg to state that Joe Mellinkopff arrived here on Friday morning, August 16th. He was sent the same day to American Stove and Foundry Co. where he was told to come to work next morning. He worked Saturday and I was promptly informed his work as laborer was satisfactory and he received $1.40 for his service. Monday he came to me and said he could not stand the iron dust as it affected his heart, and he had been examined by a physician who gave him some medicine (which was shown to me). I was subsequently informed the physician said there was nothing wrong with him, but gave him drops to humor him.

He [Joe] wanted transportation to Chicago when I next saw him on Tuesday. I sent him to the Hon. S. Livingston [the local B'nai B'rith president] and it was arranged he should go on a farm near here owned by Mr. Abe Livingston, and he expressed himself as pleased with this arrangement. This morning he came to me and said he did not want to go to the farm and work for $6.00 a month, and on my refusing to give him transportation to Chicago, wanted me to procure him goods to go peddling with. I went with him to S. Livingston's office and he repeated his refusal to go to the farm, although assured by us he would receive compensation commensurate with his work. (Farm laborers here earn from $15.00 to 22.00 per month.) He then threatened us to publish in the papers that we brought him here from New York and then failed to provide for him. He was then told if he repeated this, he would be put in jail at once. He was again told to go to the farm and show by his work what he was worth and he would get all he was entitled to. He left the office.

We later ascertained that there had been no definite wages settled upon at all, the intention being to pay him a liberal wage, and the $6.00 was his own creation.

I was informed this evening by Charley Glickstein, with whom he came here from your office, that he had received $1.50 from sympathizers on the train from New York here, and therefore had about $3.00, and had arranged with a conductor of a freight train to carry him to Chicago for $1, and that he had therefore left Bloomington.

> Very respectfully yours,
> Samuel Levy
> 815 E. Jefferson Str.
> Bloomington, Ill.

*   *   *

Aug. 24, 1901

Mr. Samuel Levy
#815 E. Jefferson St.,
Bloomington, Ill.

Dear Sir:—

In reply to your favor of the 21st, inst., we beg to say that we regret very much the trouble and inconvenience you were put to by Joe Mellinkopff, and we admire very much that stand you took, when you told him as you stated in your letter, that unless he behaved himself you would put him in jail, which by all means would of been nothing but the proper action to take if he showed no signs of taking proper advantage of the interest you intended to take in him.

According to your statement that his work as a laborer was satisfactory and the doctor said there was nothing the matter with him, there is no reason why he should not of continued working especially after having been in New York without any employment for some time. We must of course say that the recommendation we received about him was A-1, which prompted us to send him to you.

We endeavor in all cases to be as careful as possible in selecting the men upon the requisitions we receive, but you will no doubt admit that things like these will occur after they once leave the city, for which we hope you will not put blame on us.

In reference to your belief that he has gone or is going to Chicago, we think it extremely necessary, and if you will allow us to suggest to you to report this man at once to the United Hebrew Charities of Chicago, so that he may not impose upon them.

> Yours very truly,
> INDUSTRIAL REMOVAL OFFICE
> per
> George David

*   *   *

815 E. Jefferson Str. Bloomington, Illinois, Oct. 20th, 1901

George G. David Esq. Supt
Industrial Removal Office
59 Second Avenue.
New York—

My Dear Sir:—

Referring to John Weinberg, who presented your letter of the 10th inst. to me, on the morning of Oct. 12th. After giving him breakfast, I procured employment for him at the Phenix Nurseries and gave him car fare to go there with a letter of introduction. On Tuesday morning, Oct. 15th, he came to me and reported he had not worked Saturday, but did work Monday. Was to receive $1.25 per day. Work consisted of pulling up trees and digging in the ground. He said the work was too hard for him and hurt his hands, and he would not work there—and asked for transportation to Chicago. This of course I refused and told him Chicago had plenty poor and unemployed. I advised him to return to his work and with $7.50 per week and board costing him 3.00 to 3.50, he could soon save some money, and also acquire the English language, and as he became accustomed to the work he would find it easier. I told him we had no light work to give him but if he could find it for himself he could do so, but he could get neither assistance or transportation from me or my associates and strongly advised him to go back to the nurseries and resume his work there. He did not go there and I have neither seen him or heard from him since, and presume he has left the city voluntarily.

We are therefore in a position to accept another man from your office, and again require that you send a man physically able and willing to do manual labor. You doubtless understand that we cannot find light employment for an absolute stranger, whereas laborers employment we can easily supply.

If these people were sincere in their desire to work for a living and content themselves with future advancement I can see no reason why our work should fail in good results.

I have written you complete reports on all thus far received from your office, and if I or my committee have erred or you can suggest better methods for our handling them, we would be pleased to have you do so. I know your sending them here is quite an expense and are anxious that you should be rewarded with some good results, and to that end I have recommended that we continue sending for them, one at a time. Please have, whoever you send, distinctly understand what he is to expect here, viz., reasonably hard work at not less than $1.25 per day, with board and lodging to cost 3.00 to 3.50 per week, so that he cannot reproach either your office or my committee here, if we have nothing better to give him. Work as above we can easily furnish without delay—

Yours truly
Samuel Levy

*   *   *

Oct. 23, 1901

Mr. S. Levy,
815 East Jefferson St., Bloomington, Ill.

Dear Sir:—

In reply to your favor of Oct. 20th we beg to say that we are sincerely sorry that you have again had trouble with the man, John Weinberg. At the same time we wish to state that we admire the stand you take in this case in refusing transportation to N.Y. or to any other city, while the opportunity is offered by you to work and make a living. He understood fully what to expect in your town before leaving here.

He was out of work here for some time and begged most urgently to be sent away, claiming that he could not make a living and that starvation was staring him in the face. Consequently no transportation whatever, particularly to N.Y. should be granted to him by anybody.

We have complied with your request to send another man who will leave to-day. This man has a family in N.Y. and we think for that reason already, he will take better advantage of your kindness.

Thanking you most sincerely for your kind co-operation in our work, we remain,

Yours very truly,
INDUSTRIAL REMOVAL OFFICE
per
George David

LETTERS TO AND FROM JACOB FURTH, CLEVELAND, OHIO

Bohemian-born Jacob Furth (1844–1918) was a succesful wholesale grocer and communal leader.[2] He functioned as a national officer in the B'nai B'rith and was active in Jewish and non-Jewish charitable and civic organizations.[3] He also served on the national Removal Committee of the IRO, a body consisting of prominent American Jewish leaders who monitored the work of the IRO and saw to its funding.[4]

At this time, Cleveland's Jewish population numbered about 35,000 out of a general population of more than 450,000. The city contained two Reformed and twenty-six Orthodox Jewish congregations as well as a variety of philanthropic, fraternal, social, and Zionist organizations and a Jewish newspaper.[5]

January 5th, 1906

Mr. Jacob Furth
Cleveland, Ohio

Dear Sir:—

I have your favor of Dec. 30th enclosing expense account, and receipted bills for December. I am amazed at the size of the Goldstein family bill. I realize of course, that you blame us very largely for the size of this bill, but I maintain that possibly outside of the board bill for the first six days which amounts to $30.00, not another cent should have been spent by our office for them. If Mr. Goldstein was not in a position to pay rent for his family and could not get along with the furniture he had, it was the business of Mr. Richter [Furth's associate in removal work] to know that he had no right under the circumstances to tell us to send them. We are not called upon in other agencies to make an expenditure of a single penny in request cases. St. Louis takes them regularly, and we have never yet had to pay a cent for any expenditures the local community may have incurred after they reached their destination. As a matter of fact, we are not asked to pay more than $25.00 for any family sent on as a *direct* case, and here we have been put to an expense of $83.72 for one request case.

I note one bill for $17.70 of which $16.00 is for twenty-eight days' board for Ben Balamut. The receipt is dated December 31st, and upon looking up our record of this man, we find that he was sent by us on December 6th, so that he probably arrived in your city on the morning of December 8th. It would appear therefore, that he was only twenty-three days in your city at the time that the receipt was given for twenty-eight days' board. Will you kindly have Mr. Richter explain. Furthermore, I cannot understand why four weeks' board is given to this young man. He is a cloak operator and since Mr. Richter's ability at obtaining work has been advanced as a reason for his retention at a salary in excess of any that we pay to any other agent, I cannot help expressing my disapproval of this bill. If Richter could not find Balamut a position at his own trade, he should have found him something else, and if Balamut refused to accept work at anything else, there was no justification to continue paying board for him under the circumstances.

I do not wish to appear as though I were constantly criticising, but I think I ought to call your attention, particularly as you are a member of the Removal Commmittee, to the fact that in the matter of per capita expenditure, Cleveland compares unfavorably with other agencies; for instance, the per capita in Cincinnati is $15.02

Milwaukee	20.00
Detroit less than	15.00
Birmingham less than	$15.02
Rochester about	14.00
St. Louis about	16.00
Indianapolis about	$13.00
South Bend about	8.00, whereas in

Cleveland it is $26.83, this of course, exclusive in all cases of railroad transportation.

We beg to return the receipt from Goldstein for $8.00, which amount you say will be refunded by him to you.

Very truly yours,
David Bressler

* * *

January 10, 1906

Mr. David Bressler
#174 Second Avenue
New York, N.Y.

Dear Sir:—

I have your favor of the 5th inst.
I have not answered it until I had made a most careful investigation. I am now prepared to say the following:

The gist of this matter lies in the letter which Mr. Richter wrote to you at the time you asked whether or not to send the Goldstein family. Mr. Richter has no copy of that letter as he wrote it at his home, and I am therefore unable to tell whether or not he carried out my instructions.

My instructions to him were and are, never to commit this office to the sending of anybody here. He is instructed to give you all the facts in the case as we have them and to leave in your hands the responsibility of either sending or not sending the people as in your judgment you may see fit to do. This is a responsibility which you must bear.

You are engaged by the Removal Office for your intelligence and your knowledge of matters pertaining to this kind of work. If a mistake is made it must be your mistake and not ours.

In the first place this man Goldstein that you sent to us should never have been sent here. He was not a new-comer, had been in New York

23 years, had been aided by the United Hebrew Charities, and you knew or should have known all these facts.

He came here in a condition resembling a hobo. I gave him shirts to make him look respectable. We found work for him, and he came with a letter from his wife showing that she was about to be evicted and begging him to have her sent here.

With this letter before him Mr. Richter answered your inquiry. They [the Goldstein family] came contrary to our instructions and the board bill of $30 is due directly to the incompetency of some one in your employ and that you have admitted to me.

Coming here with 8 children, what were we to do? Were we to apply to the Relief Society to take care of them? Were we to leave them on the street? There was nothing else to do but to rent rooms for them and to pay their rent.

On top of this the children got measles. They had to be moved in a carriage and I could not consent to jeopardize the health of other people by allowing this man to take work into his house while his children had the measles. That necessitated a week's expense to keep the family.

It makes no difference what other communities do. Here in Cleveland the community will not allow us to bring people here to become charges on our community from the day they come here. I for one positively decline to ask this community to take charge of paupers such as Goldstein, simply because New York wishes to get rid of them.

Far from feeling hurt by your criticisms, I rather take a pride in knowing that the people that you send to me are properly cared for even if it costs a little more to do so than it is being done for in other communities.

You need not send us the people if you can do better elsewhere, but when you do send them here we will work with you on such terms and conditions as we deem fair and equitable to you, to us and last but not least, to the people that you send us.

Coming back once more to the Goldstein case. If you will send me Mr. Richter's letter and if he asked you to send this family, notwithstanding that in doing so incompetency is shown in your office, because you should have known all the circumstances in the case, Mr. Richter will of his own accord repay to us the extra expense in caring for these people.

I believe the expense was $83.72, deducting $30 for board, which you say will be charged to somebody in your office, leaves $53.72, deducting $8, which I hope he will repay to us someday, leaves $45.72. You say we should have gotten along with $25, which would leave an excess in this case of $18.72.

While I consider it absurd for you to ask that a family of ten people should be cared for, for $25, after the man had been here only a week or two, yet I am willing that this should be done and Mr. Richter will stand the differences.

An enlightened public opinion would scourge the Removal Office, were your letter in this case and your views, made public.

Now in the case of Balamut. Here is a cloak maker that you sent here when the season was over and work not obtainable. It is your business to know these conditions and to know when work slacks up in New York in this line it slacks up all over the country. This man is a tailor without any physical development and unable to do hard work. We had a place in view for him, and to put him to work carrying brick or lumber, or digging in the streets, would practically incapacitate him for his own work. We found him a place while large numbers of old employees were standing around waiting to be put to work. He was ragged and we had to buy him shoes, and my son gave him some shirts to make him look presentable in the shop. The shop where he works pay every two weeks and I arranged with Mrs. Lefkovitz that I would pay for him if he didn't pay because otherwise she would not board him. At the same time he does not know this and is supposed to pay board when he gets his wages. When Mr. Richter brought his bills to me on the last of the month he included the week's guarantee for this man so as to close up everything with Mrs. Lefkovitz. That paid Balamat's board about four days ahead.

While I am very glad to see you scrutinize the bills I want you to understand that I do so as well and that not a cent is paid unless it is justly due.

In conclusion I beg to say that so long as I represent the Removal Office, I shall do the work in accordance with what I think is right and proper to all parties concerned.

I cannot allow any arbitrary rule to stand in the way of life and sustenance of the poor people whom you send to us.

I am not going to encounter the hostility of this community simply to carry out a rule of your office. You must bear in mind that you cannot dictate to the Cleveland people and that they have as much right to their opinions as you have to yours.

Had you sent us more people our percentage showing would have been much better. You cannot make an average out of one or two families and you cannot put a family of ten in the same category as you place a family of two or three.

I have no apology to offer for what we have been doing.

You have not sent me a check for the current month.

Your action in the above matter emphasizes in my mind the necessity of a meeting of the Industrial Removal Committee. I think matters should be discussed and the situation in different localities should be known in New York.

I cannot control our Relief Association and if other communities are more liberal, they of course should be preferred when you send out people.

Yours respectfully,
Jacob Furth

*   *   *

January 13, 1906

Jacob Furth Esq,
Cleveland, O.

Dear Sir:—

I have your favor of the 10th. I am sorry that you have not a copy of Richter's letter. I enclose one. Granted that $30. expended by you in behalf of the family was due to our mistake. $28.72 was expended over and above the amount specified by Mr. Richter, necessary to establish this family properly. (Note the sentence of his letter "If you will send the family and make the usual allowance, I think I can handle the case nicely"). You say "In the first place this man Goldstein that you sent to us, should never have been sent here". I differ with you here, and point in vindication of our judgment to Richter's letter, from which I quote the following:— "He seems to be a very decent, hardworking man. . . . He has been working steadily since his arrival. The family could do very nicely if they were together."

Now let us come to the case of Balamut. Your explanation as to the apparent discrepancy in the statement showing expenditures made for him is perfectly satisfactory. I am sure that you will pardon me for having called this to your attention, as it was plainly my duty to do so. You are right in saying that we ought to know when the cloak season slackens up in New York that it slackens up in other places as well. We do know. And we explained to Balamut very carefully that other work would be found for him at which he would be employed until the season commenced again. If we should be guided by your advice not to send men of this trade out of the City of New York, excepting during the busy season, why, we would be called upon to reject all men in this trade, because when the season is on in this city such men do not apply at our office. Your advice if followed generally would shut out all persons engaged in season trades, including even some in the building trades. Would you not, as a member of the Removal Committee, rather fall in line with our policy to send such people out of New York for other work, temporarily, and even permanently, if necessary?

Even granted that the expenditures you made in behalf of these cases were necessary, I still hold that the Removal Office should not be called upon to foot the bills. These are not the first instances of excessive expenditures, but I have refrained from criticism in the hope that you might eventually bring the community of Cleveland into line with us. Frankly speaking, I cannot understand why the community of Cleveland should be so lacking in generosity and in sympathy when every other community extends to us uncomplainingly their cooperation. I cannot believe that the niggardly and narrow-minded Jews of this country have preferred to settle in Cleveland. The pride that you have taken in the fact that none of our beneficiaries has applied to the charities is not justifiable, (though it undoubtedly is a source of gratification to you personally,) for we have acted in place of the charities.

I am afraid that in assuming the responsibility for all the work in Cleveland, you misunderstood the extent of the financial backing that we were prepared to give you. Our controversy in these two cases has simply served to disclose this misunderstanding. Your expenditures have not only been excessive proportionately, they have been so actually, and in saying this, I am not going beyond what I consider the jurisdiction of my office. I am not only engaged for my "knowledge of matters pertaining to this work", but in order to supervise all the activities of the Institution in its many ramifications. Nor is the "responsibility of either sending or not sending the people as in your judgment you may see fit to do", the limit of my authority. The funds are entrusted to me and it is my duty to see that they are judiciously expended.

I cannot understand what you mean when you say, "As I am not going to encounter the hostility of this community (Cleveland), simply to carry out a rule of your office". I am sure you do not give the snap of your finger for the hostility of a community when it is directed, as you say, to a movement which commands your deepest interest and your warmest sympathy. I am afraid that you misunderstand and misinterpret the attitude of your community.

The matter resolves itself practically into this, that if the community of Cleveland refuses to lend its aid to the work of removal then the community of Cleveland must accept the responsibility for its inaction. Though we may not have the right to dictate to the Cleveland people on matters that concern Cleveland alone, we certainly have the right to appeal to the Cleveland people to give their aid to a movement which concerns all the Jews of this country and which receives their uniform support. If it is their opinion, that this work does not deserve their financial aid and moral support, then I say, though they have a right to their own opinion, the right is not one that they can be proud to exercise.

Though I am as anxious as you are to have a meeting of the Removal Committee, such a meeting need not be called for the purpose of learning the situation in different localities. We know what the situation is and if we do not know it in Cleveland, it is because its situation is unique. A discussion of conditions in Cleveland will not be very conducive to improvement of conditions in other cities, though I do not hesitate to say that the reverse may be true. Believe me, Mr. Furth, I do not say this in the slightest spirit of disrespect to you, because I realize the enormous sacrifices that you have made in the cause. I simply have come to the conclusion that you have carried out a policy and presented an attitude, locally, which it would be advisable to relinquish. In short, I feel that it is inadvisable for us to continue an arrangement whereby we assume responsibility for our beneficiaries for an indefinite period, and for expenditures over which you deny us actual supervision.

You cannot realize how badly I feel in being forced to disagree with your view of the situation. I know as well as any one how much of yourself you have given to the cause. I consequently can appreciate your feelings in having your judgment questioned in any individual case. You can yourself understand that it would have been much more agreeable to me personally to agree with you in every detail and to approve of your every decision, and in disapproving of your action in these instances, I sacrificed my personal feelings and wishes in order that I might faithfully and conscientiously do my duty as I saw it.

> Very truly yours,
> David Bressler

* * *

January 17, 1906

Mr. David Bressler
#174 Second Ave.,
New York, N.Y.

Dear Sir:—

I have your favor of the 13th inst. Acting on your suggestion, I will sever my connection with the Removal Office work in this city with the end of this month.

Mr. Richter will also discontinue so that the field will be entirely clear.

I shall send an accounting as soon as I have this month's bills which from present appearances will be very small.

> Yours very truly,
> Jacob Furth

LETTERS TO AND FROM ISAAC KUHN,
CHAMPAIGN, ILLINOIS

Isaac Kuhn owned a large wholesale and retail clothing store in Champaign.[6] He was an officer in the local B'nai B'rith chapter and active in local civic and philanthropic organizations. Kuhn also helped establish the B'nai B'rith Hillel Foundation, the international Jewish college student organization.[7]

This exchange between Kuhn and David Bressler occurred from January through March 1911 when Kuhn was assuming the position of local agent. Because of Champaign's experience with IRO men ten years earlier, Kuhn continually expresses concern about the type of men to be sent and carefully specifies the sort of persons he feels could most easily be placed. He stresses that the men and their families should be able to speak German or English because the Champaign-Urbana area, home to the University of Illinois, contained a large German-speaking population. Kuhn's letters also display his attitude toward female workers and the opportunities available to them in Champaign. The correspondence indicates that many children of Jewish immigrants did not finish school but went to work instead. This inference is confirmed by the fact that most Jewish youngsters of that generation ended their formal schooling by the eighth grade.[8] The conventional view that immigrant Jewish parents struggled and sacrificed so that their children could remain in school must be modified.[9]

Champaign, Ill., Jan. 9, 1911

Mr. A. B. Seelenfreund[10]
Chicago, Ill.

Dear Sir and Brother:

In reply to the circular of the Order, recently received, regarding placing of emigrants, we think that this community could use a few emigrants providing care can be taken of who are sent. We realize that you have to send those you may have, but unless efforts be exercised in selecting people for this community the results are doubtful. We cannot receive the same class as we did ten years ago, of which only 10% wanted to work, and the rest looked for soft snaps, of these about 75% returned to the large cities.

We write you these details so that you may give them your careful attention if you deem it proper.

Those sent here would have to speak enough German to make themselves understood, in order to secure work. We believe we could use three or four men every sixty days, until September, for farm work. In addition we could use a few for factory work, piano factory, mill work, or as apprentices, painters, carpenters, etc.

Probably, we could use a family or two every sixty days, a man and wife with two or three boys or girls, most of the children over 15 years of age, able to work. Probably we could place several families in the course of time, but it is necessary that their members speak German or English.

There are also opportunities here for young men or women capable and fitted to enter the University. There are at present fifty Jewish young men and women in the University, a great many of them working their way through school, as there are quite a number of ways in which energetic young people can keep themselves occupied.

This class of graduates from the University have all been very successful in securing good renumerative employment.

The question is whether you can send people who can talk German and are anxious and capable of working. We cannot use any peddlers or teachers or any one that is not perfectly anxious to follow some vocation that requires labor.

Pardon the length of our letter, we think it all important enough to communicate to you, even if you already have the information.

> Yours fraternally,
> Isaac Kuhn

*   *   *

Jan. 17, 1911

Mr. Isaac Kuhn,
Champaign, Ill.

Dear Sir:—

Mr. Seelenfreund has sent us your letter of the 9th inst. addressed to him. I am greatly pleased to note that your community is anxious to cooperate in the work of distribution and that you are ready to accept a certain number of men at definite intervals of time. We will be glad to send you these men, especially those who will readily fit into the work in factories, in piano factories, in mill work, or any such other places where painters and carpenters are required. We note that you lay particular stress on the essential of the knowledge of some English or of German. This condition can be met without any difficulty and we will take every care to send you none but those who can meet these requirements. We appreciate the good will manifested by Grand Prairie Lodge and would be grateful if you will kindly let us hear from you in this matter and inform us to whom we may send the men, and when we may begin the work.[11]

Thanking you for your kind interest, and trusting that the work thus undertaken by you will prove of great benefit not only to the men to be sent to you, but to your community as well, I am

Yours very truly,
David Bressler

*   *   *

January 28, 1911

Industrial Removal Office
New York City.

Gentlemen:

Regarding the letter we wrote you a few days ago, you could begin sending us the parties we asked for about the first of March, as at that time they begin to use farm laborers here, and it will probably be the best time to use all kind of laborers about March 1st.

Let us know in advance what you are going to do so we will be prepared, and oblige,

Respectfully,
Isaac Kuhn

*   *   *

Jan. 30″, 1911

Mr. Isaac Kuhn
Champaign, Ill.

Dear Sir;—

I am in receipt of your letter of the 28th inst and note that we are to begin sending laborers about March 1st. We will notify you in advance before sending any men.

Yours very truly,
David Bressler

*   *   *

February 1, 1911

Mr. David Bressler
New York City.

Dear Sir:

Prof. Varon of the State University here, also his wife, have recommended a man by the name of Altabe, who is a carpenter in New York, and I have hunted up a position for him here. He will probably come to you with a copy of this letter.

I don't know whether it is in your jurisdiction to help him some with transportation or not, never-the-less there is no harm in seeing if you can.

On account of the recommendation, I think the man must be worthy. Also he has a wife who is supposed to be a good dress maker, for whom we could also get plenty of work to do here.

Thanking you in advance,

Sincerely,

Isaac Kuhn

P.S. I think I wrote you that I expect to be away from the 10th of February until about the 28th, after which I will be home and will be ready then from the first of March to the first of April, to receive the few parties whom we correspond about sending. I trust you will select people who are willing to work and be satisfied to live in two beautiful little cities of 25,000 population, where we have all modern conveniences and are still away from city congestion, especially people who will be satisfied to work and to do as they are requested, and work their way up.

If we get such people they will certainly be a success. It will be of some advantage in sending them here to have them clothed and mannered as much in ordinary American costume as possible.

If I have taken any undue liberties in this letter, please pardon same.

Sincerely,

Isaac Kuhn

*   *   *

Feb. 3, 1911

Mr. Isaac Kuhn
Champaign, Ill.

My dear Sir:—

I beg to acknowledge receipt of your very valued favor of the 1st inst. regarding a man by the name of Altabe, a carpenter in New York, whom you recommend at the instance of Professor Varon, for transportation to your city at our expense; also Mr. Altabe's wife. When he applies we will be very glad to give the matter due consideration and we will inform you of our action.

I note that you expect to be away between the 10th and 28th of February, but that thereafter you will be in Champaign prepared to accept the few parties about whom we have had correspondence of late. It is needless to say that we shall be happy to make a start with your city, and in order to insure the success of the pioneers, I will urge that you favor me again with your opinion as to the particular kind of mechanic or mechanics you can place to best advantage. Conditions at this moment may have changed somewhat, or they may have improved sufficiently to permit you to give us wider latitude in the selection of men to be sent to your city, but at all events we want to comply with your expressed preferences. May I therefore hope to receive from you at your earliest convenience an expression of your opinion. With much appreciation, believe me,

Sincerely yours,
David Bressler

*   *   *

February 7, 1911

Mr. David Bressler
New York.

My dear Sir:

I shall try to make myself as clear as possible, regarding the information you ask me as to what kind of help we can use here.

While I have lived here all my life, over 40 years, I may be mistaken in my belief, however, I feel fairly satisfied that it depends mostly on the kind of people you send us, as I think we will be able to get work for a number of people who make the right and proper start. I feel satisfied that there are plenty of positions that can be secured providing the parties are seriously in earnest and that they are anxious to work, willing to stick to work, behave themselves in every way, and not try to dictate as to how the man should do, that engages them, or how he should conduct his business.

If you send us people that are industrious, saving, moral, and so they can make themselves understood, there is no telling how many we will be able to use. I think we can use a great many if they are this class of people.

You will pardon me if I say anything that offends you, as I don't know anything at all about the people you propose to send. The trouble has been we have run across so many who are not the right kind, not willing to work, that to a certain extent we have been discouraged. We can use any kind of mechanics, we can use people who are willing to go into the country and work as agriculturalists, which is not an agreeable life to any one not acquainted with same, however those who can adapt themselves to it, or know anything about it, are prosperous and successful in this community.

A very peculiar incident occurred recently, which I shall go into details about.

About two years ago a Yahuda schnorer drifted in, and we refused to help him unless he went to work.[12] We got him a position with the Railroad Men's Y.M.C.A. He went to work in the kitchen. To-day he is manager, does all the buying, and has full confidence of the authorities, and receives a large salary.

The manager of this Y.M.C.A. now wants us to secure two or three Jews for him to help run the place, as he says Jews are the only people to depend upon to make a success of an institution of this kind. Before this man I speak of came there, they lost $400.00 or $500.00 a year, as I understand now their profits are over $2,000.00 a year, and they attribute it solely to Mr. Cohen. Therefore we can use 3 or 4 men to fill positions in this building, where they will certainly receive good training, and respectful treatment regardless that they are of different creed.

I understand that you cannot make immigrants to order, but if there were something in the way of a training school 40 or 50 miles from New York City, for grown up men and women, as well as youth, where the rough spots could be rounded off, and they could be made to understand that all depends on themselves and upon a little knowledge of various kinds.

It appears to me that the middle West could use many thousands and they would certainly become a blessing to the community, if they are of the right character, industrious and honest.

I presume you know all these things of which I write, and I only wish to impress upon you that conditions are right in the middle West for the proper class of workers. However, if you send out a large number of shiftless, inexperienced people, it destroys opportunities, and dis-organizes the present conditions. So as I stated before, by the 1st of March you can send us several people of the right kind, and I will notify you from time to time after that, how many and for what occupations to send those we can use.

Pardon me for the length of this letter, as I am seriously interested in this matter and cannot refrain from telling you my views.

With kind regards,

Sincerely yours,
Isaac Kuhn

* * *

Feb. 15, 1911

Mr. Isaac Kuhn
Champaign, Ill.

My Dear Sir:—

I have your letter of the 7th inst. It is certainly gratifying to have before us the example of the Yahuda who could show our Christian brothers how to make a success out of a purely non-Jewish institution. We will be very happy to find two more men as assistants to Mr. Cohen to enable him to make an even greater success of the institution. But aren't you a bit fearful that too much success may result in the charge, that Cohen and company are trying to Judaize a Christian institution? Pardon my frivolity but I simply could not resist this attempt at a joke.

You write us that you can use a great many industrious, saving and moral men who are good mechanics, and also men who will make farmers, but that you do not want any shiftless or inexperienced people. You undoubtedly realize that the class of men who are perfect in character and in efficiency, do not, as a rule, find it necessary to apply to any philanthropic agency. Such men do come to us now and then, and are compelled to do so by adverse circumstances over which they have no control. But as a rule we have to do with the average run of men, some good, some not so good and some indifferent.

New York is the dumping ground for the human cargoes that come from Europe, and they bring with them their virtues and their vices, their thrift and their shiftlessness, their accomplishments and their shortcomings. We here could wish that we too were in a position to tell the European countries from which the immigrants are recruited, that we will accept only first class immigrants, industrious, saving, moral, and only those who are good mechanics. We would like, for instance, to tell the Czar of Russia that business conditions in this city are very bad, that we cannot find room or employment for any more immigrants just now, and that we would therefore appreciate it if he would send forth an order to all his minions to stop the persecution of his Jewish subjects, thereby obviating the necessity for their flight from his domain. But the wish is only father to the thought. Russia will not stop its persecution of Jews, and Jewish immigration to America will continue just as long as the pursuit of life, happiness and a livelihood are denied to them in Russia. They come to America, but after they have paid their transportation expenses, they land here practically penniless, so that what was intended as immigration to America becomes very largely immigration to New York. Had they more money, I dare say that a very considerable proportion of them would find their way into the interior of their own initiative and at their own expense. The Removal Office and its cooperating agencies and friends throughout the country are trying to supply the void created by this lack of financial means. Even then of all the Jewish immigrants that arrive at the port of New York, more than 70% take up their permanent residence here. We now have approximately a million Jews in New York City, and you will readily appreciate that the problems of poverty and non-employment incidental to so large a population, require that American Jewry put forth its very best effort for their relief and distribution. If the probem were one merely of adequate relief to the handicapped in one form or another, the solution would not be so difficult. It would mean the collection of a larger relief fund. But the problem is so much more seri-ous, in that it involves the question of employment for able-bodied men and women in no way handicapped except by lack of opportunity. No matter how good the industrial conditions may be in this city, they can never begin to offer employment for all who are here. Aside from the nat-ural increase in population as a result of births, immigration adds tremen-dously to population, and the growth of our industries have never been in proportion. Hence we always have a very large surplus of labor, and un-less opportunities are provided for them elsewhere, this class is always in danger of degenerating into dependent men and women. We therefore feel that everything possible should be done to prevent them from becoming the victims of circumstances over which they have no control. Among this class there are undoubtedly some who are not, strictly speaking, worthy or even desirable. But this can only be found out after they are given a trial. We cannot tell to a certainty that every man that comes to us is worthy, in the narrow sense of the term, but human beings, after all, are not as easily judged as commodities, so that it must occasion no surprise or even disappointment if one picked out as deserving, fails to substanti-ate our judgment.

I have written you so much at length because I want you to have no mis-conception of the task that you are undertaking, a task all the more praiseworthy because it is a difficult one. You will have your disappoint-ments, and they may be many, but you will also have the satisfaction of promoting the welfare of a great many who will prove to you that they are deserving. In this work, as in any other, an average must be struck, and if it be a reasonably high one, that is all that can be expected.

In your letter of Jan. 9th you stated that you could use three or four men for sixty days for farm work, and we shall therefore do our best to have several men ready for you March 1st. You also stated that you could use a few men for factory work, or painters and carpenters if the factory men are not available. We have factory hands as well as painters and car-penters on our lists and will be very glad to send you one or two single men, also a married man with family March 1st. In fact it will be easier for us to send this class of people than to send farmers. Please let us know whether we can make our first shipment of these people March 1st, and what class workers you prefer.

We are looking forward with a great deal of interest towards your cooperation with us commencing March 1st, and we remain with best wishes,

Yours very truly,
David Bressler

* * *

New York, Feb. 16th, 1911

Mr. Isaac Kuhn
Champaign, Ill.

Dear Sir:—

Mr. Albert Altabe presented to us last week your letter of introduction dated Feb. 1st. After investigation which included a call at his home, we told him that we would send him to Champaign if he would go with his wife and two children. He at first agreed to this, but later came back and asked to be sent alone, stating that his family would remain here with his wife's parents. We did our best to persuade him to go to Champaign with the entire family but finally yielded to him and will send him on alone to-morrow. He will take a letter of introduction to Professor Varon.

Yours very truly,
David Bressler

*   *   *

February 27, 1911

Mr. David M. Bressler
New York.

Dear Sir:

In reply to yor letter of Feb. 16, I just returned home and found Mr. Altabe arrived here and accepted a position last week. He will receive salary of $15.00 a week. He appears to like it here, and the man he is working for seems to be satisfied with him. I spoke to both of them. Mr. Altabe will probably bring his family here inside of the next month.

Regarding the emigrants to be sent here, I will let you know definitely in a couple of days what we can use. If we could get farm laborers, could use them at once, but other laborers would not be in a hurry for a week or so. You shall hear from me in a few days.

Kind regards,

Sincerely,
Isaac Kuhn

*   *   *

March 2, 1911

Mr. Isaac Kuhn
Champaign, Ill.

Dear Sir:—

We have your letter of 27th ult. We are pleased to learn that Albert Altabe is settled in your city and that we shall shortly hear from you regarding the people you are ready to receive in Champaign.

In the meantime we are wondering whether you cannot give us permission to send the family of Joseph Arnesti, who like Altabe has come to this country from Turkey.[13]

JOSEPH ARNESTI.

33 years old, married, three children, a boy aged 11, and two girls 9 and 4½ years old respectively. He was a tanner in his native country, Turkey, and has been peddling in this country and doing work as a porter. He has been here four years. He is a good man, has references, and is willing to do any sort of work. He has been idle for the last three months and his wife has been trying to support the family by sewing in their rooms. Could you not find something for Arnesti to do in Champaign, so that we can send him with his family? Remember that he is willing to do anything that you can find for him.

Awaiting with interest your reply, we are,

Yours very truly,
David Bressler

*   *   *

March 4, 1911

Mr. David M. Bressler
New York.

Dear Sir and Friend:

In reply to your letter of March 2nd regarding Jos. Arnesti, at the present time I would not consider it wise to send this party here with his family, as you say he is a tanner, and was also a peddler. We have no tanneries here of any kind, and peddling is no good in this country as the people, as a rule, do not buy from peddlers at all.

I will keep my eyes open and if you cannot find anything for him to do elsewhere, if anything turns up I will do my best to see what can be done. Will let you know later.

With kind regards,

Sincerely,
Isaac Kuhn

*   *   *

March 4, 1911

Mr. David M. Bressler
New York.

Dear Sir and Friend:

Mr. Albert Altabe spoke to me today stating that he is now ready to receive his wife, two children, and his father-in-law. If you can furnish them transportation about the 15th of this month, I will appreciate it very much if you could do so.

Mr. Altabe will make arrangements to take care of his family in good shape.

A duplicate of this letter will be sent to Mr. Altabe's wife so she can present it to you for identification.

With kind regards,

Respectfully,
Isaac Kuhn

*   *   *

March 7, 1911

Mr. Isaac Kuhn
Champaign, Ill.

Dear Sir:—

We thank you very much for your letter of March 2nd and your postal of March 3rd, giving us permission to send the following workers to Champaign:—

2 Bushelmen, or tailors, who can alter first class ready-made clothing. young or middle age men to earn $10 to $15 a week. 4 Strong men, German speaking, who can work on farms.

We have already sent you, yesterday, one man, David Goldberg, 24 years old, single, who has been doing general labor work in this country where he has been four years, a man who is strong, and who tells us that he will be contented to work on a farm. We shall send you three more farm laborers, and hope for the other three to be able to find for you men who have had some experience on farms.

2 Painters and Paperhangers, and if we cannot find men who can do both work, we can send two of each.
2 Carpenters

We have today sent you one carpenter, Nathan Runetsky, a worthy man, who lost a good position in Brooklyn because he was unwilling to work on Yom Kippur.[14] We shall send you one other carpenter and will pick out for you a good man with family.

We note with pleasure that all the above men, with the exception of the farm hands, can be sent on with families.

3 or 4 young men to work in piano factory.

You ask for two girls who can do office work, good in arithmetic and correspondence, also two or three stenographers. We are sorry, but we do not ordinarily send young girls unaccompanied by their parents, but will do our very best to select for some of your requisitions men who have daughters who can qualify for these office positions.

We note what you write about train service, and also about work on Saturdays, and in closing want to assure you that we shall do everything in our power to send you worthy people who will appreciate the opportunities to be found in Champaign.

Sincerely yours,
David Bressler

*   *   *

March 7, 1911

Mr. Isaac Kuhn
Champaign, Ill.

Dear Sir:—

We have your letter of March 4th regarding the Altabe family, and are today writing to Mrs. Altabe asking her to call at the office. When she comes we shall arrange to send her to Champaign the first of next week so that she will arrive by the 15th.

We note from your letter regarding Arnesti and family, that it would not be advisable to send these people to Champaign at present, and we thank you nevertheless for your good intentions in the matter, and remain with best wishes,

Yours very truly,
David Bressler

*   *   *

March 9, 1911

Mr. David Bressler
New York City.

Dear Sir:

In reply to your letter of March 7th, Mr. Goldberg and Rientsky arrived here without any notice. However, one of them will go to work in the morning, the other one will have a position this coming week as carpenter.

You had better withdraw the application for four strong men who can speak German, for farm work, as farm work is overloaded now.

The painters and paper hangers are alright, but please reduce the piano factory men to two, as one of the men we already have is going to work at the piano factory.

Regarding the girls for office work, I did not expect you to send girls by themselves, as that is a ridiculous proposition. What I wanted was for you to send some family that had girls who could do that kind of work. We could also use plenty of girls for house work. They could come with families. So the parties we are asking you to send, if you can send with these girls or young men, it would be better to select such families.

We cannot use too many families at once, and please let me know a few days in advance, as this is not a large community where we have opportunities to place so many. If you will come at us so we can handle things we will get along alright.

Trust you appreciate that we are writing you in a spirit of kindness, and we will do the best we can and we know you are trying to do the same. With best wishes,

Sincerely
Isaac Kuhn

*   *   *

March 10, 1911

Mr. Isaac Kuhn,
Champaign, Ill.

Dear Sir:—

No doubt by the time this letter reaches you, you have seen Morris Gold, the young man who is very anxious to work on a farm near Champaign; and also Harry Berman the house painter whom we are sending you with his family.

And we have no doubt but that you will find both of these two men as willing and worthy as the enterprising schnorrer who made a place for himself in the Young Men's Christian Association, of your city.

Both Gold and Berman are cheerful enthusiastic men who realize the opportunities that await them in your city.

We hope to have some other good people for you this coming week, and we remain, with best wishes,

Yours very truly,
David Bressler

*   *   *

March 13, 1911

Mr. David M. Bressler
New York.

Dear Sir:

Mr. Gold and Harry Berman and family arrived yesterday morning, and I must say it was a hardship for a man with his children, to lay around on the road as long as he laid around, as you did any railroad connections for him. I received your letter after the parties got here, so they had to stay around the station for three or four hours after they reached here, after having had no sleep for hours.

These things could be obviated if you would write us a day or two in advance.

With the two exceptions below noted, please do not send any more people here until we notify you, as I have my hands full now getting these people started and located.

You wrote that you sent a couple of men to work on a farm. Both men sent had no experience in farm work and would not be satisfied on a farm. They had no conception of what a farm is like.

We could use a man to work on a dairy farm at the edge of town, one who knows how to milk cows, do chores around the place and that kind of work. Start to work at 4:30 A.M. to 6 P.M. $25.00 a month, with board and room. Plenty of work but the man must understand and be perfectly willing. Must be strong and healthy, cannot take any substitute or any man who does not understand how to milk cows. Will have to milk 8 to 12 cows.

If you can send a paper hanger who has a daughter who can do office work, you might send him with his wife. Outside of this kind, do not send any more parties until we have a little more time and you have the right parties we want. You have been sending people we find are not competent.

Respectfully,
Isaac Kuhn

*   *   *

March 14th, 1911

Mr. Isaac Kuhn
Champaign, Ill.

Dear Sir:—

We were glad to hear from your letter of the 9th that Goldberg was put right to work and that Rientsky will find work this week.

In accordance with your request we cancelled call for the men for farm work and are reducing the call for piano factory men to two.

We understand what you mean about girls for office work, but are unable to find amongst our applicants men who can qualify for other jobs, and who at the same time have daughters suitable for office work.

You tell us that you cannot use too many families at once and that you would like notice a few days in advance of sending a family, and hereafter we shall not send you a family without notice in advance. We are sorry however that we must disappoint in one more instance, because this morning before your letter reached us we had already selected for Champaign a carpenter, Rubin Hamburg, who was sent home with instructions to pack up at once all ready to go to your city with his family tomorrow. Rubin has five children, but Max the oldest son 16 years old has been working in tailoring shops in the city and can doubtless find employment in Champaign. If necessary, David, age 14, who has been in school, will go to work.

Hamburg is a Union man, in good health, and comes to us well recommended. We would have been glad, in accordance with your letter, to have him wait here a few days longer before going to Champaign, but before your letter reached us we instructed him to hurry up his packing, for fear that the place for a carpenter might be filled before his arrival in Champaign.

Before taking up another subject, we want to assure you that we do appreciate the fact that you write in a spirit of kindness, and we want to tell you that you are doing splendid work for us in your city. You are certainly doing your share to help ameliorate the condition of our unfortunate co-religionists.

Now in regard to the Altabe case, Mrs. Altabe presented your letter of introduction a few days ago, and we asked her to return with her parents which she did this morning. It seems that her husband asked the wife to come with the two children and with the father-in-law, but not with the mother-in-law. We carefully explained to these people this morning that it would be impossible for us to break up a family by sending the father-in-law and not the mother-in-law. The mother-in-law wishes to be here in the city until after another married daughter gives birth to a child, which will probably be in three months. We suggested that Mrs. Altabe and her two children go to Champaign now and expressed our willingness to provide transportation. And we added that when the mother-in-law and father-in-law are ready to go to Champaign together, we would endeavor to help them. But Mrs. Altabe refused to go without the father-in-law, at least until after she hears from her husband. If the husband comes to you about the matter, we would like to have you explain that we endeavor to unite families and are very much opposed to separating families. That is why we would gladly send Mrs. Altabe and children at once, and that is also why we cannot send Mrs. Altabe's father unless the mother goes along.

We remain with best wishes,
Very truly yours,
David Bressler

*   *   *

March 15, 1911

Mr. Isaac Kuhn
Champaign, Ill.

Dear Sir:—

When we send the next people to your city, we shall take up matters carefully with the man who has charge of our railroad tickets to make sure that the routing is proper, and that there will be no unnecessary hardships, as in the case of Mr. Gold and the Berman family, which we assure you we sincerely regret.

We agree with you that the difficulties will be obviated if you were notified in advance before we send people, and we shall be very careful to do this in the future.

We did not understand that the men you wanted for work on farms must be experienced farm-hands, but we do understand it now and our mistake will not be repeated. You specified comprehensively just what kind of man you want for work on the dairy farms, and to make sure of filling the bill properly, we shall call to our assistance the Jewish Agricultural Society.

In accordance with your request, we shall not send you anybody else without receiving further permission, other than this man who can work on a dairy farm, and a paperhanger who has a daughter who can do office work.

While we are perfectly willing to try and find a paperhanger such as you specify, we have grave doubts as to the probability of success, and wish very much that you would give us permission now to send you

DAVID RIMSON

English speaking, having been in the country eight years. He brings us references showing that he is not only honest and industrious, but also a good paperhanger. He is 31 years old and in good health. He lived in London 2 years before coming to this country. He is married and has two children, one three years old and the other five months old. If you can use Rimson, we shall let you know in advance as many days as you might specify, about sending him on, so that you will be ready to receive him when he comes to Champaign.

MORRIS SINGER

5 years in the country and English speaking, 25 years old, would like to go to Champaign with his wife. Singer is a plumber and tinsmith, but is willing to do any kind of work that you can find for him. It is but fair to tell you that his wife expects to give birth to a child in three months.

He has some factory experience, and if you cannot find him work as a tin-smith or plumber, perhaps you can get him a job in the piano factory.

CHARLES POTASHNIK

Speaks some English, having been in the country 3½ years. He is a young man, 31 years old, of pleasing personality, has had a little factory experience, and would like very much to obtain employment in the piano factory in your city. If he gets along well, he would like to bring to Champaign his wife and child whom he left behind in Russia.

Before closing, Mr. Kuhn, we want to express our regret at the difficulties you have been encountering and to make sure that in the future we send you just the kind of people you want, we shall first submit, as we have been in this letter, a brief description of the applicants.

We hope that you will give us permission to send you the three above mentioned cases, and remain with best wishes,

Very truly yours,
David Bressler

*　*　*

March 16, 1911

Mr. David M. Bressler
New York.

Dear Sir:

Mr. Hamberg and his family layed in the station here from 9 P.M. all night like cattle, and this morning about 8 o'clock, I was notified and tried to do my best to take care of them.

I know you have your troubles but I want to express to you my dissatisfaction and annoyance which you have caused me by not paying strict attention to my orders.

These people arrived here and not a house in town to be had. I have been running around all day trying to find a location for them, and finally I found a house this evening, and I had to spend about $50.00 furnishing and fixing it up so they could live in it, as they could not stop in any hotel here as they don't take families with children.

You have not the slightest idea of the trouble you have caused me. Had you notified me two or three days in advance, who you were going to send, I could have made some arrangements.

Furthermore I will not be able to secure any work for this man for probably a week.

With the Altabe family, you have made a mess of that also. As difficult as it was here to find places, I finally secured a splendid place for Mr. Altabe, only through a personal friend who otherwise would not have taken a family of children. He agreed to give Mr. Altabe four rooms in his own house, second floor, where he had a bath, steam heat and every convenience at $19.00 a month, right near a school for his children, in a good neighborhood, which is a very important thing to get a family like this in good hands to Americanize them as speedily as possible.

You don't need to tell me anything about dividing families, we have the same sympathies and intelligence that you folks have. The family had arranged to come here with the father. I had work for the father, and if you want to saddle the mother on this family, it would also probably bring another daughter and children. This man could not take care of this bunch of people.

Had I known anything about this affair in the first place I would not have rented the quarters. At the last minute I have to face my friend and tell him the trouble, and I shall be very careful hereafter that I have no more conflicts, because I absolutely refuse to take any more people, under any circumstances, until I clearly know in advance who is coming, and when I will be ready for them.

I know you have your burdens, but there is no use creating trouble here for me, and I have no one to help me take care of these people, besides having my hands full with business.

I was out all day Sunday in the worst of weather, looking for a place for Mr. Altabe, and not until Monday evening could I secure something, and as before stated, I promised a friend to take the place after another party had already spoken for the same, so you have put me in a very unpleasant position, as I never yet, made any promises to any one here but what I tried to live up to them. I will probably have to pay a month's rent, $19.00, in advance, or at least offer it to the party, and Mr. Altabe can look out for himself, in future.

You must not think I am touchy, I am willing to overlook a whole lot of things in emigrants, but when I am dealing with people who should know a little about diplomacy, I cannot have an unlimited amount of patience, unless I had nothing else to do but this kind of work.

Respectfully,
Isaac Kuhn

P.S. Please do not write me anything more about the Altabes, they will have to look after themselves here after.

* * *

March 17, 1911

Mr. David M. Bressler
New York.

Dear Sir:

In reply to your letter of March 15, as stated yesterday, we do not want you to send any more help until we let you know. I will take the matter up regarding the parties named, next week, and if I can find places for them will let you know then. Under no circumstances send any one until we inform you, and then we want you to write us at least two days in advance.

Mr Altabe wrote his wife last night that she should positively come Monday, so I trust you will send her without fail on that day. Wire me what time she leaves New York, and if she will come via Indianapolis or Chicago.

There is probably something wrong with the house hold goods you shipped to Mr. Berman, as it was shipped over a week ago and has not been received.

If you could ship all the goods by M.D. via Big Four, or Erie Despatch, Train 77, if these fast trains will take house hold goods it would be delivered here in three days.

Please send tracer immediately after Mr. Berman's goods, also after Mr. Hamberg's goods, otherwise we can never tell when they will be here and a tracer will hurry them up. Mr. Berman's bill of lading is dated March 10th and 11th, there are two of them. Same was delivered by Fried's express. R. Hamberg's goods was shipped March 14th from Brooklyn, N.Y. and were shipped by H. Teplitz. Trust you can get a tracer sent after these goods.

Respectfully,
Isaac Kuhn

* * *

March 21, 1911

Mr. Isaac Kuhn
Champaign, Ill.

Dear Sir:—

We have your letters of the 26th and 17th, the former written before you received our letter of March 15th, in which letter we assured you of our sincere regret at the mistake we made in sending you two families without first giving you information in advance, so that you could have things in readiness for them at Champaign. You doubtless realize, Mr. Kuhn, that if I personally could have attended to the matter, we would not have made the errors which we did, and you know from your own business experience, even with the most careful supervision, things which are, of necessity, left to subordinates, are sometimes not handled in the way the management desires. We do want to assure you, however, that we are doing the very best we can, and on one point at least you may be certain—we will never make the same mistakes twice. Instructions have been issued so that in the future no one will be sent to Champaign without your first giving specific permission, and furthermore no one will be sent to Champaign without your receiving ample advance notice. We know very well that you are not "touchy" as you call it, and that you are broad minded enough and of great enough vision to take in the entire situation, and we do not think that you will again have cause to feel that we lack the diplomacy and are careless of detail.

In regard to the matter of routing, we have been endeavoring to send your people on direct routes, but are not always able to insist that the railroad companies, from whom we receive concessions, carry out our wishes. The Trunk Line Offices here endeavor to distribute our people along different routes, and it often requires a great deal of fighting to have our people sent the way we want them to go.

We have made note of the fact that household goods in the future should be shipped "M.D. via Big Four, or Erie Despatch, Train 77", if these fast trains take household goods.

In accordance with your request, we are sending tracers after Berman's and Hamberg's household effects.

After all the trouble you went to in the Altabe matter, we, of course, understand your disappointment when you received our letter informing you that we were not willing to send the father-in-law with the wife and two children unless the mother-in-law went as well. But we can see from your post script in which you tell us that you explained to Mr. Altabe the seriousness of separating father-in-law from mother-in-law, that in your heart of hearts you agree with us that families ought to be united and not separated.

Well, to cut the matter short, just as we were about to send out a messenger for Mrs. Altabe this morning, she appeared, and when we told her we could not send her father unless her mother went along, she reconsidered her decision of the 14th and agreed to start at once with her two children, and as we telegraphed you this afternoon, she will reach Champaign Wednesday morning at 6:30, Illinois Central Depot.

It is splendid of you, Mr. Kuhn, after all the difficulties you have encountered, to be willing, as you express in your letter of the 17th, to accept the other people we wrote you about, provided that you could find places for them.

We hope that we shall shortly receive permission from you to send on the other people, or a portion of them, and assure you that these future cases will be so handled that you will have no reason to complain. Instead of disppointment we believe that you will be more than satisfied, and will see in these people to come, duplications of the success which followed the advent into your city of the "schnorrer" who made a success of the Y.M.C.A.

Yours very truly,
David Bressler

PART TWO

The Immigrants

CHAPTER 4

Interactions with the IRO

This section presents specimens of the most common types of letters that removals sent to the IRO's New York office: letters of gratitude, request, and complaint. Often letters contained more than one element, such as a thank-you followed by a request, usually for a relative to be sent.

Most of the immigrant letters were originally composed in Yiddish. In all cases when I translate Yiddish letters, I try to capture the spirit, flavor, and syntax of the original. To increase readability, however, I introduce paragraphs and punctuation and eliminate obscure or unclear references.

Letters of Gratitude

In this group of letters, the removals express their gratitude to the IRO for having sent them out of New York. The letters selected come from Wichita, Kansas; La Crosse, Wisconsin; Detroit; Columbus, Ohio; and Cincinnati. In each instance, the letters were written by immigrants who succeeded or were satisfied with their new surroundings.

LETTER OF CHAIM ZADIK LUBIN

Since biblical times, Jewish law and tradition has mandated that the more fortunate members of the community must assist their less fortunate brethren.[1] Chaim Lubin's experience with his friends and family members in New York appears to contradict this ethic.

Lubin wrote to the IRO in Yiddish.[2] At the time Wichita, Kansas, contained approximately 150 Jews out of a general population of 45,000. Russian immigrants constituted more than 60 percent of the Jewish population. Wichita's Jewish community supported one Orthodox and one Reform congregation, a Hebrew school, and a chapter of the B'nai B'rith. The Mr. Mann alluded to in this letter was B. L. Mann, a businessman, community leader, and local IRO representative from 1905 to 1913.[3]

Wichita, Kansas
March 16, 1906

Dear Brothers of the Jewish Removal Office:

I beg you to forgive me for not thanking you when you sent me to this city a year ago, or when you sent my family to me six months ago. Now I come to thank you for me and my family, from the bottom of my heart.

I see that you are the real doctors, bringing people back to life again. You need not look far, but take me as a living example. The day I came to your office, asking you to help me leave New York, I felt like a dead person. I told myself that if you refused to send me, I would commit suicide. Those five weeks that I was out of work in New York seemed to me like 15 years, because I was without money.

My best friends from Europe, those who met me when I landed, humiliated me and made me feel as though I was being stuck with needles whenever I asked them for a piece of bread. In order to keep away from my so-called friends, I was forced to go to a free kitchen to get something to eat. Just imagine, my own brother-in-law reproached me and made me choke with every morsel he gave me.

Now dear brothers, you sent me here to a person named Mr. Mann. He tried his best for me and found me a job. You can just imagine how thankful I am. I worked and made a living. Then, with your help, I brought my family here. And, thanks to God, I am making a respectable living.

I do not forget you for a single day, and my family and I always pray for you. I wish all of you, who work for such a good cause, health and long life. I only wish other Jews can be helped the way you helped me a year ago. Now I have contributed some money to our society's fund to help our suffering brethren in Russia.[4]

From me, your best friend,
Chaim Zadik Lubin

My wife, whom you sent to me, is named Chaye, and my three-year-old son's name is Zvi Hersh.

LETTERS TO AND FROM CHARLES ZWIRN

The IRO sent Charles Zwirn to La Crosse, Wisconsin, in 1911.[5] He found the city to his liking and made a life for himself there. In May 1913, Zwirn visited New York to spend Passover with his parents. While in New York, he composed this letter to the IRO offering his thanks, a sketch of his initial experiences in La Crosse, and tips to prospective removals. Although he addressed the letter to the IRO, Zwirn directed it to the immigrants, giving the IRO permission to publish or use it in any way the office chose. Zwirn typed his letter in Yiddish.

In 1913, the city of La Crosse contained a general population of about 30,400. The Jewish population numbered one hundred, most of whom were eastern European immigrants. The Jewish community supported one Orthodox and one Reform synagogue, a local B'nai B'rith lodge, and a benevolent organization.[6]

May 13, 1913

Mr. Seman
Assistant of the Industrial Removal Office
174 Second Avenue
New York

Worthy Sir:

I beg to inform you that I just arrived from La Crosse, Wisconsin, to visit my parents for Passover. I ask you to kindly devote a little of your time to listen to my expression of thankfulness to you for all that you have done for me. I feel that I ought to be of some service to the Removal Office. But for the present I am not able to do anything else but tell the hundreds of applicants my impressions. I hope that this will be of some use to them.
MY TRIP TO THE WEST THROUGH THE REMOVAL OFFICE—
WHY SOME PEOPLE SUCCEED AND OTHERS FAIL—
MY IMPRESSIONS OF PEOPLE SENT BY THE REMOVAL
OFFICE—THOSE WHO RECEIVE THEM, ETC.
Day in and day out, I used to walk in New York looking for jobs. But being unable to find anything, I went to the park and sat there day after day. I lost all my ambition and energy. The few dollars I had, I spent.

I saw that if someone does not come to my assistance, then my future is lost.

Gathering together my last bit of courage, I wrote a letter to the Removal Office. I explained to them my condition and begged them to do something for me. Immediately the following day, Mr. Seman wrote me to call upon him. After I filled out an application, he promised to send me for half the fare, although I had money to pay my own expenses. The third day after I filled out my application, I was sent to La Crosse, Wisconsin. A letter was given to me, addressed to Mr. Goldfish of the same city.

Sunday at three o'clock in the morning, I took my satchel and went to the stated address. Instead of his residence, I found there Mr. Goldfish's office. I then made my way back to the depot. To my surprise, I was met there by a gentleman, who was about 40 years old. I was surprised when he asked me my name and told me he was Mr. Goldfish.

He took me into his house and gave me a very nice welcome. He then led me to the synagogue and introduced me to all the members. Mr. Goldfish is a Jew with a real Jewish heart. He is religiously inclined and is the biggest businessman in the city. If any controversy arises, it is always settled by Mr. Goldfish. Recently, a divorce suit between Mr. and Mrs. Malowitz took place, and the judge suspended the trial until he could consult with Mr. Goldfish upon his return to the city. To this man the Industrial Removal Office sends its applicants.

Mr. Goldfish then took me to a shop and they paid me $6 more than I earned in New York. When I wanted to thank him, he said that the only thing he expects of me is that I conduct myself properly and go on the right path so I can eventually succeed. This, he said, was the best reward I can give him. I did as he told me and saved a few hundred dollars. And now when I go back, I intend to become independent in business.

In order to succeed, the best way is not to bluff when you make application to the Removal Office. When the truth is told, it gives them a chance to decide properly and use proper judgment. As long as an applicant does not become impertinent, he is treated in the most respectful manner. Men who come through the Removal Office receive kindlier treatment than other newcomers. Upon my inquiry as to why it is so, Mr. Goldfish told me that the men sent by the Removal Office are an honest class of people who seek to improve their condition. The office investigates their character and only sends respectable people.

Only those which I shall enumerate hereafter could not succeed here. A family was sent here from New York. They were welcomed and given a furnished house. Mr. Goldfish supplied the husband with a job where he could earn a decent living. The family was kept in that same house for a period of three months and supplied with light and heat without a cent of cost. The husband was well satisfied, but the wife could not break away from ghetto life. She did not want to bake her bread and she did not have a world full of neighbors as in New York. She so aggravated her husband, that he left her and settled in a large city. He eventually sent for his family. There his wife could get everything on order, even ready-made noodles. And she knows everything about her neighbors, even what they are cooking in their pots. The husband, on the other hand, is the real slave who has to work hard in a shop to make a living. On my way out here, I met the family and the husband cried bitterly for having taken this step.

Another man sent here had been in the country two months. He then applied to your office. He declared that he was willing to do any kind of work. He was sent to Mr. Goldfish, who found him a job sorting corks for $2 a day. This man then told Mr. Goldfish that he could not remain in La Crosse. He said that a fortune teller in New York told him that he will find his luck while traveling. And since he did not find his luck in La Crosse, it did not pay for him to work for $2 a day. He then left.

By the way, when I return to La Crosse would you be so kind as to send to me a boy to drive a milk wagon on Mr. Jacob's farm and an older man to work at junk? They must be honest and respectable people, for they have a chance here to advance themselves.

For the present, I have no more news. I thank you and send you my regards. And if you want to publish this letter, you can do it with my permission and you can mention my name.

> Yours very truly,
> Charles Zwirn
> c/o A. M. Goldfish
> 430 Lax Street
> La Crosse, Wisconsin

* * *

May 16, 1913

Mr. Charles Zwirn
c/o A. M. Goldfish
430 La Crosse St.,
La Crosse, Wisc.

Dear Mr. Zwirn:

We are in receipt of your very interesting letter of appreciation for services rendered to you by this office. What we have done for you,

Mr. Zwirn, is no different than what we are making every effort to do for every applicant that comes to us. As you very clearly stated, the success of the applicant does not depend on the Removal Office anywhere near as much as it does upon the individual who applies for its services. It is most pleasant for us to receive a letter of the kind you have sent, for while many of our applicants who have had the same experiences as yours might feel exactly the same as you do, yet they have not put into writing their appreciation. Letters of this sort indeed are a service, for they are a testimony as well as an encouragement to many thousands of unfortunates in the city of New York who have lived under similar conditions that you have lived under, and encourages them to make an effort to try life anew under entirely different environments. We are in possession in our office of thousands of letters since our existence, carrying a message of similar tone to the one contained in your letter. We appreciate your privilege to use your name, and if we desire, to publish your letter, and should the proper opportunity present itself, we will take advantage of this.

We likewise notice that you can use an elderly gentleman to work in a junk shop in La Crosse as well as a young man to drive a milk wagon and do general farm work. We will make every effort to find among our applicants such who will be able to do the work your requisitions expect.

With very kindest regards to yourself and Mr. Goldfish, we are,

> Very truly yours,
> INDUSTRIAL REMOVAL OFFICE,
> Per
> Philip Seman

LETTERS TO AND FROM LOUIS FRIEDMAN

In April 1907, Louis Friedman sent the IRO an effusive letter praising his new home, Detroit, which he described as an economic mecca.[7] It may have been so for him, but not for everyone. Detroit, like other American cities, was hard hit by the Panic of 1907, and thousands of persons lost their jobs.[8] The letter indicates that, after having suffered in New York, a removal's exuberance at finding a home and a job could affect the way in which he perceived his new surroundings. Friedman wrote his letter in Yiddish.

At this time, Detroit's Jewish population numbered about 25,000 out of a general population of approximately 420,000. The Jewish community supported one Reform and fourteen Orthodox synagogues; two religious schools; and numerous social, cultural, and charitable institutions.[9]

April 5, 1907
Detroit

Worthy Sirs of the Removal Office!

I thank you many times for all the good you do with people and have done with me, by sending me and my three children to Detroit. I thank you for your noble deed which gave us the opportunity to tear ourselves away from oppressive New York. In Detroit, where you sent us, we can breathe more freely and make a respectable living. I can inform you that as soon as we arrived and showed your letter to Miss Pick, she straightaway provided us with accommodations, food, drink, and lodgings for eight whole days and secured work for everyone at his trade.[10] In New York, I, a man with no trade, walked around for three months and could not find work. Now, when I came to Detroit, Miss Pick also found me a job, and I earn nine dollars a week. And it is a steady position. The person who worked in my place before me was employed steadily for fifteen years and was not laid off even for a day. And each of the children works at his trade and earns good money. I have rented three nice rooms for six dollars a month and have bought a few pieces of furniture, and so far I and the children are managing quite well.

As it is Passover, Miss Pick supplied us with matzoh and we are very satisfied. Blessed is Detroit where, if only one wants to work, there is no shortage of work. And there the working class does not live in foul, airless rooms as in New York because the rent is cheaper here.

Detroit is to be marveled at for her freedom and for her clean air, which is like that found in a park full of beautiful trees!

Therefore, I beseech you to send me my family, as listed with you, as well as my son-in-law and daughter. I also beg you to send my two nephews, Shayeh Chmelzitski and Idshize Weiner, who are struggling in New York and cannot find work. I have confidence in myself now and am convinced that we will make a better living here than in New York! However, I have come to ask you to send them with a letter to the office where Miss Pick provides the newly arrived people with work and help.

I thank you in advance and remain your best friend and wish that time will help the Removal Office advance its noble work of helping our needy Jewish brethren! Friedman!

April 19, 1907
No. 239 East High St.
Detroit, Mich.

Mr. L. Friedman
c\o Miss Birdie Pick

My Dear Sir:—

I was most agreeably surprised to receive your letter of April 5th, and am happy that success has come to you so quickly after your removal from New York. I sincerely hope that you will continue to prosper. As soon as we can make the necessary arrangements, we shall be very glad to comply with your request to send the remaining members of your family to Detroit.

Yours very truly,
David Bressler

LETTERS TO AND FROM M. GOLDSTEIN

By 1900, New York held more than 500,000 Jews, the largest Jewish population of any city in the world.[11] But despite New York's rich and varied Jewish religious, cultural, and social life, thousands of Jewish immigrants found the city nightmarish. M. Goldstein was one of these.[12] In 1907, he applied to the IRO, which sent him to Columbus, Ohio. Goldstein loved Columbus and communicated his feelings to the IRO. In his letter, he vividly contrasts his former existence in New York with his present life in Columbus. He wrote his letter in Yiddish.

In 1907, the Jewish community of Columbus numbered about 3,000 persons. They supported one Reform and four Orthodox congregations, a Hebrew school, and a variety of social and charitable organizations. The Mr. Silber referred to in the letter is Rabbi Saul Silber (1881–1946), who was the IRO's local agent from 1905 to 1908. Silber subsequently moved to Chicago, where he became president of the Hebrew Theological College.[13]

10/13/07

Worthy Sirs of the Removal Office:

I have the honor to inform you, and at the same time it is my moral duty to do so, about everything that has happened to me.

After seven weeks without work in the sucking whirlpool of New York, and being a greenhorn, you can just imagine how I suffered—hunger, thirst, torn and insulted from all sides. I somehow managed to survive. But in truth, I was in agony.

And now? I would impudently scoff at all those who dissuaded me from leaving until I had undergone all these miseries. Now I would accuse such people, including the Yiddish press, of spreading falsehoods.

Oh, if I were only able to prove to those people, who are hindering the work of the Removal Office, how false their accusations are and how they misuse facts. I, too, have run around half-starved, from 5 o'clock in the morning until evening, looking for work that pays a meager wage. And did I find anything? Yes! A bench in Hester Park.

But now, after being sent here by the Removal Office, on the 2nd of October, to a beautiful and clean city, I feel as if newly born. My head no longer pounds from the elevated. My feet no longer shake from the subway. On Saturday the 5th of October, I secured work in a railroad shop for $2.30 a day.[14] After working three days and not finding the position suitable, I left and went to work in a place where I earn $2.00 a day and have much easier work. (I am a carpenter.) I now feel like I am beginning to live, after so much suffering.

I also wish to tell you that your agent here, Mr. Silber, is a noble person, a man with a splendid character, a man who sympathizes with the afflicted and is happy when his friend is not in need. He treats the people like a father. He provided me with all the necessary tools, gave me a position, and has guided me everywhere.

From the bottom of my heart, I want to thank all the officials of the Removal Office and also the Columbus agent, Mr. Silber.

With a Jewish greeting,

M. Goldstein
427 E. Mound str.
Columbus, O.

*   *   *

October 16th, 1907

Mr. M. Goldstein
427 Mound Street
Columbus, Ohio

Dear Sir:—

We beg to acknowledge receipt of your favor of the 13th inst., and thank you most sincerely for the kind expressions contained therein. It is, as you say, unfortunate that there should be any doubt as to the nature of the work of the Removal Office and the advantageous results accruing to people who place their trust in the representations of our society. I am very glad indeed therefore that you have satisfied yourself that we keep the faith with those who have faith in us, and I trust that the future may bring ever increasing proof of the fact that we are doing everything possible to better the conditions of our unsuccessful coreligionists in New York.

With best wishes to you, we are,

Very truly yours
David Bressler

LETTERS TO AND FROM JACOB FINKELSTEIN

The IRO sent Jacob Finkelstein to Cincinnati, Ohio, in 1912.[15] For him, Cincinnati was a breath of fresh air. He found a job, enjoyed the city, and expressed optimism about the future. He wrote the IRO an effusive letter praising it for the way in which removals are treated and for preserving their dignity in the process. The letter is translated from Yiddish.

Cincinnati in 1912 contained about 28,000 Jews in a general population of 590,000. The Jewish community supported seven Orthodox and three Reform congregations, two settlement houses, two branches of the Workman's Circle, two Jewish social clubs, and numerous Jewish fraternal orders and benevolent organizations.[16]

Cincinnati, Aug. 5, 1912

Industrial Removal Office
174 2nd Ave.
New York City

Worthy Sirs and Friends:

I consider it my sacred duty to express to you my hearty thanks for what you have done for me. I was thinking all the time and finally came to the conclusion that the work you are doing on behalf of the poor cannot be repaid. It is not the free transportation you are giving. No. This is the least of it. It is as though you send a good samaritan to accompany the one you ship out, to warn him from making a false step. He is taken off the train and given food and shelter with the greatest friendliness so that he does not feel in the least embarrassed—does not feel that he is get-ting charity. The main thing, however, is the fact that employment is pro-cured for him. And if he is not lazy, he can make a nice living for himself and his family. This is more, much more, than one can accomplish with his own means.

As for me, I hope that you will be glad to hear that I have a good job and get $4 per day. I hope to make a nice living here. And I have you to thank for all this. You, because I would never have thought of coming here of my own accord.

I intend to bring my family here because we have double expenses liv-ing separately.

My wife will come to your office, and I appeal to you to enable her to join me as soon as possible.

Thanking you for everything, I remain with great respect,

> Yours truly
> Jacob Finkelstein of 128 Allen St.

Who was sent by you July 16, 1912
My present address is:
Jacob Finkelstein, 543 Hoppkins St.,
c/o Mulberg, Cincinnati, O.

* * *

August 6, 1912

Mr. Jacob Finkelstein
543 Hoppkins St.,
c/o Mulberg
Cincinnati, Ohio

Dear Sir:

It gave us great pleasure to receive your letter of August 5th wherein you express your hearty appreciation of the efforts put forth in your be-half. We are very glad indeed to learn that you are pleased so far with your lot in Cincinnati, and only hope that your present state of satisfac-tion will grow with time and that before long you may be in a position to send for your family and reestablish your home in your new environment.

Letters of the kind that you have written are a great encouragement to us. We know and we feel the things that you make mention of in your let-ter, and while we do not expect all of our applicants to thoroughly un-derstand our real motive, we are very often much gratified by communi-cations like the one we are in receipt of from you.

Again hoping that you may continue to be thoroughly satisfied and that by-and-by we may help you to receive your family, we are,

> Yours very truly,
> INDUSTRIAL REMOVAL OFFICE
> per
> Philip Seman

Letters of Request

The largest single category of immigrant letters are those that request something from the IRO. Most often, the removal asked the IRO to ship relatives, friends, or belongings to him. The following three letters, from Detroit, Oklahoma City, and Chicago, characterize the letters in this category.

LETTERS TO AND FROM JACOB SCHIFFMAN

In 1907, the IRO sent Jacob Schiffman and his family to Detroit.[17] According to Schiffman, he had a terrible time adjusting to the city. When his situation became unbearable, he sent his wife and children back to New York and began peddling for a living. After a time, he wanted his family to rejoin him. His wife and one of his children did so, but she left their other two children with her parents in New York. This prompted Schiffman to write to the IRO and ask for help in bringing his other two children back to Detroit. Although sympathetic to the plight of the children, Bressler expressed skepticism about Schiffman's tale of woe. Nevertheless, he did agree to assist Schiffman by contributing one-half of the fare. Schiffman's letters were written in exceptionally good English; he either was literate in the language or, as was likely, had someone write the letters for him. His letters illustrate how removals appealed to any sentiment to get Bressler to assent to their requests.

Detroit, 2/11/09

D. Bressler Esq.

Dear and honored Sir—

You will perhaps recollect my name at the foot of this letter. I was the recipient of your kindness about two years ago when you assisted me to remove with my family to this city. During this short period I passed through a great many vicissitudes, starting under very favorable auspices and finishing in absolute destitution and misery. With the advent of the Panic [of 1907] all my little capital and all my resources vanished, and I was reduced to such a pass that my wife and the three boys had to return to New York in quest for shelter with her poor old parents. A few months ago she returned with the youngest boy, and I have started peddling with tea and coffee, eaking out a meagre living. I should nevertheless feel comparatively contented if I had all my family together under one roof, and precisely this ardent desire of mine prompts me to appeal to your charitable feelings again. Your institution ought to do something towards gathering together the members of a scattered family, especially when two mere boys in the tender age of 8 and 10 respectively come into question. Moreover, the elder of the two has been ailing for the last month or so, which called for his frequent attendance at the dispensaries and Mount Sinai Hospital, thus pushing the patience of his aged and infirm grandma to the utmost limits. The untoward climax of all this is that an operation has to be performed on him, which would require the attendance and care of parents only. I venture to hope that all these unfortunate circumstances considered, your sentiment of pity will be aroused and you will give orders that the two boys be shipped to this city with all possible speed. The annals of your institution have scarcely had a more meritorious and pressing case than this one.

The names of the boys are Isaac, 10 and Leo, 8, and they live with their grandfather Mr. Michael Ganapol, No. 15 W. 118th Street, N.Y.

Thanking you most kindly beforehand I remain,

> Dear Mr. Bressler
> most respectfully yours
> Jacob Schiffman
> 312 Winder Str.
> c/o Mr. Abraham August

* * *

Feb. 15th, 1909

Mr. Jacob Schiffman,
c/o Abraham August
312 Winder St.
Detroit, Mich.

Dear Sir:—

I have yours of the 11th inst. I regret that things have not prospered with you. I recall you perfectly, and would be more than pleased to comply with your request if I felt that the circumstances entitled you to that consideration. But I am sorry to say that I do not feel so. We are not responsible for your having returned to New York, nor are we responsible for your having left two of your children here while the rest of the family returned to Detroit. As a matter of fact there was no particularly good reason for you to return to New York in the first place, because, if I remember rightly, your reason for wanting to leave New York two years ago was because you could not possibly make a living for your family here. The Removal Office does not send people away from New York a second time.

Regretting our inability to serve you in this matter, I am,

Yours very truly,
David Bressler

* * *

Detroit, 2/21/09

Dear Mr. Bressler:

Your kind letter of the 15th inst. whilst couched in the most courteous and judicious terms is at the same time the disappointment of my life. If you are a father, you will perhaps feel what is going on in my sore heart for my two tender aged boys thrown on the mercy of an aged and infirm couple, one of them sick and requiring an operation. You seem to be under the erroneous impression that I had gone back to New York but the fact is that only my wife with the boys went then to escape from starvation, whilst I remained here. I earnestly hope that this circumstance will appeal to you and that you will see your way to mite [sic] out mercy instead of justice. I fully appreciate your situation and your scruples, but here is an exceptional case which ought to induce you to sidetrack all the rules of the institution and let mercy prevail.

You are all powerful and you can do as your good heart dictates you. But I hope that even the honorable [Removal] Committee will approve of your favorable decision and sanction your good deed. It is the earnest and humble petition of distracted parents craving for the sight and presence of their two tender boys, who had seen better days and for the sake of their faith have been reduced to utter misery. I beseech you once more with folded hands not to disappoint me but to comply as speedily as feasable [sic] with my earnest request and may almighty Jehovah bless you and your belongings.

Soliciting an early and favorable reply I remain dear and kind Mr. Bressler most respectfully yours.

Jacob Schiffman
c/o Abraham August
312 Winder Street

* * *

Feb. 24, 1909

Mr. Jacob Schiffman,
c\o Abraham August
312 Winder St.,
Detroit, Mich.

Dear Sir:

I have yours of the 21st inst. I do not wish to enter into a protracted discussion of the merits of your request. I am perfectly willing to concede that you are badly in need of assistance. The point, however, still remains that your present plight is of your own making. You sent your two children back to New York for the reason, as you state, "to save them from starvation". At the time we sent you to Detroit, the very same reason was given by you for sending you and your family to Detroit, only that time you wanted to save them from starvation in New York. If you are out of employment in Detroit, I fail to see how sending your wife and children to New York would improve their condition. If you had friends here who were willing to provide for them, those friends should likewise provide your children with transportation, particularly since it means that their care will be taken off their hands. It seems rather strange to me that you should subsequently send for your wife to return to Detroit and leave such "tender aged children" with people not their natural guardians. Whatever your reasons were they do not appeal to me as good, but it is not our purpose to mete out punishment. We have in mind the welfare of two young children who are not responsible for the mistakes of their parents, and on their account we are willing to render some assistance, provided you can raise one half the amount of money for tickets to Detroit.

Yours very truly,
David Bressler

*   *   *

Detroit, 2/26/09

Dear and honored Mr. Bressler.

In respectful reply to your kind favor of the 24th inst. I perfectly coincide with you that there is no use entering into any polemics regarding the merits or demerits of my personal case. Maybe that I am not faultless, that I am to blame, but can anybody tell my sufferings? Although a sincere and warm-hearted Hebrew, yet did I ever fail to see the justice of visiting the sins of the parents on their offspring even to the 3rd and 4th generation!! The more heartily do I appreciate your kind and generous decision of making a concession in behalf of my poor innocent boys who are guilty of nothing and are suffering for no blunders of their own. The condition, however, which you impose upon me is a very hard one under prevailing circumstances, and whilst admitting the full justice thereof I scarcely see my way how to comply with same. My rent falls due next Monday and my landlady although a poor woman herself agrees to wait for some time yet, and suggests that I remit you the $5 bill instead of paying it to herself. Next Monday then I shall send you the said amount, and I earnestly hope and trust that this arrangement will turn out satisfactory. It is my desire that my boys be dispatched from there on Saturday next so that they land here on the feast of Purim, which will turn out a real joyful day for me.[18]

Thanking you once more for your great kindness of heart I remain, dear Mr. Bressler

> Most respectfully yours
> Jacob Schiffman

* * *

> Detroit 2nd March 09

Dear Mr. Bressler.

In pursuance of my respects on Friday last, I now beg to enclose m.o. value $5. Sincerely trusting that no hitch will intervene in my two boys being put under way for this city next Saturday so that they may land here on the Feast of Purim. Kindly notify Mr. Michael Granapol #15 W. 118th Str. to that effect, asking them to get everything ready for Saturday night.

Thanking you once more for your great kindness, I remain

> Dear and honored Sir, most respectfully yours,
> Jacob Schiffman
> c/o Abraham August
> 312 Winder Str.

LETTERS TO AND FROM JOSEPH LIPETZ

In 1903, the IRO sent Joseph Lipetz to St. Louis, Missouri.[19] Lipetz stayed in St. Louis until 1906, when he relocated to Oklahoma City, Oklahoma. Meanwhile, his wife remained in Russia. After he moved to Oklahoma City, Lipetz brought his wife to New York. Some weeks after she arrived, he wrote to the IRO and asked it to send his wife to him. David Bressler wondered why Lipetz had brought his wife to New York but not to Oklahoma; nevertheless, Bressler sent Lipetz's wife to him. The correspondence then resumed one year later. By this time, Lipetz owned a "Gent's Furnishing Goods and Jewelry" store in partnership with his brother and had changed his name to Joe Lee.

When he wrote the first letter, Lipetz had been in the United States for four years. The series exemplifies typical requests and demonstrates how quickly some of the removals Americanized and achieved success. Like Schiffman's letters, these were composed in English. Although the language use is far more rudimentary than Schiffman's, there is no clue as to whether Lipetz wrote them himself.

Oklahoma City in 1908 contained seven hundred Jews in a total population of about 63,000. The Jewish community consisted primarily of German and Russian Jews who maintained a Reform and an Orthodox synagogue, a local B'nai B'rith chapter, and two charitable organizations.[20]

> Oklahoma City, Oklahoma
> May 4, 1907
> Industrial Removal Office
> 299 11th Street
> New York City, N.Y.

Dear Sir!

In 1903 I was shipped out from New York City by you. It means by the Removal Office to St. Louis, Mo., where I stayed until 7 months ago, and then moved to Oklahoma City, Oklahoma.

All the time I was trying my best to make a honest living by common labor and now here I'm seling dry goods and make my living, but didn't sucseeded yet to save some money. But I hope I'll sucseed. I'm not long in this country only 4 years. 9 weeks ago my wife Anna Lipetz came over from Russia to the United States and she is now in New York City, 56 Gouverneur str. c/o A. Cooper.

Mrs. Cooper is the sister of my wife and very very poor and in miserable condition and my wife is compelled to live with her in dirty room and is suffering terrible.

I would like to have my wife Anna with me here in Oklahoma City and live together. I'm anxious to see her after 4 years beeing far away from her.

I beg you be kindly and corteously to my wife and to me and bring us together—for if I would have the money my wife wouldn't bother you at all.

Hoping you will do the duty of a man as a gentlemen, I remain

> Yours truly
> Joseph Lipetz
> 120½ Sout—Broadway
> Oklahoma City, Oklahoma

* * *

Oklahoma City, Oklahoma
May 6th 1907

Dear Sir!

Nearly 10 weeks since my wife Anna Lipetz came from Russia to New York City and for all the time I wasn't able to send her money for Railroad ticket to Oklahoma City. She, my wife is suffering undescribable living with her poor sister 56 Gouverneur Str. She aplied to you many times for help—to send her to me, just to ship her to me and to give her the same free transportation as you gave to me 3½ years ago, sending me to St. Louis, Mo.

I appeal to your good feelings and beg you in name of humanity and justice to do some thing for my poor good lady whom I did't see for 4½ years.

Respectfully
Joe Lipetz
120½ S. Broadway, Oklahoma City, Okl.

*   *   *

May 10th, 1907

Mr. Joseph Lipetz
120½ South B'way,
Oklahoma City, Okla.

Dear Sir:—

We have your favor of the 4th. inst. and in reply thereto beg to assure you of our deep interest in your welfare. When we sent you from New York, it was because we were desirous of giving you an opportunity to earn your livelihood away from the cut-throat competition of New York City; that we have succeeded in this endeavor, your letter amply proves. We feel that after giving you this opportunity, for which we cheerfully footed the cost, you have no further claim upon us. You knew at the time you sent for your wife that you were in Oklahoma, and that it cost considerable money to go to Oklahoma. Notwithstanding that, you sent her money to get only as far as New York, relying upon us who had already done you a good turn to take up the burden that is justly yours. While we appreciate your anxiety to be together with your wife, we want to call your attention to the fact that you allowed almost three and a half years to elapse before sending for her, and that therefore you could have waited a month or two longer, or until such time as you had sufficient money to pay for her transportation to where you are at present located. We feel that we are going out of our way in offering her our assistance to the extent of sending her upon a contribution of $20. We can do no more.

Very truly yours,
David Bressler

* * *

Gentlemen! Do you really thing I'm well suplied with money but don't want spend 35–40 dollars Railroad fare and therefore send my wife to the Removal Office to beg for free fare?——

If I would have the nessesary money I would't let my wife to suffer whole 9 weeks in her sister's hous in poverty.

My wive wrote me in a letter that you offered her a half a ticket when she'll pay the rest #20.00.

Believe me I have't the 20 dollars to spare. I shall go and rent a little hous and buy a couple pieces of forniture and It'll be hard for me to get the money but I'll do the best. But where can I find 20 dollars in cash to send to my poor—poor wive.

Truly I'm mad!! Can't you understand the circumstances? Or you thing there is some fraud? When I applied to you 3 years ago to send me away from New York City you shipped me in the same day (look in your records and you'll find it). And now when my wife is appealing to you for the same purpose—to send her to the South West to her husband whom you shipped out—You ask money (#20.00).

Joseph Lipetz

* * *

June 30, 1908

Industrial Removal Office
174 Second Ave.
North-east Corner 11th Street
New York City, N.Y.

Dear Sir:

Your favor of June 26, 1908 to Mr. Abraham Lipetz—at hand.

In reply I beg to inform you that Abraham Lipetz is my brother, his name is now Abraham Lee and a partner of mine in the business conducted by us. He was shipped out by you last year from New York City.

My wife Anna Lee was shipped out by you in 1907 and my self came to St. Louis, Mo. in 1903 through your New York office.

Our business is growing. I need a shoemaker badly; and therefore I beg to send me at once a good shoemaker who will have a steady place to work—piece work,—it is understood that I don't bound my self with any obligations to the man you'll send me; it is up to him to succeed or not.

I'm ready to assist you all the time in your work giving you the best information about Oklahoma City and vicinity particularly and the Southwest generally.

Hoping to hear from you very soon, I remain

Yours very truly
Joe Lee

*   *   *

July 3rd, 1908

Mr. Joe Lee
114 So. Broadway
Oklahoma City, Okla.

Dear Sir:—

I have yours of the 30th ult and am pleased to learn therefrom that you have succeeded so well since we have sent you away from New York. I am doubly pleased that you are now in a position to offer employment to some one who may be in need of it, but I cannot send any one to you unless you state definitely what terms you are willing to make. You cannot expect us to expend a whole lot of money to send some one to you, if you are not willing to bind yourself to a certain extent. Suppose we should send some one out to you and then you should find that you do not care to employ him. Our money would then be wasted and the man's trip for nothing. That would hardly be fair. If you will specify just exactly the kind of man you want, and tell us the smallest sum you will guarantee him per week, we will endeavor to help you.

Very truly yours,
David Bressler

LETTERS TO AND FROM BENNY FINKELKRAUT

During the early part of the twentieth century, New York's Jewish community experienced a worrisome rise in prostitution among eastern European immigrants.[21] Contemporary and later sources agree that for much of the prewar period Jews, not Italians, were most often identified as procurers, pimps, madams, and prostitutes.[22]

David Bressler and other Jewish community workers were acutely aware of the problem. Because the IRO sent thousands of immigrants across state lines, office officials exercised extreme caution lest the organization be accused of transporting Jewish women for immoral purposes.[23] Consequently, Bressler made certain that the IRO did nothing to place immigrant Jewish women in dubious or compromising situations. As a matter of policy, the IRO refused to send unaccompanied unmarried women or women who were not relatives to persons who requested them. Thus, the IRO's assistant manager, Philip Seman, sent an unusual response when he agreed to Benny Finkelkraut's request (in Yiddish) to send him his fiancée.

Minneapolis in 1913 had a Jewish community of about 15,000 persons in a general population of 300,000. Russian and Romanian Jews were predominant. The community sustained seven Orthodox and one Reform synagogue, three Hebrew schools, a number of Jewish fraternal and social organizations, and a unified Jewish philanthropic association.[24]

Minneapolis, April 30, 1913

To the Removal Office in New York.

Fully three months have passed since I was sent to Minneapolis, Minnesota, through your office. I therefore take great pleasure in informing you about my welfare. I am, in the first place, highly satisfied and am obliged to give you my heartiest thanks and best wishes for your noble work. I also wish you success in your undertaking.

Now, dear friends, I have another favor to ask and I hope you will not refuse me. Before telling you what I want, I shall give you a little of my past in New York, mentally and physically. I was in New York for sixteen months, and for sixteen months I suffered. In fact, I was disgusted with my life. I am a young man of 29 years of age, and I definitely saw no future for myself in New York. The most I ever earned there was from $5 to $6 a week. I had no trade, for in the old country I was a clerk. However, I have a lot of ambition and energy. So I decided to apply to you to leave New York, for in a smaller place there is a greater chance to get on to something.

You sent me to Minneapolis, Minnesota. I arrived safely at my destination and immediately found employment at $9 a week. I left this position and secured another one at $12 a week. After a short time, I gave up this position and secured a job as assistant machinist with the Chicago, Milwaukee, and St. Paul Railroad Company. I work 8 hours a day and earn $60 a month. This is a steady position. The work is not hard, and my hours are only up to 4 o'clock in the afternoon. I enjoy this place very much. I have good friends here and have met some very nice people. I feel I am progressing in the right direction.

However, I have one regret. And that is that I did not tell you the truth when you asked me whether I was engaged to be married. I told you that

I was not. In truth, I am engaged to a young girl in New York, whom I love more than my life. And when I told you an untruth, I did not intend in any way to run away from her. She did not want me to leave New York. But since I had resolved to no longer remain there, I thought it best not to mention to you the fact that I was engaged to a young girl. She was probably under the impression that if I left New York, I would sever all my connections to her. That is why she objected so strenuously.

Now, dear friends, I ask you kindly to send her to Minneapolis as quickly as possible. As soon as she arrives here, we will set a date for our marriage. Unfortunately, I am not yet in a position to send her a ticket. So I ask you kindly to finish your good work and send my bride to me.

She is at the following address:
New York
Mr. H. Singer
204 E. 99 St.
c/o Sadie Freeman
My address, where you can send your answer, is:
Mr. B. Finkelkraut
Minneapolis, Minn.
1521 6th St. So.
With best wishes to all the staff of the Removal Office,

Yours truly
B. Finkelkraut

*   *   *

May 7, 1913

Mr. Benny Finkelkraut
1581 6th St. So.,
Minneapolis, Minn.

Dear Sir:—

We have your favor of the 30th ult. wherein you inform us that you are very well satisfied at having been sent to the above city and that you will never forget our assistance in your case. In reply we beg to state that we are indeed glad to hear of your success and welfare. Regarding the transportation of your fiance, we beg to refer you to our representative, Miss Anna L. Fox, 14 Fourth St. No. in your city, who will no doubt inform us as to your request.[25] Also, please write your fiance to call at our office and file an application.

Very truly yours,
Industrial Removal Office
per
Philip Seman

LETTERS TO AND FROM H. SCHREIBER

In July 1916, the IRO sent Mr. H. Schreiber to Chicago.[26] After two months in the city, he wrote to ask for his family. As part of its procedure, the IRO asked removals to contribute something toward tickets for their family. In this case, Schreiber pleaded poverty and an inability to contribute anything toward the cost. Schreiber's letter is unique in that he invoked almost every stratagem—flattery, appeals to conscience, agreeing to undergo investigation, and threats—to get the IRO to assent to his request. It worked. After reading his letter, the IRO agreed to pay the entire fare.

The letter was composed in fairly polished English—most likely translated for the IRO from the original Yiddish or written for Schreiber. I have added punctuation to enhance readability.

At the time Schreiber wrote his letter, Chicago's Jewish population numbered about 200,000 out of a general population of more than 2 million. Almost 80 percent of Chicago's Jewish citizens were Russian-born. The Jewish community supported fifty-five Orthodox and five Reform congregations; two Jewish settlement houses; more than one hundred Jewish fraternal, educational, and cultural organizations; and more than fifty benevolent, charitable, and relief societies as well as a city-wide Jewish Aid Society.[27]

* * *

Chicago Ill. Oct. 20th 1916

My Dear Sir Esq.

My wife writes me that the charity of New York City are insisting upon my poor wife of giving them fifteen dollars towards that transportation.

Dear Sir, I think it is the most greatest sin and crime being committed towards humanity for trying to bleed a poor helpless woman with three small children and demanding fifteen dollars from her, when the only means of their existence depends upon the few dollars I can send her, and I can send her the utmost from five to six dollars per week. I am earning fourteen dollars per week. My board is five dollars per week besides my dinners, laundry, and other expenses. I need at least from seven to eight dollars per week for myself in which, if my family would be here, I would have enough for my family to live on.

I am only two months in Chicago, and I bought furniture for sixty-five dollars in cash. I am paying my rent for four rooms since Oct. 10th 1916. My rent is only seven dollars per month. I have done my utmost to accomplish a complete home for my family and have sent her money to live on with the children.

Dear Sir, you can honestly believe me, if I could loan anywhere those 15 dollars I would let you people have it at once. But unfortunately I have no possible means or ways to help myself.

Dear sir, I honestly swear to you as soon as God will help me to get on my feet, I will refund every penny to you people for advancing this money towards my families transportation. So you see, I have good intentions. I will not accept that great favor as a charitable term, but merely as an extended loan. I will return that money to you at my earliest convenience, after a thorough investigation by the Jewish Aid Society of Chicago and provided the assurance of the Jewish Aid Society of Chicago proving to them I am able to support my family. My employer signed a guarantee to that extent. Everything is all completed now. I have preserved a good home for my family and paid for a months rent and have prepared every thing, and am anxiously waiting and longing for the arrival of my family.

I received a letter from my wife stating that not unless she will pay fifteen dollars towards that expense, my family cannot be transported to Chicago. Dear Sir, you no doubt are a father of children. Do you think it is fair or human for a charitable institution to impose upon a poor devil like me to contribute such a large sum of money in order to receive my family. It is absolutely impossible for me to contribute a single penny at present. But as I have stated above, I will return every penny to you at my earliest convenience. In the meantime, I think it would be an outrageous crime against God or humanity to keep a poor woman with three children, torturing them to death and keeping them in constant misery, penniless, and having starvation staring them in their faces. And their father and supporter is drifted one thousand miles apart from them merely because the present unfortunate circumstances does not allow me to donate that money. And for the sake of those few dollars you are creating misery, poverty, and tearing away a loyal father of three helpless children. Don't you think for a moment that my heart is bleeding for them after I have done my utmost of providing a good home for them. Supposing I will get discouraged now and will sell everything for a few dollars and will ignore my family and throw everything off my mind? Don't you think my family will fall a great burden upon the shoulders of the United Hebrew Charities of New York, and will have to support them and will create a lot of trouble for the Desertion Bureau of New York to locate me as their supporter to transport me to New York and legal action will be taken against me for non support? I will certainly defend myself in law, proving the facts that you people are the cause of my disappearance, and through your negligence four poor victims had to suffer the consequences. And the public news papers would publish a big article about the United Jewish Charities of America being mean and selfish toward the poor element in time of need.

You can honestly believe me, it is a very bitter pill to me to approach you people to assist me at present. But I hope I will be able to return that money to you within a very short time. So I beg of you, dear sir, as a good hearted soul and a man of intelligence, kindly act as a good samaritan and see to it that we shall not—God forbid—have to go to our grave in our young days through your negligence, as we are in the best prime of life. So I beg of you, kindly take immediate action upon this matter and see to transport my family at once. It is a very urgent necessity for me to have them here at once, and let five young people lead a life of happiness, instead of leading a life of misery and in darkness.

Hoping that my anxious desires and my longings for my family, my heart will soon be filled with joy. In that behalf, God will reward you people for it. He will bestow the blessings of heaven upon your genuine hearts with health, luck, and success.

Kindly honor me with an immediate reply and best results. Best regards and success to all. I remain yours fraternally,

> H. Schreiber, c/o H. Sobel
> 1422 S. Central Park Dr.
> Chicago, Ill.

*   *   *

Oct. 23rd, 1916

Mr. H. Schreiber,
c/o H. Sobel,
1422 S. Central Park Ave.,
Chicago, Ill.

Dear Sir:

Replying to your letter of the 20″ inst., we desire to inform you that as soon as your family can get ready to leave, we will forward them to Chicago.

> Yours truly,
> INDUSTRIAL REMOVAL OFFICE

Letters of Complaint

Most complaint correspondence contained grievances about the IRO's New York operation, the place to which the removal was sent, or the treatment the removal received at the hands of the local agent. The immigrant's objections about the place and the local agent often appear in the same letter, as does praise for one aspect of the IRO's work and a protest about something else. Of the selections that follow, one criticizes the IRO, three complain about the new setting, and three denounce the agent.

LETTERS TO AND FROM MRS. SAMUEL FRIEDMAN

Although she appreciated the IRO's help, Mrs. Samuel Friedman resented Bressler's attitude toward her when she applied for assistance.[28] Her letter highlights the misunderstandings that could exist between the immigrants and those charged with assisting them. What the administrators of many American Jewish philanthropies perceived as efficient and modern procedures the immigrants often saw as insensitive, impersonal, and heartless. Bressler considered his questions, intended to ascertain the financial status of the applicant, a necessary formality before granting a loan. Mrs. Friedman, however, saw them as humiliating and demeaning. This letter was written in English.

September 15, 1912
823–15 Ave S.
Minneapolis, Min

Mr. Bressler;
Industrial Removal Office,

Dear Sir:

Inclosed please find ten ($10), the balance of the debt, which we contracted for my transportation to this city.

Allow me to thank you for your kind favor, which can really be called, 'good deeds'. You are reputed to be an educated and clever man, therefore you will not resent criticism that is extended to you. I mean to give mine in good intention.

There are different ways of doing things. The most important is courtesy, if the party that is looking for a favor should be refused gently, he will feel better then if he were granted the request and treated as if he was not among those that can be classed as human, and spoken to as if that party did not know the meaning of insult.

When I applied to you for transportation, I told you everything, and the truth only. Yet, it was not enough. You humiliated me by asking why I do not pawn my jewelry, which was pawned for the last five years, why I do not borrow of friends, and when I told you I owe everybody, you suggested that I should leave my child some place with strangers and go to a hospital to have my second baby. At last, when I told you I intend to pay it all back as it is only a loan, you made me sign a note for $20. My husband had it all arranged with Miss Foxe to pay her $15 as soon as we are in position to do so.[29]

Sir, I do not complain! In fact I am very grateful to you. But the reason I mention it at all is because, you should not think everyone that comes into the office to ask for aid must be a cheat, a liar and ignorant. The few hours that I sat waiting, I had a chance to study the characters that came in. Some may be such I admit, but there are exceptions and a man like you ought to know the difference.

You will excuse us for not settling the bill as promised, because we paid the bills in turns. We are now clear from all debts. Nevertheless we are not less grateful to all our friends and good people, for their kindness.

Mr. Friedman would like to have the note if possible.

Respectfully yours
Mrs. Samuel Friedman

*   *   *

September 19, 1912

Mrs. Samuel Friedman,
823 15th Ave. S.
Minneapolis, Minn.

Dear Madam:

We are in receipt of your kind favor of the 15th instant with check for $10. as a balance in full of the loan made to you some time ago by this office. Thanks for your suggestions contained in your letter. We beg herewith to return your note signed by you Nov. 10, 1911, duly receipted.

Yours very truly,
INDUSTRIAL REMOVAL OFFICE
per
Philip Seman

LETTERS TO AND FROM MOSES GOLDSTEIN

The IRO sent Moses Goldstein to Chattanooga, Tennessee, in March 1913.[30] One month later he wrote to complain about his situation, primarily the cost of living. The cost of living in Chattanooga, however, compared favorably with other Tennessee cities, notably Memphis and Nashville. Surveys by IRO agents in all three cities in 1912 showed that Goldstein's salary of $15 per week corresponded closely to the wages of skilled workers in other trades.[31]

Goldstein's letter illustrates the frustration and anger some removals felt when their expectations were not fulfilled. Because traveling agent Abraham Solomon had recently canvassed Chattanooga, the IRO passed Goldstein's letter on to him for a reply. Solomon's rejoinder is sensitive to Goldstein's anguish. The Mr. Daneman referred to in the letters was a local merchant who served as the IRO's agent in Chattanooga.

In 1912, Chattanooga's Jewish community numbered about eight hundred out of a general population of 60,000. The community supported two Orthodox congregations and one Reform, chapters of two national Jewish fraternal organizations, a Zionist organization, a YMHA, a Jewish social club, and a single community-wide charitable organization. Most of the city's Jews were of Russian origin and engaged in some form of merchandising.[32] The original letter was written in Yiddish and translated by the IRO. That translation appears here.

Chattanooga, Tenn.
April 2, 1913

Worthy Sirs of the Removal Office:

As I was sent by the Removal Office to Chattanooga, Tennessee one month ago, I believe you would be interested in knowing the situation of the unfortunates who are sent here by your office.

My name is Moses Goldstein, of 53 Groftin Street, Brooklyn, N.Y. My family still lives at this address.

During my first week in Chattanooga, I immediately saw that this is no place for a workingman to make a living. In the first place, everything is so expensive it is impossible to earn enough to live. Things are more expensive here than in the largest city in America. A shave costs 15 cents, the price of groceries is exorbitant, and rent is outrageously high. Every family has to pay for water each month, the same way you pay for gas. Just imagine, every child has to bring their own school supplies and books to read from home.

Mr. Daneman persuaded me to bring my son and said we would find him work. Now my son has been going around without work for three weeks.

I also want to inform you that those men sent here by you have all left Chattanooga, for the same reasons I give in this letter.

You should know that I am working for Mr. Daneman, and I get $15 every week, for six days of 9 hours work a day. That is still not such a bad wage for Chattanooga. Today, if I had to look for work some place else, I don't know if I could find anything for $2 a day.

Do you remember a carpenter you sent here by the name of Kopowitz? He worked for Mr. Daneman for 10 days and got sacked. He couldn't find any other work so he had to leave Chattanooga.

So, worthy sirs, as you can see, under these conditions, it is not possible for me to bring my family to Chattanooga. My expenses are $6 per week, and I eat dry bread and herring.

You should know that I have to support a wife and 6 children, so you can understand the terrible situation in which I find myself. Therefore I am writing to you in the hope that you won't let me stay in the middle of this terrible situation in which I find myself.

> With warmest greetings,
> Moses Goldstein

N.B. Dear friends of the Removal Office, I want to tell you that if you're thinking of sending working men to Chattanooga, don't do it. Chattanooga is fifty years behind civilization.

> M. Goldstein
> General Delivery
> Chattanooga, Tenn.

* * *

New York, April 9th, 1913

Mr. Moses Goldstein
c/o General Delivery
Chattanooga, Tenn.

Dear Sir:

Your letter of April 2nd. with your criticism of the city that you are now a citizen of, was referred to me for reply because I was in Chattanooga very recently. Of course, you have been in Chattanooga only a very short time, and you will realize that your opinion of that city on so short an acquaintance may not be altogether correct. I was only there for three days, but I saw enough to convince me that Chattanooga is not fifty years behind civilization. In fact, I noticed that it is a growing industrial town; that the Jewish population is very happy and contented; that men like Mr. Koblentz and Mr. Fine and Mr. Daneman have all started without a button on their coat, and today are respectable and respected citizens of the community, and successful business men. What you say about the price of a shave will apply to almost any city. The cheapest shave to be gotten in New York is ten cents. If you tip the barber five cents that brings it up to fifteen cents. I have noticed quite a few ten cents barber shops in the City of Chattanooga, and you can easily find your way to one of them.

I can sympathize with you and know that the change from a large city to a relatively small one is pretty hard in the beginning. But everything adjusts itself, and if you will constantly bear in mind that it is up to you to make good and become self-reliant, all other good things will follow.

As to your son, I hope that he has by this time been placed in work.

Hoping that you will be of good heart, and that you will put your shoulder to the wheel, and assuring you that we are always interested in your welfare, we are,

> Very truly yours,
> INDUSTRIAL REMOVAL OFFICE
> per,
> A. Solomon

LETTERS TO AND FROM MARY RUBIN

In 1905, the IRO sent the Rubin and Rosenthal families to New Orleans, where they experienced many difficulties.[33] Mary Rubin and a member of the Rosenthal family composed a bitter and sarcastic letter blaming the IRO for their plight. A second letter was sent by Rubin alone. In it, she threatened to publicize the organization's failures. Although David Bressler took her to task for the tone of her letter and her threats, he promised to look into the matter.

Rubin's letters were written in English. The first is obviously a cooperative effort because the narration moves from first to third person. The second was written by or for Mary Rubin alone.

New Orleans in 1905 contained about 5,000 Jews out of a general population of 280,000. Most of the Jewish population consisted of German Jews whose families had settled in the city in the nineteenth century. The Jewish community supported two Orthodox and three Reform synagogues, a YMHA, and a number of charitable and fraternal organizations.[34]

New Orleans La. Feb. 21, 1905

Mr. Bressler,

We thank you very much for the kindness for which you have shown us, and send us to New Orleans. You have send us out here to starve for hunger and live in the streets. You have told us, before you have send us, that you will try the best for us. And I suppose thats the best you could do. We have arrived in New Orleans about 12 o'clock in the night, and there was knowbody to await us there, and we had to go around alnight and look for the address which you have given us. And when we did find it, Mr. Cohen told us that he had nothing to do with it and he won't let us in. So we had to look for somebody else where Mr. Cohen has send us. When we have found him, they put the nine of us all in one room, with out a bed or a pillow to sleep on, that was all done well. Then they took Mr. Rubin and his wife [Mary Rubin] up to the cigar factory and gave them both a job. Mrs. Rubin is getting about four ($4) a week and Mr. Rubin five ($5). Now we will ask you if a family man can make a living with that. And Mr. Rosenthal they told if he wants work he will have to look for it himself. So he had to go out looking for work himself. And when he found work, and they told him to bring his tools and come to work. He went to the office and asked for the tools; they told him that he can't have them.

Now we will ask your advice, and let us know what we are to do out here. Thursday when we have been on the depot, the expressman from the office, Mr. Saltzman, told us that the furniture was not paid for yet, and that you have send him for the receipts, and that they will send them to us through the office. And we have not received them, yet we will also hold you responsible for the furniture.

> From
> Mrs. Rubin & Mr. Rosenthal.
> answer at once,

They have also told us that you did not tell them that we had any furniture, and that they can't get any rooms for us. We are still in your lowly lodging house.

534 (South) Ramport St.

New Orleans La.

I will again ask you to answer at once.

*   *   *

New Orleans Mar. 6, 1905

Mr. Bressler,

I have written you one letter, but did not get any answer on it, but I will try and send you a second one, hoping that you will answer this one.

You have send us out here, as I've said before, to starve. We came here, and they claim that we have furniture, and that they can't do anything for us. Now you knew well enough that we have furniture and everything else; and if you knew that they have know use for a respectable family, you had no right to send us here. They need a lot of beggers out here, that could go every day to another society [charity] and beg, but we are not use to that. We have lived in N.Y. for over 13 years and have not received one cent from the charity, and we can't do that now either. So we beg of you to try and do something for us. And if you can't do anything with us in N.O., then we want you to take us back where you have taken us from. They send mama to be a cook for $4 dollars a month, which she had never done before, and if she wanted to be a cook in N.Y. she could have gotten 3 times that much or more, but it did not suit us to let our mother be a cook, and now we should have to do. I beg of you again to take us back to N.Y., because if you don't we will come back anyway, and there is sure to be trouble then. We will sell every bit of our furniture and come back; so you need not think that we will keep still over it, because we are poor but respectable. And if we have to sell our furniture out here, it will cost you twice the amount when we get there. Still more, I will have your charity house published in all the papers and I don't think it will be very pleasant for any of you that belong to it. So far every family that you have send out here, they have all been arrested. And why, because they go to the charity committee and beg for work, to keep them from starving for hunger. They have also given my husband a job in a cigar factory to run an elevator for $4 dollar a week. Now I will ask you if two familys could make a living with that. So he had to go out looking for a job him self. And now he is the only one working and supports the family, and his salary is not much $9 dollars, and he works on the boats, which is worse than a prisoners work. And if you knew that it was such a town, I don't see why you send us here, Kindly answer at once.

> From Mrs. Rubin
> 731 Dryades St.
> New Orleans La.

P.S. answer

* * *

> March 13th, 1905

Mrs. Mary Rubin,
731 Dryades St.
New Orleans, La.

Dear Madam:—

We beg to acknowledge receipt of your favor of March 6th. I cannot for the life of me understand what the trouble is. In sending you and your husband away from New York together with the other members of the family, we did so upon your own request and with the best intentions in the world, for we had assurances that efforts would be made to furnish you the means for a livelihood. You recall what I told you before you left that the working members of your family would have to be ready to accept work at anything, as I could not guarantee that positions at their trade could be obtained at the very outset. Your husband is working now making $9.00 a week, which is a great deal more than he made in New York for a long time. You say that he is working very hard, but then that must be expected; when he is known a little better in New Orleans I have no doubt he will succeed in finding a more congenial position. As for your mother working as cook for $4.00 a month, no one compels her to do that. I haven't the least doubt in the world that if she is willing to remain as cook she can easily get three times that amount right in New Orleans. You must simply await your opportunity.

The tone of your letter is such that you can hardly expect any sympathy, for threats of the kind you make are wasted on the desert air and do not influence us one bit, so I would suggest the advisability of ceasing such useless tactics, for they certainly will not avail you anything. We have tried to do the best we could for you and we are still desirous to continue doing so, but you must meet us in a fair spirit. I have written to-day to a gentleman in New Orleans, asking him to inquire into your case and you will soon hear from us again.

Very truly yours,
David Bressler

LETTERS TO AND FROM ISRAEL GINSBURG

Because Chicago had a large Jewish community and many of the same urban problems that New York did, the IRO rarely shipped removals there. In 1905, the year Israel Ginsburg wrote his letters, Chicago's Jewish population stood at about 80,000.[35] Most of the city's Jews congregated on the West Side, which was dubbed "the Chicago Ghetto." Russian Jews formed the majority of Chicago Jewry.[36]

Removals who ended up in Chicago usually migrated there of their own volition. Israel Ginsburg was different. The IRO sent him to Indianapolis at the end of June 1905. According to Ginsburg, after ten days of not being able to find him work, the Indianapolis IRO committee shipped him to Chicago. Indianapolis sometimes reacted like this, when it could not quickly place the removal.[37] Ginsburg also encountered adversities in Chicago, so he wrote to the IRO asking for help.

In his letters, Ginsburg blamed the Indianapolis IRO committee for its actions and criticized the IRO for having sent him to Indianapolis in the first place. He claimed that the IRO office intentionally misled him as well as other immigrants. After cataloging his grievances, he lectured the IRO on how to behave toward those who came for help. He asked the office to find him a job or return him to New York, threatening otherwise to publicize the IRO's actions in the Yiddish press.

Ginsburg originally wrote his letters in Hungarian, and the IRO had them translated into English. With some slight editing to enhance readability, these translations appear here.

19 July 1905 Chicago

Removal Office of the City of N.Y.

Dear President.

I, Israel Ginsburg, was sent by you, on the 28 of the last June, to Indianapolis. It was supposed, that this way my plight will be improved. The result is: I am abandoned in an unknown place. I came to Indianapolis with your letter to Mr. Wolf.[38] He registered my name in a book, gave me lodging and boarding. I was there ten days. They couldn't find work for me and have sent me away to Chicago without resources. Now I am in Chicago. I wander around hungry and I cannot find work. I don't know to whom to appeal. I live on a little piece of bread. My forces leave me. The heat is unbearable. I actually go crazy. Although I lived only on 5 dollars in N.Y., yet I pulled through. A man from your office on 2nd Ave. persuaded me, and in the Tageblatt it was assured, that your Office is to be trusted.[39] But I have seen others in Indianapolis who were sent to Virginia. They became like savages, hungry, excruciated, and worn out. That's what I have seen.

And as far I am concerned, I don't grasp what you have done with me. I wanted to go to Indianapolis. One of your Office persuaded me it would be all right. A friend of mine was sent there too, and every trace of him is lost. If there is no place for newcomers, why should they be sent there. In New York I worked at 21 E. Houston, sheet trimmings factory, Berlin & Trossky [name of company]. I could work there until now.

And now I don't know what to do. I don't find work in Chicago. I have no means to go back. I have sold everything. Although I didn't call at the Charities in Chicago, I was told they don't send people back to New York.

For me it is best to go to New York, to live at least half hungry, not hungry entirely. I therefore ask you to do something for me. Write them to send me back to New York. Write to them and to me some brief [letter], to show them.

If you knew what I have had to suffer. And it is a shame to me before the people in New York. They write me: "We told you before hand not to trust the Office"—although it is not your fault that work cannot be found for me in Indianapolis.

Dear Sir, I think you will not mind that little sum of money, what my return may cost you. You'll save me and I'll thank you the moment I'll come. There are people here who advise me to go to Christian charities. But I find it more fit to apply to my previous benefactors and don't want to evoke the reproach on the part of the gentiles. All the more, we are "merciful children of the merciful." I expect your immediate answer upon receiving my letter.

With respect, Israel Ginsburg
My address: Chicago, Ill.
529 W. Taylor St. Mr Black
for Israel Ginsburg

* * *

August 2nd, 1905

Mr. Israel Ginsburg,
c/o Mr. Black
529 W. Taylor St,
Chicago, Ill.

Dear Sir:—

We have your favor of the 19th. ult. contents of which we have read. We are sorry to hear that you have suffered. We have received a report concerning you from Indianapolis which conflicts with your story. A position was obtained for you at the Big Four Railroad Yard as car repairer for $1.25 per day. You say you could still have obtained the position you held at 21 E. Houston Street where you earned $5. a week. This is not what you stated when you were at our office. You said you had been out of work for four weeks and could find no job. Surely you should have been happy to obtain the position as car repairer at the Big Four Yard where other men sent by this office are working steadily. We are sorry you do not realize how much harm you are doing to others by your conduct. We can do nothing more for you.

Yours very truly,
David Bressler

* * *

Chicago 5 August 1905

Industrial Removal Office N.Y.

Your favor from 2 August I received. I don't really know what to write you. I didn't expect from you such an answer. I thought you'll send me a ticket, and you have sent me a letter, written in a refined literary English language. It was very pleasant to read. Vive la langue anglaise. You wrote to Wolf, and he answered you, I don't know how. God is with him. I'll only bill you. I could not consent to do what Wolf offered me for 1 dollar 25 cents a day, to carry all kind of goods, old iron, etc. In a word, to do things the Englishman doesn't want to do for any price.

I have calculated this way: 1.25 car fare to the work and back, 4 dollars for board and lodging. You need a special clothing for this work. Besides it is without prospects. Is it worthwhile? There were two other Jews working there. I discussed with them the subject. They curse the day they took up this work. And even if they were satisfied, are all people alike, and can everybody do the same work? He [Wolf] kept me 10 days before they got me work. I could this way spend time in New York. I told your people everything to the detail. I looked for their advice, as that of intelligent men. I told them I can easily get work in New York in two weeks, and I shall get 7 and 8 dollars. But they waved only their hand at the idea of staying in New York, and told me a young man can easily make 12 and 13 dollars a week, and in time he can push forward. This is the conversation I had with the employees of the Office on 2 Ave. One has spoken and the other seconded. And when I have applied to the office on 174 2n Ave for information, your people were full of praises, showing me the Tageblatt. And the chief trump [reference unclear] of your office, when I tried to ask about details, he raised his voice and said he doesn't want to have long talks with me. He raised his voice with the gravity of a governor. This way he caught the little fish on the hook. You as employers are trying to do more work in order to make a better show, and you forget that you are killing human lives in order to serve your personal ends. I have seen another man, who was sent the same day, but not to Indianapolis. He is in Chicago, wandering, crying, and cursing you. One young man more, from Hungary, was sent by you. He is walking along the streets of Chicago, bootless and breadless. His only dream is to get back to New York. I am not the only one. All are crying and grumbling. I think there is no reason to send people away without the proper foundation.

The luck presented to us by those various Wolfs we can get right in New York. All this kind of work we can get for 1.75 instead of 1.25 a day. Looking at your formalities, I was really sure there is something in view, something better. One more of my acquaintances, Corogin, who was in Indianapolis is now in Hospital. He hurt his leg and burned his hands and is sick. But that is enough as to the deficiencies. I think it is not so much your fault as the fault of your agents. They take 50 dollars a month and they find only work to carry foul lumber or something else of this kind. And your fault is that you don't tell the people exactly how the matter stands in order that the people may have a clear idea what confronts them. You know only one answer: Ich weiss nicht [I don't know]. This is the whole misfortune. If you'd say, this is our work, who would go?

If you'd ask me how I lived in Chicago these two weeks since my first letter, I can tell you. I asked help from my acquaintances in New York. You may ask Mrs. D. Levitan, 550 E. 116 St. She collected a few dollars and sent it over to me in Chicago. If not for this help, I'd die from hunger. I try to find work. This week I earned 2 dollars working for a Polish man. That's all.

And now I appeal to you with the same request. Or please give me a job in Chicago, but not a common one, or send me back to New York, because you sent me away. Otherwise I'll ask for help in publicity. If you don't send me a ticket I'll appeal to the Forward, the Tagblatt, and all those who have a warm Jewish heart, because I am entrapped and was deceived. Are you really so reserved with such a trifling sum of money, or you don't want your name to be spoiled? And for this reason you are staking my soul and I am personally so insignificant to you. How much pain and humiliation this brings to my heart, when I recollect that I've made a mistake and it is so difficult to correct it.

I ask you again. In the name of God and his saints, and in the name of all that is sacred—please either give me a job or ship me back to New York. And I'll know for the future what America is and how to talk to American Jews. The American philanthropy is only a matter of show, of advertising, to pose before others as benefactors.

I don't find any more to write you, because my head refuses to continue in its service. I'll ask you only one thing. If you are persistent in your cruelty at this time too, and you are not sending me a ticket and 1 dollar for expenses, please answer me this very day and don't wait. I must know what to do. I'll think out something else. But I don't think that you'll send me an expression of sorrow on paper.

Be healthy and lucky and well inclined to send me the ticket.

> Israel Ginsburg
> address: 529 Taylor St. Mr. Black for Israel
> Ginsburg. Chicago, Ill.

Sent on the 28th of June to Indianapolis, Indiana

LETTERS TO AND FROM JOSEPH DAVIDOWITZ AND FROIM KRAVITZ

Once the removal reached his destination, the local IRO agent was the person with whom he had the most contact and upon whom he depended most. The local representative found the removal lodging, provided him with food and sometimes money, and helped him find a job. If things went well, the removal praised and blessed the agent; if things went badly, he cursed him and complained to the New York office. The remaining letters in this section all protest the behavior of the local agents.

The exchange between Joseph Davidowitz and David Bressler illustrates the antagonism that could develop between a removal and the local agent. Although Bressler and the traveling agents toured various communities and monitered the work of the local agents, they were not always aware of problems. In this instance, Bressler acknowledged that the criticism might be justified, suggesting that Davidowitz contact another Memphis Jewish businessman who could help him.

In his letter, Froim Kravitz reinforced Davidowitz's complaints and even mentioned him. Kravitz also threatened to commit suicide. Although many removals included this threat in their correspondence, Jewish law forbids the taking of one's own life: a Jew who commits self-murder is deemed to be outside the pale of the Jewish community. As such, he or she forfeits the rituals due to the deceased.[40] The eastern European immigrants, most of whom came from traditional backgrounds, employed this threat because they believed it was the only way to gain sympathy and wring concessions from the IRO's German Jewish managers. The threat of suicide reflected the ongoing lack of communication and trust that existed between the Americanized German Jews and their eastern European clients.

Bressler did not reply to Kravitz. Both Davidowitz's and Kravitz's letters are translated from Yiddish.

In 1906, the Jewish community of Memphis contained approximately 2,500 persons in a total population of 120,000. The community sustained three Orthodox congregations and one Reform and a variety of benevolent, social, and fraternal organizations, including a Hebrew Ladies Benevolent Society, a United Hebrew Relief Association, a YMHA, a B'nai B'rith lodge, a Zionist Society, and the exclusive Memphis Club. Memphis's Jews engaged in a variety of occupations, but most worked in some form of merchandising.[41]

Best and Dear Caretakers:[42]

(merciful sons of merciful men)

You send people to make a living in Memphis, and you also tell them that your ideals are to make Jews live in all parts of the land and have them make a decent living. Yes! It is true! Jews can make livings if your agents would only try and devote themselves earnestly to their work and not care for themselves only. They mock and laugh at the people sent to them. They give jobs from which no living can be made.

Here you have sent me. (My name is Davidowitz.) I have a wife and three children in Russia who live in fear of the Russians. I am in Memphis and don't earn anything. And when I ask the agent to give me a position and help me make a living, he tells me that it does not concern him.

If you don't want me and the other people to make a living, don't send the rest of them out. And if you do help us to make a living, we shall pay you back every cent. It is just a waste of money if it is used the way it is at present. I know that the money sent to Russia for relief has also the same purpose and has come to nothing.

> Joseph Davidowitz
> c/o Heyman
> 361 No. 2nd Street
> Memphis, Tenn.

*   *   *

March 9, 1906

Mr. Joseph Davidowitz
c/o Heyman,
361 No. 2nd Street
Memphis, Tenn.

Dear Sir:—

We have your favor of recent date, in which we regret to read that you have not as yet been satisfactorily established in Memphis. We cannot understand why, because we know that our agent does his work conscientiously and is personally interested in all of the people that we send to him. We have sent a translation of your letter to our Committee, with the request that they look into it.

> Yours very truly,
> David Bressler

*   *   *

Memphis, Tenn.
March 13, 1906

Sirs:

I have received your letter and am very much grieved at the fact that you have no knowledge of what takes place here.

Maybe it is possible for you to send here a man incognito, a man of righteousness, to ascertain every fact. He will see that only those to whom food, a dollar or so, and a suit of clothes are given by the agent are the ones to be satisfied. I will give you Mr. Rosenthal as an example. Two months have already elapsed, and he still makes no living. But for him it is profitable because he earns $3 a week and is supplied with all the necessary expenses by the agent. And so he is satisfied.

As for the rest of us, we cannot make a living. Sinowitz was sent away, but we do not know to where.

I protest against the way I am treated, but the agent, in order to get his revenge, laughs and taunts me. I earn nothing and therefore want you to take me back to New York, where I will feel better. If not, I shall be forced to walk back on my own.

Joseph Davidowitz

* * *

Mch. 27th, 1906

Mr. Joseph Davidowitz
c/o Heyman,
361 No. 2nd St.,
Memphis, Tenn.

Dear Sir:—

We have your letter of Mch. 13th. I suggest that you call upon Mr. Emil Nathan, 66 South Main Street and tell him your grievance. I am quite sure that you will receive courteous and satisfactory treatment from him.

Yours truly,
David Bressler

* * *

Memphis, Tenn.
March 29th

Honorable Sirs:

I wish to ask you to put an end to the game which your agent, Mr. Buzik, plays with us. I would rather go back to Russia and be persecuted and ill-treated by the Russian anti-Semites than to be badly treated by a Jewish anti-Semite. Mr. Buzik is an anti-Semite. He rejoices when he sees us suffer. Nothing is done for us unfortunates.

I begged him to send to Chicago for $15 worth of merchandise from which I can earn a livelihood. I told him he could keep the goods in his possession and only advance $5 worth of stock to me. He refused to do so because I could earn 50 cents. If Mr. Buzik wants me to do business, give me goods so that I can earn something.

In other words, it costs our Jewish people much money, but with no good results, only losses.

Sinowitz returned through the assistance of English workmen.

Joseph Davidowitz

* * *

Memphis, Tenn. Apr. 27, 1906[43]

Dear Sir and Manager:

Your words with which you console the person, during the time you hand him food, when he is about to get on the express, to ride out of this crowded city of New York, these words ring harmoniously in his ears. They are clear and comfortable words meant for a good purpose and meant to accomplish much. True, your idea to spread people over the U.S. is a very good one, but the results of it are very sad.

I will take myself as an example. I called at your office and asked you to send me away. I also told you the real truth about my profession, and you have also inquired as to its truth. I brought you the necessary references and gave you all the information desired.

Now, I ask you, why do you take so much responsibility upon yourself, that a family should cry because of you. I told you I was not in a position to bring my family to New York, and you sent me to this place where you said I could make a living. But it is not so.

Not only have you caused misfortune to me and my family but to other people as well. From the time I arrived in Memphis till now, I have not seen any future for myself. I have not a cent. All I had, I spent. The thought that something may turn up was always in my mind, but my patience was in vain. Your agent does nothing for me. And now the only thing left for me to do is to throw myself in the Mississippi River.

Is this what Baron de Hirsch intended? That on account of his money, people should be forced to commit suicide? I don't even have 5 cents in my pocket to write a letter to my wife to let her know about my troubles. I therefore wish, gentlemen, that you send me to St. Louis, because St. Louis is a larger city, and more business is done there than in Memphis.

In New York, I was able to take a pushcart in order to make a living. And here I can not even do this. Send me to St. Louis and save me and my family from starvation.

Here is a list of people you sent here. Kindly notice what happened to them: Mr. Skokolsky cries and curses the day he arrived here. Mr. Zavinstein has fortunately found some nephew of his and was taken to his city. Abe Rosenthal and Mr. Silberman were idle for many weeks until, finally, Mr. Emil Nathan found jobs for them, as bottle washers, in his own store. The two painters have no work here. You sent two greenhorns, one a Russian and the other a Hungarian. One is at present working in a shoe factory and earns 3 dollars a week. The other shovels dirt and carries heavy loads. Davidowitz told me he wrote you a letter letting you know about all his troubles with your agent Mr. Buzik.

Kindly see what you can do for me and have pity on my wife and child who are in Russia.

Froim Kravitz

LETTERS TO AND FROM HARRY LISS ET AL.

The following letter (in Yiddish) was signed by five removals who had been dispatched to Spokane, Washington, in 1909.[44] They complained bitterly about the local agent, who, according to them, had no time for them. David Bressler may have suspected that there was some truth to their complaint because he asked them to contact another member of the local IRO committee. Whatever the merits of this particular case, a number of local agents found that they simply did not have time to do more for the removals than they were already doing. The removals, however, expected more. These differing perceptions could lead to misunderstanding and conflict.

In 1909, Spokane contained about seven hundred Jews, mostly Polish and Russian, out of a population of 100,000. They supported one Orthodox and one Reform synagogue, a chapter of the B'nai B'rith, two charitable societies, and a Zionist organization.[45]

Spokane, Dec. 28, 1909

To the worthy Mr. Bressler:

Dear Mr. Bressler:

We, the immigrants sent to Spokane, thank you heartily for your action. You have tried your best to send us to a place where we should earn a respectable livelihood for us and our families. But in one thing you have erred. You gave us letters to one Mr. Pross, that he should find work for us. You have done your share of the work, and we believe that you intended to do everything for us. But Mr. Pross has done nothing for us. And to say that he is not a gentleman would be saying too little. A gentleman would not make a comment such as "All immigrants who come to Spokane should be burned." And all for the simple reason that we asked him to find us something to do. It did not matter if the work was not in our trades. Anything would be satisfactory.

Mr. Pross has a private business, a secondhand furniture store, which he has to attend to. He has no time to engage in this work. There are immigrants who have been here for 2, 3, and 6 weeks and still do not have jobs.

Therefore, I, Harry Liss, went to the mayor's office and asked him to find work for me because I can't feed my family and I have nothing to live on. Pross said that the society [the local IRO committee] has done enough for me and that the two weeks' board that I was given is enough.

The mayor asked me how I came to Spokane, and I told him the truth. Afterward it was published in all the newspapers that Pross does nothing for the immigrants. You can see by the clippings that quite a few of the men have been to the mayor's office. We have also applied to Kussner, chairman of the Relief Committee, and also to Feuchtwanger.[46] They told us that they can do nothing for us. They referred us to Pross, and Pross can only be found in the saloons.

We beg you, Mr. Bressler, to write to us about what to do. Spokane has no factories. It is only a city of hotels and saloons. We don't know what kind of a living we can make here. And we don't know why you send people here. The man who is in the building trade can make a living. But the common laborer has no chance to make a living here.

Mr. Bressler, we advise you to engage someone with more feeling to be the agent here. A man who can sympathize with his Jewish brethren and who is more competent than Pross. Then will your work be crowned with success. Thanking you in advance,

> Harry Liss, Sam Seligman, Hyman Stenbock, Joe Cohen,
>   Louis Nauterman
> Please answer us at the following address:
> Mr. Harry Liss
> 1105 4th Av.
> Spokane, Wash.

*   *   *

January 5th, 1910

Mr. Harry Liss
1105—4th Avenue
Spokane, Wash.

Dear Sir:—

I have your letter of the 28th ult, and am very much grieved to learn that you and those who sign the letter with you are so much dissatisfied with the treatment accorded you by the agent, Mr. Pross. I am glad that you appreciate that we have done everything in our power to improve your condition, for we can assure you that we would not have sent you to any city where we believed you would have cause to complain of conditions. I think possibly your whole difficulty at the present moment is due to a misunderstanding, which I am very hopeful can be remedied. I have today written a long letter to Mr. Feuchtwanger, who is one of the most prominent gentlemen in Spokane, and who I know has endeavored to do everything in his power for the relief and welfare of our coreligionists.

Call upon him again and state your case fully. I am quite sure you are mistaken as to your information that there are no opportunities for employment in Spokane, because I have been there myself and have ascertained that opportunities are not lacking for able-bodied men, anxious and willing to earn their livelihood. The one thing that they need is some person to introduce them to these places. I am hopeful that my letter to Mr. Feuchtwanger will result in correcting any misapprehension or misunderstanding by which you may have inadvertently suffered.

Yours very truly,
David Bressler

LETTERS TO AND FROM JAKE LIBOFF ET AL.

The following letter from Gary, Indiana, was another group effort.[47] In this instance, however, a local food and liquor merchant, E. A. Gross, also wrote to the IRO endorsing the men's allegations. These removals distrusted the agent and accused him of heinous conduct toward them—another case in which procedures that the IRO viewed as efficient and modern were seen as ruthless and callous. David Bressler and Philip Seman expressed reservations about the removals' allegations and backed their agent, a local attorney named Leon Gould. The removals' letter is translated from Yiddish.

Gary, Indiana, in 1913 contained 40,000 people, of whom approximately eight hundred were Jews. Most of the Jews were of Russian, Hungarian, or German descent. The town accommodated two Orthodox synagogues and one Reform, one Jewish benevolent society, and a number of Jewish fraternal organizations.[48]

Gary 20 July 1913

Memorable Chairman of the Removal Office:

We, the undersigned, first of all, consider it our duty to thank you for having sent us here.

But we have charges to make against your representative Mr. Gould. He met us at the train upon our arrival here, and the first question he asked was whether we had any money with us. The majority of us were penniless. But some had some change, which was promptly taken from them by Mr. Gould.

Then he took us to a restaurant and placed at our disposal, as a lodging, a cellar which was dark and damp. This cellar had been occupied by a married man, a certain Mr. Isidore Muller, who contracted there consumption and was sent to Chicago to receive medical treatment.

The food which we were given was horrible. It consisted of rotten swine meat, which made all of us sick in the stomach, and we were compelled to call a doctor.[49]

Mr. Gould compels us to sign a paper authorizing him to receive our pay. And for this service he charges each of us a dollar a week.

To three of your removals—Siglin, Jacobson, and Koff—who came here penniless, Mr. Gould gave only 50 cents for supper and dinner.

Whoever comes with a letter from Mr. Gould to ask for a job is refused because the employers know that Mr. Gould receives their wages, and naturally they are not very anxious to deal with such working men.

We are all greenhorns, and Mr. Gould is doing with us whatever he pleases. Mr. Isidore Greifer was three days without food. Mr. Gould gave him only 10 cents during these three days. Then he placed him to work in a restaurant, and for three whole months Mr. Greifer did not see a penny of his wages. Mr. Gould held up $50 of his wages, although Greifer owed him only $22.

When a working man is in need and comes to Mr. Gould, he does not want to speak to him. Mr. Gould is a lawyer and of course does not understand the working man, his needs, and troubles and does not sympathize with him.

We appeal to you to do something for us because our position is unbearable. We work here 12 hours a day in a steel factory near fire. And at the end of the day, we cannot move our limbs. In addition to that, we have no proper food and lodgings, although we pay for it more than enough.

For how long will we last? We are getting weaker and weaker from day to day.

Worthy sir, we hope you will look into this matter. Otherwise we will be compelled to make it known to the world.

I. Meltzer

Sam Shlingbaum

Jake Liboff

Isidore Greifer

I. Rushevsky

Israel Polner

Baruch Boik

Harry Epstein

Ignatz Goldberg

Jacob Jacobson

Sam Glowatzky

Max Katz

Sam Siglin

Jonah Rishes

Answering Address:
Mr. Sensebrach for Jake Liboff
1965 Broadway
Gary, Ind.

*   *   *

July 29", 1913

Mr. Jake Liboff
c/o Sensebrach
1945 Broadway
Gary, Ind.

Dear Sir:

We have your letter of a few days ago wherein you and some thirteen other persons seem to complain about the treatment you have received at the hands of our representative in Gary. We desire to say in general in answer to your letter that every single man that has been sent to Gary knew and understood very thoroughly, (because he was personally instructed by myself,) that the work in Gary is unusually hard, and that nothing could be expected from our agent except that he would make every effort to find employment for those sent. Likewise, that he would recommend a boarding house, and that each individual would be expected to sign that the amount advanced for a period of three weeks would be deducted from the wages received from the factories. We have on repeated occasions received very excellent letters of appreciation for what has been done for persons sent by this office to Gary.

Personally, I have made a visit a few months ago and saw a large number of men sent by us. In the majority of the cases the men were perfectly satisfied with what our representative did for them; they also showed me bank books, proving without any doubt that any man who is sent to Gary, who is physically strong enough and willing to work, that he can make a good living and if he is thrifty, can save some money. What surprises us particularly is the fact that your letter has been written on the 20th of July and a number of the persons who have signed this letter only arrived in Gary on the 19th. This is a fact in two cases, that of Sam Glowatsky and Harry Epstein. On the other hand, Jake Lubin, who was sent to Gary on Dec. 23, 1912, Ignatz Goldberg sent January 8th, 1913, Jonah Rishes sent March 12, 1913 and Issy Greifer sent May 8th have absolutely no reason for complaint. They have been in Gary long enough to satisfy us that it is about time they were in a position to look after themselves without writing letters of complaint now. Our advice is to you and the men who have signed their names to the letter that you get busy, go to work, and never mind writing letters. We are convinced and know positively that there is more work in Gary for willing men than the factories there can be supplied with.

We again urge, for your own good, that you throw aside your petty excuses and in earnest make good, for it was our sincerest hope that each and every one that was sent from this office to Gary would, in a short time, be instrumental in bringing over other of his friends, as has been true in a number of cases.

Very truly yours,
INDUSTRIAL REMOVAL OFFICE
per
Philip Seman

* * *

June 6, 1913

Removal Office
New York City

Gentlemen:

A number of the Jewish men you sent here for the last few months in care of Leon Gould of this city have asked me to inform you that Mr. Gould is not fit to have your confidence. These people tell me tales that I do not want to put in writing over my signature.

These people seem to be good hard working people and the way Mr. Gould takes advantage of them has made me to write to you, to kindly send some one to investigate this matter.

Hoping to hear from you, I remain yours

respectfully,
E. A. Gross

* * *

June 9, 1913

Mr. E. A. Gross
The Pure Food Liquor House
Gary, Ind.

Dear Sir:

We have your favor of the 6th instant in which you state "that Mr. Gould is not fit to have your confidence"; further, that "these people tell me tales that I do not want to put in writing over my signature".

Although the statement against him is of a general nature, it is so worded that, if unfounded, it does a grave injustice to Mr. Gould. Realizing that you do not want to be a party to any injustice to anyone any more than we, I would suggest that you ask the complainants to write to us themselves stating specifically the nature of their complaints, and since you have shown your interest to the extent of writing us in the matter, might I request your further cooperation in indicating your opinion of the character and trustworthiness of the complainants.

You will appreciate our caution in the matter, since the sending out of an investigator to Gary upon a general and unverified complaint might leave us open to charges of extravagance, not to say of wastefulness. Our Assistant Manager, Mr. Seman, who was in Gary only a short time ago, personally came in contact with quite a number of the men who were formerly sent out by us, and he was strongly impressed with the progress they had made in the short time they were in your city. They had all the opportunity in the world to complain had they felt justified in doing so, because Mr. Seman invited their confidence; but outside of three Turkish Jews who complained that they did not get any cigarette money from Mr. Gould, they all spoke in terms of praise and appreciation of him. Perhaps you may not know that Mr. Gould has expended so much time and money on our protegees; that he has resigned upon three distinct occasions, and it was only after considerable urging that he consented to continue.

Awaiting the favor of a more definite statement, and with much appreciation, I am

Yours very truly,
David Bressler

CHAPTER 5

Economic Adjustment

Immigrant memoir literature is filled with stories of economic success and failure, as the letters to the IRO also show. A survey of the correspondence shows that a removal's decision to remain where the IRO sent him, generally hinged on whether the removal had made it economically.

LETTERS TO AND FROM NATHAN TOPLITZKY AND MIRIAM HART

The following writers were both from Detroit. The first letter, written in Yiddish, describes Nathan Toplitzky's tragic encounter with factory work. The second correspondent, Miriam Hart, was a young social worker who served as the local IRO representative. She wrote to Abraham Solomon, a traveling agent who also worked in the New York office, to relate the success story of a removal. She and Toplitzky present contrasting perspectives of the economic life of removals in Detroit.

By 1913, Detroit contained about 500,000 residents, 34,000 of whom were Jews. Seventy-five percent of the Jewish population were eastern European immigrants. Detroit's Jewish citizens supported one Reform and fifteen Orthodox congregations; a community-wide Jewish philanthropy organization; a settlement house; a Hebrew day school; and numerous religious and secular fraternal, social, and Zionist organizations.[1] Because of its growing manufacturing base, Detroit was a favorite terminal for the IRO.

Detroit, Mich 3/30/08[2]

Dear Sirs and Friends of the Removal Office:

I, Nathan Toplitzky, sent to the above city 5 months ago, wish to inform you that a great misfortune has happened to me. Your committee has placed me to work in a machine factory where I have earned $.75 a day, and being unskilled I have had 4 of my fingers torn from my right hand.

I now remain a cripple throughout my life. For six weeks my sufferings were indescribable.

When the condition of my health improved a little, I called on the Committee and they advised me to go back to the old employer. I went back to him and he placed me to work at the same machine where the accident occurred. Having lost my fingers I was unable to operate the machine which made me a cripple. I now call daily at the office of the Committee and beg them to give me another job, but they do not want to hear me. I am alone in the city without a cent, without a friend, whereas in New York I have many friends.

Kindly write to your Committee to find a position for me, for you cannot realize how unfortunate I am.

Nathan Toplitzky
128 Napoleon St., Detroit

* * *

April 2, 1908

Nathan Toplitzky
128 Napoleon St.,
Detroit, Mich.

Dear Sir:

In answer to yours of the 30th ult., I regret very much to learn of your mishap, but trust you will in a very short time have recovered. I have no doubt that our agent in Detroit is doing all she can for you and if you are not employed now, it is not because she is not willing to find employment for you, but because it is impossible to do so. In any event call upon her and I am sure she will give you due consideration.

Respectfully yours,
David Bressler

* * *

Detroit, Mich., October 20, 1913[3]

Mr. A. Solomon
Industrial Removal Office
New York

Dear Sir:

The following case appeals to us as being most interesting and covering so much of the work being done by your office and its agencies.

About eight months ago we received, as a direct case a man who had no trade, spoke but little English and seemed anxious to secure employment no matter of what description. We secured work for him in one of our large factories where he was assistant porter and helped in the dining room at noon. After being here about a month, he received, through your office, his wife and family, the eldest a boy of twenty. This young man was given work with his father in the dining room and both were earning about fifteen dollars a week. After a few weeks the father and boy were given entire charge of the dining room and the boy had sent for his chum who had been idle for some time, in New York. The wife received, also through your office, her own people and today the father and son are operating a lunch stand near the factory where they were first employed, and the superintendent tells us that the competition is quite a strong one. The man is now making a very good living and tells us that he is going to bring "all of his friends" to our city.

Very truly yours,
Miriam H. Hart

* * *

Oct. 23, 1913

Miss M. H. Hart
Detroit, Mich.

Dear Miss Hart:

We have your letter of the 20th instant with the account of a notable direct case, for which please accept our thanks. If some time you should run across a similar case, we would appreciate data.

Very truly yours,
Industrial Removal Office

LETTERS TO AND FROM MORRIS WEINKRANTZ

In 1912 the IRO sent Morris Weinkrantz to Des Moines, Iowa.[4] Weinkrantz remained in Des Moines for a year and never managed to succeed.

He left the city in 1913 for Wichita, Kansas. After one year, he opened his own business, the Morris Hat Store, which featured $2.00 specialty hats. The letters he sent to the IRO chronicle his tribulations in Des Moines and his success in Wichita. The correspondence covers two years, and all of his letters were composed in English.

Des Moines, Iowa, in 1912 contained 105,000 inhabitants, of whom 5,500 were Jews, predominantly of Russian descent. The Jewish community supported four Orthodox synagogues and one Reform, a city-wide federated Jewish charity, and four Jewish fraternal organizations.[5]

In 1912, Wichita, Kansas, had about two hundred Jews out of a general population of 66,000. The community contained one Orthodox and one Reform synagogue, a number of Jewish fraternal organizations, and a Jewish charity.[6]

Des Moines, Iowa
May 16, 1912

Mr. Seman
174—2nd ave.
New York City

My dear Mr. Seman,

No doubt you received the post card I sent you telling of my arrival in Des Moines.

I have had an interview with Mr. Marks, and also a friend of his here in this city by the name of Mr. Leon.

They have both taken an interest in my behalf but as yet have not secured anything for me. I have gone around myself in the various shops trying to locate something, but to my sorrow have not succeeded as yet.

I have hired a room with a Jewish boarding house but the rates are very high here. It will cost me approximately $8.00 per week to live here.

If I could only get settled I shall try to locate a place with a private family.

I shall appreciate if you will put your best efforts in seeing what you can do for me. Do you think it advisable in going to St. Joseph, Mo. I have very little money so I must get to doing something and it must be immediately.

Trusting you will look into this at once, and advise further, I beg to remain, with kind regards to yourself and also Mr. Bressler.

Faithfully yours,
Morris Weinkrantz

c/o General Post Office
Des Moines, Iowa

* * *

May 18, 1912

Mr. Morris Weinkrantz
c/o General Delivery
Des Moines, Iowa

Dear Sir:

I am in receipt of your letter of the 16th and am glad that you have been well received by Mr. Marks and his friend Mr. Leon, but I am indeed sorry that you have as yet not found any employment. I am sure, though, that Mr. Marks and Mr. Leon will do their very best in finding some employment for you very soon.

If you find that you cannot find employment in Des Moines within another week or ten days and you feel that you have given the thing a thorough test, I would suggest that you talk with Mr. Marks very frankly and tell him that I have likewise received a letter from St. Joseph from Mr. Feffer, and that Mr. Feffer asked you to come to St. Joseph and promised to interest himself very kindly in your behalf. Should Mr. Marks feel that it would be better for you to go to St. Joseph, let me know at once and I will send you a copy of the letter that Mr. Feffer wrote me and also a letter of introduction to him, and then go there. But remember, do this absolutely with the advice of Mr. Marks. I would much prefer that you give the Des Moines proposition a fair test.

Wishing you every success and hoping that you will find yourself very soon, I am

Very truly yours,
INDUSTRIAL REMOVAL OFFICE
per
Philip Seman

* * *

General Delivery
Des Moines, Iowa, May 23, 1912

Dear Mr. Seman:—

I am in receipt of your welcome letter of the 18th inst.

In reply, I wish to say that I have succeeded in securing a position with the United Cigar Stores Co.

Although this kind of position was not my intention of coming west for, I had to make the best of it under the circumstances. They treat you here with that company just as bad as in New York. The hours are very long (12 hours daily and Sunday is included) but I shall look around if possible and see what else I can do. The hours and confinement would not bother me, were I to see any possible chance for advancement for the future. It's a position that you possibly cannot rely on, and with no prospects.

Anyway I shall take your advice and do nothing without first consulting Mr. Marks.

Sincerely yours,
Morris Weinkrantz

c/o General Delivery
Des Moines, Iowa

*   *   *

May 27, 1912

Mr. Morris Weinkrantz,
c/o General Delivery
Des Moines, Iowa.

Dear Sir:

In answer to your letter of May 23rd, I am glad to see that you have found something, even though it merely means a position with the United Cigar Stores Co., which is not altogether to your liking. I sincerely hope that within a very short time you will be able to find yourself in Des Moines with the help of Mr. Marks. I think the spirit you show by being willing to accept anything, even though it is not the kind you intended to do, is illustrative of the fact that you will make good.

Wishing you every success, I am,

Very sincerely yours,
INDUSTRIAL REMOVAL OFFICE
per
Philip Seman

*   *   *

627 West Third st.,
Des Moines, Iowa, Sept. 4, 1913

Mr. Bressler
174 Second ave.,
New York City

My dear Mr. Bressler:

If you will look up my case, you will find that about a year ago last May I was up to see you with regard to sending me away west, and you also will remember me by telling you that I met you in Des Moines last November.

Up to the present time I have been employed by the United Cigar Stores Co. I have been discharged by them for violating one of their rules, and at present am out of work. Mr. Marks, who is your agent in this city, is out of town, and won't be back I understand for two or three weeks.

I remember when you wrote letters to a number of people regarding me. You got an answer from a certain party from St. Joseph, Mo. Would you advise me to go to St. Joe?

I assure you Mr. Bressler that I have committed no crime with the United People and want you to feel that I am the same fellow who is willing to work in order to make good.

I have about $250 saved up, so you can see that I was taking care of what I earned.

I shall be happy if you will talk this matter over with Mr. Seman and take your advice.

Trusting to hear from you very soon, I am

> Very respectfully and obediently,
> Morris Weinkrantz

* * *

Sept. 8, 1913

Mr. Morris Weinkrantz
627 West 3rd Street
Des Moines, Ia.

Dear Sir:

We have your letter of Sept. 4th addressed to Mr. Bressler and in answer to same we beg to say that it would be advisable for you to wait until Mr. Marks returns to the city and confer with him as to the advisability of your leaving Des Moines for St. Joseph. It may be possible that Mr. Marks is acquainted with persons of influence in St. Joseph and will offer you whatever friendly advice he can.

> Very truly yours,
> INDUSTRIAL REMOVAL OFFICE
> per
> Philip Seman

* * *

627 West Third St.
Des Moines, Iowa, Sept. 10, 1913

Mr. Philip Seman
New York, N.Y.

My dear Mr. Seman:

I am in receipt of your letter of the 8th inst. and in reply will say that I shall act with your advice in not leaving Des Moines before I see

Mr. Marks. I expect to see Mr. Marks next Monday, on which day he is expected back from his vacation.

Will let you know what course I will follow. Thanking you many times for your kindly interest, I am with regards,

Very truly yours,
Morris Weinkrantz

*   *   *

104 E. Douglas Ave.
Wichita, Kansas, May 1st, 1914

Mr. Bressler
174 Second Ave.
New York City, N.Y.

My dear Mr. Bressler:—

Perhaps at first thought you will not remember the name of the writer of this letter, but if you will recollect or refreshen your memory, you will remind your-self that you sent me to Des Moines, Iowa, to Mr. R. Marks in that city, nearly two years ago. I went to work for the United Cigar Stores Co., and had been with them for quite some time.

At present Mr. Bressler I am in business for myself. I took your advise in keeping my eyes open for an opportunity, and now with the help of Mr. Marks, I am running a $2.00 specialty hat store.

I opened on Feb. 21st 1914 and am happy to advise you that I am doing better than I really expected. In fact I had a very successful spring season and anticipate a good straw hat season.

Now Mr. Bressler, I have a very dear friend of mine in New York city, who writes me that he would like to come west if there was any chance for him in this part of the country. I would send for this friend of mine if there was the slightest chance for an opening here, but as the case is, it is very slow here with the merchants at present and from inquiry, I am afraid to advise my friend to come to Wichita. The next best thing I thought my friend could do in order to get away from New York was to get your help, and so I have written to him to go up and see you and get your advice in the matter. His name is Mr. Abe Edelstein, and comes from very fine people.

I would appreciate very much if you could do any thing for him, as I know if he were given an opportunity, that he would make good.

When you wrote to your various people in my case, you received a letter from a party by the name of Mr. Pfeffer, of St. Joseph, Mo. Mr. Pfeffer's letter came after that of Mr. Mark's so that is the reason that I did not go to St. Joe, but I thought that if you would write this Mr. Pfeffer and perhaps Mr. Marks and any other people that you think this boy can go to that you will get some favorable reply.

Thanking you many times for what you have done for me, and trusting that you will be able to do something for my friend, I remain, with best regards,

Yours very sincerely,
Morris Weinkrantz

*   *   *

May, 1914

Mr. Morris Weinkrantz
104 E. Douglas Ave.,
Wichita, Kansas

Dear Sir:

We have your letter of the 1st instant and are very glad indeed to hear of the success you are making, which we hope will increase steadily. As regards your friend Edelstein, we will, of course, be willing to be of service to him, but it seems to me that since you are permanently established in your city and have familiarized yourself with conditions and opportunities there, that you ought to be able to advise him as readily as we can.

With reference to Mr. Pfeffer, we think it would be advisable for you to take the matter up with Mr. Marks direct.

Wishing you the best of luck, we are,

Yours very truly,
INDUSTRIAL REMOVAL OFFICE
per
Abraham Solomon

LETTERS TO AND FROM ALEX GRUBMAN

Alex Grubman worked in the IRO's New York office examining immigrants who wished to become removals.[7] What he really wanted, however, was to go into business for himself. Before coming to the IRO, Grubman had opened a clothing store in New York; but the competition proved too difficult, and he failed. After a time, he asked the IRO to send him to a place where he could build a new life. Acceding to his request, the IRO sent Grubman and his wife to Portland, Oregon, in 1905.

Grubman began his career in Portland working in a dry goods store. Within a short time, he and his wife opened their own clothing business. His wife managed their store, while he continued working for the dry goods company. Grubman's career path—working at a job, saving money, and then opening his own business—typifies the ambition of many men sent out by the IRO.

In 1905, Portland's Jewish community numbered about 3,000 out of a total population of more than 100,000. The city contained three Orthodox synagogues and one Reform, four B'nai B'rith chapters, three charitable relief societies, and a social club.[8]

> 274 Sheridan St.
> Portland, Oregon, Nov.24—05

Dear Mr. Bressler:—

Having been settled in our own rooms, I write you how fortunate I am in being placed in one of the largest dry goods houses in Oregon by Hon. Sig Sichel who worked hard to place me with a good house.[9] He went personally with me until he procured the present position for me as inside salesman and to start at $60 per month. It is the 4th week tht I am employed and have been OKed by the manager of my department.

The start is a very good one and now I will strive to advance myself in the commercial line in which I could get no chance in New York City.

Mr. Bressler, many of the people here who were sent out by the I.R.O. came to me having heard of my arrival and knowing that I was one of the investigators of the I.R.O., wish me to thank the I.R.O. for helping them to success in their various occupations by transporting them to Portland.[10] Many of them are in business. The following are a few names. Mr. Aaron Zaik a recent arrival has a large 2nd hand furniture store. Mr. Lvov or Lvovsky, a tinsmith sent out direct 2 years ago has a stove and hardware store. M. Kaplan a tailor is earning $20–25.00 a week.

Mr. Nathan Siegel who arrived only a few days ago is already employed as a clerk earning $10.00 for a start, and many others too numerous to mention have succeeded well in a short time. They all thank the I.R.O. for helping them to get out from the city of misery [New York]. I also send my thanks and am only sorry that I did not come here a few years ago.

Kindly give my compliments to Mr. Waldman, Mr. Bero, the young ladies and gentlemen of the I.R.O.[11] With this I remain

> Yours respectfully,
> Alex Grubman

* * *

December 4th, 1905

Mr. Alex Grubman
#274 Sheridan Street
Portland, Oregon.

Dear Mr. Grubman:—

I am very pleased to learn from your letter of the 24th ult., that you have a permanent position as salesman at $60.00 per month. This is excellent. I have no doubt that you will in the course of time command a much better salary; at least if conscientious work and ability counts for anything, you will get there. You have my very best wishes and my entire office staff joins me in them.

With best wishes, I am

Yours very truly,
David Bressler

*   *   *

192 Gibbs St.
Portland, Or. May 13—06

Dear Mr. Bressler and Mr. Waldman:

We are not dead yet. The earthquake did not hurt us in the least.[12]

Hope that such accidents do not happen again.

The cause of our silence is produced by our strenuous life we lead. I am still working for the same firm but have made a trial by opening a small dry goods and gents furnishing store which my wife manages. It is hard to tell at present whether its going to be a success. It is the third month since we have opened the store and have made our expenses. I'll give it another two mos. trial and if by that time we see no improvement, I will have to give it up.

We will try hard as we done to make it pay. I believe that we are too near the large department stores to make our shanty a paying business. Otherwise we are well and happy with an acception of my being home sick.

I had no chance to see Mr. Sig Sichel. He was in San Francisco with his wife when the earthquake happened, but both escaped injury.

You no doubt think that I had forgotten my debt to the I.R.O. I wish to assure you that I am worried a bit by not being able to send some part of the money, though I will try to remit some of it soon. This country is now blooming, we have very few rainy days. It is not very warm here in the day time though quite cool in the evening. All in all it's pleasant to live here. Hoping to hear from you soon. I remain,

Yours respectfully,
Alex Grubman

P.S. My compliments to all of the staff.

*   *   *

May, 21st, 1906

Mr. Alex Grubman
192 Gibbs St.
Portland, Ore.

Dear Mr. Grubman:—

I have yours of May 13th. and am glad to learn there from that all is well with you. I suppose you are best qualified to judge as to the advisability of holding on with your store or giving it up. In a general way, however, I would counsel not to be hasty. It takes a little time to work up a good trade, and if you are meeting expenses for the first few months, you are doing all that can reasonably be expected. Inasmuch as you are earning your livelihood, apart from your store venture, I think there is an additional incentive for you to hold on with your store as long as possible. So far as refunding to us the amount of money which we laid out for you in the matter of transportation you need not make yourself any undue anxiety on that account. We are quite sure that the money will be eventually returned to us, even if we have to wait a little longer. Just you go ahead and make a success of your business and make that your first consideration.

Wishing you well, I am, with regards,

Very truly yours,
David Bressler

LETTERS TO AND FROM BARNET MARLIN

The IRO sent Barnet Marlin to Atlanta in 1905.[13] After some initial difficulties, he began to succeed as a peddler. Marlin's story reflects a classic pattern among nineteenth- and early-twentieth-century Jewish immigrants. The Jewish founders of some of America's greatest department stores, including Filene's of Boston, Gimbel's of Philadelphia, Kaufmann's of Pittsburgh, and the Riches of Atlanta, began their careers as peddlers.[14] Marlin's letter indicates that he was becoming Americanized; he had already anglicized his first name. The Dr. Wildauer referred to was

Benjamin Wildauer, a policeman turned dentist who served as the IRO agent.[15] The letter was typed in English. Most likely it had been written for Marlin or translated for the IRO from the original Yiddish.

Atlanta's population in 1905 numbered about 120,000, with a Jewish population of approximately 3,000. By 1905, most of Atlanta's Jews were Russian-born. The Jewish community supported one Reform and four Orthodox congregations, a religious school, and a number of charities and fraternal organizations. Despite the four Orthodox synagogues, the community was non-Orthodox in its religious behavior.[16]

March, 2″, 1906

Friends of the Removal Office

As you are interested to know the welfare of the people whom you sent away and the progress they have made, I Barnet Marlin, one sent away to Atlanta 5 months ago, to work as a trunk maker, hereby lets you know all about himself.

Upon reaching Atlanta, Dr. Wildauer secured a place for me to work, at wooden trunks. I worked there, and received a dollar for the first two days. As they have given me a weeks board and lodging, so I was in the hopes that later on, I shall be able to pay my own board and receive a larger salary. But I was mistaken, I was waiting for the time to have a chance to work myself up, but the time never came. I could not earn more than 60 cents a day and was working harder than a horse. I was fortunate that the employer should give me piece work for the second week, but there, I could not earn more than I did.

I must call your attention to the fact that Atlanta does not pay to work, especially for a foreigner. The days that I received free board past away and the time arrived when I was forced to pay my own lodging and board. My evenings did not exceed the cost for board, and the expenses were also very large. Several weeks past by and at the end I was in debt for $7.00.

I went to Dr. Wildauer, and told him about my condition. He spoke to my employer but nothing was accomplished. Dr. Wildauer went with me to other places, but he could not find anything better than the position I occupied. My position was embarrassing and so I was forced to apply to Dr. Wildauer for aid. Of course it took some time before a meeting was held.

During that time I became acquainted with a jewish policeman and he was the only one who took pity on me.[17] But what could I have asked from a strange person. I sent to New York to my brother for aid and he sent me his last $15.00, which I returned to him long ago, when he was out of work; but what was I able to do with $15.00. A meeting was held by the committee and they helped me pay my lodging bill, after which Dr. Wildauer said to me that he can do nothing else for me and also gave me the privilege to do what ever I pleased.[18]

I told my friend the policeman that I had $15.00 (sent to me by my brother) and he advised me to go out peddling.

He took me to a store and told the storekeeper to furnish me for over $30.00 worth of goods. He also acted as my reference and prepared me with everything.

I went out peddling and gradually I earned enough money to pay all my debts; and so I kept on peddling. I earned enough money and bought a horse and wagon. I now convey goods from the city to the country and sell them there.

I thank you very much for sending me to Atlanta because the future will seem to be better than the past. I have already made a return payment of $1.50 to the committee that helped me out before. Now I hope you will help my brother who is in New York and works very hard to come to Atlanta. I again thank you for sending me to Atlanta.

Respectfully,
Barnet Marlin

* * *

Mar. 2nd, 1906

Mr. Barnet Marlin
Atlanta, Ga.

Dear Sir:—

We have your recent communication, and though we are sorry to hear that it took some time before you were established in your new home, we are glad to hear that you are now comfortably situated. We will be glad to send your brother, provided we have the consent of our representative Dr. B. Wildauer.

Yours very truly,
David Bressler

LETTERS TO AND FROM MAX FRUCHTMAN

In 1908, Max Fruchtman, who had been an unemployed tailor in New York, acquired a job in Pensacola, Florida.[19] Since he had no funds to get there, he approached the IRO for assistance. In November 1908 the office shipped Fruchtman and his family to Pensacola.

After one year, Fruchtman found that conditions were not what he expected and complained that his boss behaved harshly toward him. In a letter to David Bressler, Fruchtman said that his employer exploited everyone who worked for him. He asked Bressler not to send anyone else to work for this individual for two reasons. First, the new man would take Fruchtman's place, thus leaving him jobless. Second, his employer would more than likely exploit the new man as well.

Fruchtman exhibits a strong worker consciousness and shows no reticence in demanding what is due to him. His stance indicates that he may have been active in the labor movement or been a member of a garment worker's union in New York. Bressler was sympathetic to Fruchtman's charges, but before taking any action he wanted to consult with the local IRO agent, Rabbi Jacob Schwartz. This was standard procedure whenever a removal wrote to complain about his employer.

Fruchtman's letter was written in English. The language use is fairly sophisticated, but there are a number of misspelled words. Because this was the only copy in the file, there is no foolproof method of judging whether Fruchtman wrote it or had someone else write it for him or whether it was the IRO's translation from the Yiddish original. If the IRO had the letter translated, the syntax and spelling indicate that the translator was also not a native speaker of English. Aside from adding some punctuation, I have transcribed the letter exactly as it appears in the file.

About the time Fruchtman wrote his letter, Pensacola's Jewish community numbered approximately four hundred people, the majority German-born or American-born children of German Jewish parentage. Most of Pensacola's Jews worked as merchants in the wholesale or retail trade. The community supported one Orthodox and one Reform synagogue, a number of fraternal organizations, a Hebrew Ladies Benevolent Society, and an all-Jewish social club.[20]

Pensacola, Fla.
Sept. 28, 1909

Mr. D. Bressler, Manager of the Removal Office
New York

Dear Sir:

I, Max Fruchtman, who excepted a position as a taylor by Mr. A. Friedman, Pensacola, Fla.

Presently is my way a few difficulties, for which my wife, two little children and I compeled to appeal to you for help!! The help which I beg of you is not from financial stand point of view. But for you not to send some-body, who would substitute my position, which is just the same to me as taking away all the necessaties of life from my poor and weak family.

Here, I am going to characterise my present situation. When last No-vember I learned that Mr. Friedman is looking for a ladies taylor, who is willing to pay $15.00 per week. I excepted tha offer and was send through the removal office at Pensacola, Fla. to Mr. A. Friedman.

Landing at this location I had learned that a sertain Mr. M. Rosenberg, employed by A. Friedman, was brutally treated and refused to continue the work under the same conditions. Then Mr. Friedman tried to employ me as a scab. Fortunately, Mr. Rosenberg, as my countryman, who finded out my economic condition, gave me a permmision to work there.

Working 3–4 days, Mr. Friedman made me an offer of $20.00 per week. I was perfectly sadisfied and tried the best for him. Consequenly, working there a considerable length of time, I learned that Mr. Friedman is not a gentleman to his word, because I heard pretty near daily, him ac-cusing in not holding his promises. I as being told by my friends, and also impressed with the mistreaties to the people, formed an opinion to ask for a contract of one year. In response to which he said: that his word is more valuable as a contract. I then was forced to take his word.

During the season I worked six months, much more harder as in New York in the shops, from 8 in the morning till 10 at night, and Saturday till 11 at night, having only one hour for dinner. But I never kicked; always fulfilled his desires, and was as a slave, even several times had been hited with a stick in the face. But I stood and never contradicted. My only con-selation was that I am getting $20.00 per week all year around.

At last I was not mistaking. He, Mr. Friedman anonced that he only can pay me $15 per week from June the first. But promised to pay from Au-gust first, $20.00. Yet I am working till October the first and he still did not increase my pay.

O, My dear sir! If you only could know the condition in which I am. That is truthful, that being perfectly ignorant of the conditions of the south, where the life is very high, everything is dear, and with $20.00 per week you hardly making a living; I mean only to have a place where to slip, and have something to eat. But where is a shoe, a skirt, and some-thing for the little kiddies and for myself. Consequently I went deep in debt to furnish me a house and something to wear because he himself [Friedman] told me to wear good and dicent close.

And when I learned that I am getting only $15.00 I was a pefect dead man. Four months my family had not a pice of meat in the house, and our diet consists of bread, potatoes and water, and chip sardines. I have to pay $4.00 per week rent, $4.00 for furniture. If not, they will take it away from us. So I would be satisfied to get in New York $8.00 per week then here $25.00.

To day, 28th of September, I quit to work there. And I ask him to give me $20 per week; (2) one year contract; (3) to pay me back for the 16 weeks, and not at the reduced sum; (4) a human treatment; (5) to pay for working after 6 p.m. This are my conditions. Dr. Rabbi Schwartz is representing me in this action, and he is perfectly agreed with me.

This is my favor which I am asking you; not to send any body to Mr. A. Friedman, because this man has ruined already three families. He made every one of them to bring their families and employing them through the busy time. And during the summer reduces the prices, which makes for them to make a living impossible.

My dear sir, if you are not taking my word you could ask your represenetive Rabbi Jacob Schwartz, and any reliable person of Pensacola. But I am asured that he will get another man through the removal office, or by paying a full price for the transportation. I am going to ask you another second favor, which consisits only in giving me an advice where to go from Pensacola.

Presuming that Friedman gets another taylor, then is for me here positively nothing to do. And my family and my self have to starve. Therefore if you know that any body in this vicinity wants a taylor, then let me know as soon as you can. I realy prefer Memphis, Tenn., or Birmingham, Ala., or Cincinati, O. Even if you have not a demand for a man, write what is your opinion about these three localoties.

Trusting that you will pay attention to my favor. I remain very truly yours,

Max Fruchtman
117 W. Goveman St.
Pensacola, Fla.

*   *   *

Oct. 4th, 1909

Mr. Max Fruchtman
117 W. Goveman St.
Pensacola, Fla.

Dear Sir:

I have yours of the 26th ult and regret to learn of your difference with your employer. You must understand that your employer was of your own selection, and that we had nothing to do with it, and naturally we could not interfere in your disputes, much as you may have justice on your side. At the same time, it is only fair to point out to you that we have heard only your side of the story, and therefore it would not be altogether fair to Mr. Friedman to accept your statements without hearing what he has to say. If, therefore, you will show this letter to Rabbi Jacob D. Schwartz and he will thereupon write me a letter assuring me that you are altogether in the right, we will absolutely refrain from sending any one to work for Mr. Friedman, but please see to it that we get this letter. As for other positions, we do not know of any particular ones in the cities you mention, but we hear that good tailors are in demand in nearly every fair sized town in the South.

Yours very truly,
David Bressler

CHAPTER 6

Social/Cultural Adjustment

A large number of immigrants wrote the IRO about the trouble they experienced in acclimating socially and culturally to their new environment. This segment contains the letters of four removals and correspondence from the secretary of the National Desertion Bureau.

LETTERS TO AND FROM RAPHAEL GERSHONI

The first letter recounts the ordeal of Raphael Gershoni, a removal who had been sent to Atlanta, Georgia, about the same time as Barnet Marlin (see the previous chapter).[1] Gershoni's encounter with the city, however, was vastly different: he likens his situation to that of a prisoner in Siberia. David Bressler expresses skepticism regarding Gershoni's complaints and rebukes him for his unrealistic expectations. The J. J. Saul mentioned by Bressler was a businessman who served on the board of trustees of the Jewish Educational Alliance, a settlement house that catered to the needs of the city's Russian Jewish community.[2] Gershoni's letter is translated from Yiddish.

Atlanta

Friends!

First thing, please excuse my calling you friends. My reasons are that you do much for the Jews, and there is among you more than one man who works to better the situation of our Jews. I don't know to whom to address my letter since I only know the name "Industrial Removal Office." To me everyone is the same, rich or poor. Of the poor, I certainly have nothing to be ashamed of because I am also poor. You yourself know this very well since I am one of those who came to you for help. And I certainly have no reason to be ashamed of the rich because I was once rich myself. By that I mean I made a nice living and I was healthy. For all of the above-mentioned reasons, I call you friends!

I would write to you in English, but I don't know the language. I would tell someone else my troubles, but I cannot do it, and it is not becoming. But in Yiddish—I think there are people with feelings in your office who will understand me.

I heard that Dr. Wildauer received a letter from you saying that my brother in New York protested against the office. I say to you that my brother had full right in this matter because the office's name is known all over the world. I was forced to apply to the office instead of to my brother, a poor worker who barely makes a living for himself and who must study so that he can enter college. He has been in this country less than a year. He must help himself, and now I come to him for help. He feels my pain. He knows that I am not lazy. He understands quite well that if I had to ask him for a ticket, then I must be suffering in Atlanta.

It is very foolish for me to write about all this. I don't feel that I know what I'm doing. My head is spinning and feels like it's going to split in half. But what concerns me is the future.

Only one thing I want to know: why do you send people to Atlanta? You give them eight days worth of food and then you let them starve in the street among Negroes. You know very well that the people who go through your office haven't a cent in their pockets. You can ask the man who took us from the office to the train and the man who took our baggage to the train. They both stood and saw how two men didn't have five cents to pay for car fare. I took my last pennies and gave the men ten cents. I think that they won't deny this.

It is very nice of you to send a letter to the doctor [Wildauer] about my brother's protest. But why should you ask the doctor? Ask the one who is sick. Anyway, it is not my business. As the music plays, so we must dance.

It is true that I was given help in Atlanta. I was given a job to work in a restaurant kitchen, to wait on Negroes, and to clean the Negroes' closets, for three dollars a week. I think the doctor will not deny that.

I began to protest and to write, asking what people had against me. All I want is to live my life in this world. It was at this time that I wrote to my brother. I told him to sell everything and send me a ticket because I am in exactly the same position as a Russian political criminal who is banished to Siberia and can't return.

I told the doctor everything, about how the local board refused to help me and that I wrote to my brother asking him to send me a ticket so I can go back to New York.

I was then given ten dollars for goods so that I might go around and peddle in Atlanta. But out of this ten dollars, I have to pay four dollars for lodging and three dollars a month for a place just to lay my head. This was when I had been in Atlanta exactly two weeks. And everything here starts from a nickel; you don't hear about a penny. And the doctor already helped me. From the three dollars' worth of goods, which in New York can be had for one dollar, one has to make a living from sales of 15–20 cents a day.

But thank God I received money from my brother for a ticket. I didn't buy a ticket but used the money to try and make a living. I bought a stand, and my expenses are ten dollars a month. You can ask the doctor about this. I sell thirty cents worth a day, excluding Saturday. In the meantime, I am eating up my goods and eating up myself. And I only have enough goods to last me for a week. I attend to my stand for half a day, and the other half-day I go around with my pack, so much so that my feet become swollen. And still I can't make a living.

It is hopeless to work in Atlanta. The highest wage is 75 cents a day. And for what kind of work? The Negroes go around with their mouths shut. And the competition is difficult here. Why should anyone hire a white greenhorn when they can get a black Negro, who is strong as iron and works like a horse.

Everyone says that the only choice here is to go out into the country-side and peddle. But one needs 40–50 dollars worth of goods. How do I get the money? It is very bad. I only want your advice. What should I do?

I would like to ask you to help me out. Help me to crawl out of black Atlanta and go to Chicago. There I have friends and can make out better, or I will peddle. I don't want to go back to New York. I want to make a living, and I hope you will help me. Here in Atlanta I have nobody to appeal to because they helped me once.

Forgive me for writing. If my letter interests you, write me a few words about what I should do. Then, if you like, I will describe for you the whole situation in Atlanta, from top to bottom. I hope my letter will not be torn and you will answer me. And if not, I also don't care. Because the office is not the tsar of Russia, and Atlanta is not Siberia. I won't die in Atlanta. I will be saved. Money was sent to me for one ticket, and money will be sent for another one as well.

Your acquaintance,
Gershoni
Address = Atlanta, Ga.
150 Decatur St.

September 14th, 05

Mr. Raphael Gershoni
150 Decatur Street
Atlanta, Ga.

Dear Sir:—

We have your letter which was carefully read. We also have a detailed report of Dr. Wildauer concerning you, and I wish to inform you that your statements and Dr. Wildauer's report are altogether at variance. From past experience and from my own personal knowledge of conditions in Atlanta, I am almost convinced that the true version is the one given by Dr. Wildauer. It is no one's fault if you expected to make a fortune the minute you got to Atlanta. You were informed at this office that you would have to work and work hard, and it was upon that condition that you were sent there. We have made you no promises which were not kept, but you have not kept yours. If you are dissatisfied, it is because you expected too much. If however, you still feel that Dr. Wildauer has not treated you right, I would suggest that you call on the president of the Committee Mr. J. J. Saul. Tell your troubles to him, he is a just and good hearted man and you will receive justice from him.

Yours very truly,
David Bressler

LETTERS TO AND FROM DAVID SELECHANOK

The following letter from David Selechanok depicts the difficulties facing an immigrant who could not speak English.[3] In Selechanok's case, however, the language handicap proved to be a temporary barrier because of the good will and patience he encountered in Columbus, Ohio. His good experience in that town echoes that of removal Morris Goldstein (quoted in a previous chapter), who also communicated his gratitude for having been sent to Columbus. The letter was originally composed in Yiddish.

Columbus, Ohio, June 1, 1906

To the People of the Removal Office.

Today it has been 13 months since the time I left New York and was sent to Columbus.

On the first of May 1905, I was sent out of New York by the Removal

Office, and I don't regret it. One thing I do regret is not informing you sooner about my satisfactory welfare and, at the same time, express my thanks for the good you have done for me and my family.

It is not in my power to express my thanks on paper. But I will try to acquaint you with my mode of life in New York and here in Columbus, and you may judge for yourself how far my thanks ought to extend.

In New York, being a man of no trade, I was forced to peddle in order to make a living. Every time I tapped at different doors, it was similar to receiving wounds in my heart. Even then there were no chances of making a living. For several nights, hunger drove me to shovel snow in the streets, and my future was like darkness. Such was my distressful condition in New York.

On the other hand, from the very first day I arrived in Columbus, I felt much better and more comfortable. Your letter I handed to the agent. He treated me kindly and advised me to learn a trade. He selected the paperhanging trade in preference to others since its season had just begun. I informed him that in my possession there is no more than four dollars. This is not a very large sum to start in a new life. His reply was not to worry but to rely upon him. Two days later the same agent led me in to a wallpaper store and left me there to learn the trade. I was a very good apprentice, and in a week I was able to paper a room. But as I had no knowledge of the language, I was forced to forfeit the position.

I was left in a destitute condition, so I returned to the agent. He again treated me kindly and promised to get me another job. He got me a second wallpaper job. From this job, I earned $8.00 the first week. My salary was later increased to $12.00 a week until the season ended. This left me again without work.

I was ashamed to notify the agent about it again since I knew that it was his duty to aid me only once, and this was already the third time. I determined to look for a position myself. But as I cannot speak the English language, I found it very difficult. I spent five days without work or money and finally was bound to go to the agent for the last time.

At first I thought he would refuse me, but he promised to do his best. Six days went by, and the agent called at my boarding house and took me to a place called "Champlin Printing Co." I remained at that place, and they respected me.

The boss told me that as soon as I learn the language, he will make me foreman of the place.

During the season I usually earn $20.00 a week, and it is a steady position. Last year I put $450.00 into the bank besides the money I sent to my wife and children.

This is my long story, and this is the difference between New York and

Columbus. I again thank you and also everybody of the Removal Office. I beg you not to publish this letter in the newspapers for certain personal reasons.

> Yours,
> David Selechanok
> 301 Donaldson
> Columbus, Ohio

*   *   *

> June 21st, 1906

Mr. David Selechanok
301 Donaldson St.,
Columbus, O.

Dear Sir:—

We have your favor of the 1st. and are very happy to hear of your welfare. We trust you will continue to prosper. We shall at all times be glad to hear from you.

> Yours truly,
> David Bressler

LETTERS TO AND FROM SARAH GOLDENBERG

Many letters sent to the IRO describe the strain that immigrant Jewish families were under in America.[4] Ashamed of their inability to provide satisfactorily for their families and unable to cope with their diminished status in America, many immigrant Jewish husbands abandoned their wives and children.[5] The following letter from Sarah Goldenberg provides an example of the problem.

Sam Goldenberg, his wife, and their three children arrived in Brooklyn from Russia in 1903. Goldenberg supported his family by knitting sweaters. In 1905, the factory he worked for went bankrupt, and he lost his job. Goldenberg went to the IRO and asked to be sent someplace where he could earn a living at his trade. In January 1906, the IRO sent him and his family to St. Louis, but he was unable to pursue his craft there and could not find a job approximating his vocation. He remained unemployed for three months and sank into a deep depression. In March 1906, Goldenberg's wife, Sarah, wrote to the IRO to report that her husband had abandoned his family, and she asked for help. Her letters were written in Yiddish and translated into English for the IRO.

In 1906, the Jewish population of St. Louis numbered approximately 40,000 in a general population of 750,000. Most of the city's Jews were of Russian origin. The Jewish community supported thirty-six Orthodox and four Reform congregations, chapters of all the major Jewish fraternal organizations, as well as an extensive network of Jewish social and benevolent organizations.[6]

St. Louis, Mo. March 22, '06

Industrial Removal Office

Gentlemen:

You send a family, M. Goldenberg with a wife and 3 children, to St. Louis from Brooklyn, N.Y. He is a knitter by sweaters, and this trade isn't in St. Louis at all. He was 3 months in St. Louis. He would be glad to do any work, but he couldn't get any. And we was suffering with great trouble, and Mr. Bienstock positively didn't do anything for us.[7] My husband lost his patients and couldn't get any advice to make a living, and could not see his children suffer. So he sold my watch and his over coat, and he left me a letter on the bureau with 2 dollars.

He said in his letter that he leaved St. Louis. Where he is going, he don't know himself. He wrote in his letter when he will come on a place, he'll let me know. Now my 2 dollars is gone and I have nothing to eat. I was today in the Relief and they said "they wont do anything for me." Thats all they will do for me, they will send me back to the Industrial Removal Office. They said they will send me from whom I was send. Now the question is, if I'll come back to Removal Office and maybe I will get a letter from my husband that he is somewhere else. Then you will have to send me back to my husband. I suppose it is not right. I suppose it is better to stay in St. Louis till I'll hear from my husband where he is, but I need to live. Gentlemen I beg your pardon, and give me an advice what to do. I should come back to your office, or to help me here, till I'll hear from my husband,

Yours respectfully,
and hoping for an answer
Mrs. S. Goldenberg.
904 Biddle St.,
St. Louis Mo.

* * *

Mrs. S. Goldenberg,
904 Biddle St.,
St. Louis, Mo.

Dear Madam:

We have your letter of Mch. 22nd. and are surprised to learn that your husband has gone to another city. We cannot believe that he had any justification for doing so, as we know from reliable information that your family was looked after, even if your husband may not have been earning as much as he thought he should have earned. You will remember that we were unwilling to send your family when you first applied to us and only consented to do so when your husband gave us a solemn pledge that he would be prepared to accept work of any kind, for we informed him that there was very small likelihood of his obtaining employment as a knitter. The only thing that you can do is to induce your husband to return to you. I am quite sure that Mr. Bienstock will find him employment.

Yours truly,
David Bressler

* * *

St. Louis, Mo. March 30th/ 06

Removal Office,

Dear Sir:

Your letter at hand. I feel very much grieved when you ask me to write to my husband to return to St. Louis, at a time when I myself do not know his whereabouts.

I received a letter from him from some place in Ohio, stating that he was going further, but did not even state the name of the place where he wrote this letter, but I noticed the envelope was marked Ohio. He also wrote me that he will not write me until he gets a steady position. I did not hear from him since. Maybe you can find out his whereabouts much quicker than I can.

In regard to your statement that I should write to my husband to return, if Mr. Bienstock would have tried for him before, I would not be in such a destitute condition.

I wish that some one from your office would come here and see all the good Mr. Bienstock accomplished for all the people you sent here, whether he even secured work for one of them.

If you would know what Mr. Bienstock accomplishes for the people you sent him, you would not send any families together with their furniture. On such a foundation you ought not to have sent the entire family.

If you could just picture to yourselves the sufferings we had to undergo during the three months since we arrived at St. Louis, you would not have written me to bring my husband back to St. Louis at a time when I do not know where he is.

Now I wish to ask your advice. What shall I do? At present the Relief Assn., refuse to do anything for me. They only want to have me return to your office in New York. The question is—shall I return immediately, or shall I wait here another week or two. Maybe my husband will, in the meanwhile, write me where he is, at which time I will know where to go, because it is a very hard job for me to travel with small children and mostly not knowing whether that will be our permanent settlement.

I am positive that my husband did not abandon me—because he is angry with me. He tried enough for his family, and we suffered so much that he became discouraged and made this step without my knowledge of it.

I therefore wish to ask you gentlemen to answer me at once, whether I shall return to your office, or whether you will notify the Relief Society that I have to remain here for about two weeks. Maybe my husband will let me know his wherabouts within that period.

Hoping to receive an early reply, I am

Respectfully yours,
Sarah Goldenberg

LETTERS TO AND FROM MONROE GOLDSTEIN

By 1911, the problem of husband desertion had become so serious and widespread that Jewish communal leaders created the National Desertion Bureau (NDB) to find the errant spouses and bring them to justice.[8] As part of its effort, the bureau published photographs and descriptions of the husbands in the Yiddish press and set up investigative agencies within local Jewish charities. Because many of the deserters fled to towns where the IRO operated, the bureau enlisted its help in locating the men.[9]

The correspondence between the NDB, the local IRO representatives, and the New York office illustrates the cooperation between the agencies as well as the process of finding a deserter.

One of the more absorbing cases of family desertion involving the IRO concerned the Gordon family of Brooklyn, New York.[10] Sam Gordon abandoned his wife, Dora, in September 1912. Posing as a single man, he approached the IRO and asked them to send him out west. Believing his story, the IRO shipped him to Toledo, Ohio.

The NDB received information that Gordon had gone to Toledo under IRO auspices. Monroe Goldstein, the bureau's secretary, communicated this fact to Philip Seman and received permission to contact the IRO's agent in Toledo. The following series of letters consists of Goldstein's letters to the local agent, Maurice Newman, and to Philip Seman as well as Seman's reply.

Oct. 18, 1912

Mr. Maurice Newman
116 Michigan Street
Toledo, Ohio

Dear Sir:—

An applicant of this Bureau, Mrs. Dora Gordon of Brooklyn, New York, was deserted and abandoned by her husband, Sam Gordon on or about September 30, 1912. He left her in a pregnant and destitute condition. Our applicant became acquainted through a professional match maker and after a short acquaintance married about six months ago. From the information received at this end, we are of the opinion that the husband is a professional marrier. Mrs. Gordon possessed $500.00 prior to her marriage and shortly thereafter her husband through various contrivances succeeded in securing this sum from her.

The Bureau has been in consultation with the Industrial Removal Office and it is at the direction of Mr. Philip Seman that I am now writing you. It seems the Removal Office has a record of a Mr. Sam Gordon, who posed as a single man and who is reported to have journeyed to Toledo at the same time that the above desertion occured. The Bureau is under the impression that this same Sam Gordon is no other than the missing husband we are seeking. We have no photograph to assist in the identification, but the following description will be sufficient to identify him. He is about 25 years of age, of Russian nativity and arrived in this country in 1906. He is about 5 ft. 6 in. in height, is light complected, has blond hair, dark brown eyes, has reddish eyelashes and is clean shaven. He may be recognized by his rapidity in speech. Under our law, mere wife desertion is defined as disorderly conduct, a quasi-criminal offense and therefore does not subject the offender to process of extradition from another state. Under the circumstances, if there is any prosecution to be had, it can only be instituted at the place of the husband's location, whereat a charge of non-support might be instituted against him upon the theory that the domicile of the husband is the domicile of the wife, if she so elect.

The circumstances of the case are unusually aggravating, inasmuch as the deserter has not alone caused great harm to our applicant, but is likely to endanger the moral welfare of many other innocent women, who perchance will yield to his influence. For the present we are merely desirous of verifying the information as to identity and location, nothing more. Great caution should be exercised in the investigation, as Gordon would no doubt abscond should he become aware that an inquiry concerning him was pending. The Bureau has received further information that he is living with another woman, a Miss Clara Tellon, with whom he absconded from Brooklyn so that you will be doubly careful in not interviewing her.

Assuring you of our appreciation for your kind cooperation and awaiting your early advice as to the above inquiries, I am

Yours very truly,
Monroe Goldstein

*   *   *

October 23, 1912

Mr. Philip L. Seman, Assistant Manager,
Industrial Removal Office,
174 Second Avenue,
New York City

My dear Mr. Seman:—

You will recall the telephone conversation we had with reference to the case of one Sam Gordon who secured transportation to Toledo through your office. Acting upon your advice, the Bureau directed an inquiry to Mr. Morris Newman, copy of which is herewith enclosed. This morning the following telegram was received in reply thereto:—

> "SAM GORDON IS HERE. ANSWERS TO ALL YOUR DESCRIPTIONS. BOASTED TO OTHERS OF HIS DESERTION. IS UNDER IMPRESSION HE FOOLED INDUSTRIAL REMOVAL OFFICE AND IS BEYOND REACH BY LAW. ADVISE WHAT ACTION TO TAKE."

The braggart evidently knows a thing or two and there is some truth that he is beyond the reach of the law. Wife desertion, as you know, is merely construed to be a quasi-criminal offense and is therefore not extraditable. However, Gordon could readily be brought to account by way of the institution of a non-support proceeding at Toledo. Mrs. Gordon should journey to that city, where she could prosecute him.

The matter is now submitted to you, with the suggestion that you agree to make allowance for the transportation of Mrs. Gordon to Toledo for the purpose aforesaid. Men of this stamp should not be permitted to roam at large and I feel that you will do all in your power to check their machinations. Deterrence must be established and there is no more efficacious method than publicity and prosecution. What are your views and what is your disposition?

Very truly yours,
Monroe Goldstein

* * * .

Oct. 24", 1912

Mr. Monroe M. Goldstein,
356—2nd. Avenue, City.

Dear Mr. Goldstein:

   I beg to acknowledge receipt of your letter of Oct. 23rd. and copy of your letter to our Mr. Newman, re Sam Gordon. I have carefully gone through your letter as well as the copy of the letter to Mr. Newman. As far as this office is concerned, I cannot see how we can send Mrs. Gordon, except if we receive permission from the United Hebrew Charities of Toledo. I would, therefore, advise that you take this matter up with the United Hebrew Charities of Toledo, and if you can get permission from them, it will be much easier for us to furnish transportation to her. I believe, however, that it might be a very much better plan if this matter were settled amicably. I do not personally think very much of litigation in family desertion cases, especially in a matter of this sort where the woman has no family dependent upon her. I think, if our Mr. Newman and Mr. Hirsch were to bring this to the young woman's attention, and you were to scare him up by writing him a good, strong letter, stating that he can amend all this difficulty by sending for his wife, the results would be much more satisfactory. What do you think about this plan?

Very truly yours,
INDUSTRIAL REMOVAL OFFICE
per,
Philip Seman

LETTERS TO AND FROM LETA CHLANIN
AND NACHUM GEISHEN

Although many removals included a threat of suicide in their pleas to the IRO, few of them actually carried it out.[11] Nevertheless, suicide was not unknown among eastern European Jewish immigrants. The major reason was despair at failing to adjust economically, socially, or emotionally to

America. Dr. Maurice Fishberg, a prominent physician and the medical examiner for the United Hebrew Charities of New York, noted that, while suicide was infrequent among Jews in eastern Europe, "in New York City it appears to be growing among them." In fact, he said, "we hear of Jewish suicides quite often." [12] Later research has validated Fishberg's observations. [13] The correspondence that follows is unusual because it includes an authentic suicide note. Although not addressed to the IRO, the letters ended up in the IRO files. [14]

In 1905 the IRO sent Nachum Geishin to Cleveland. He had never made a decent living in New York and fared little better in his new home. Worse, in Cleveland he felt lonely and bereft of family and friends. Disconsolate, he wrote to his beloved friend Leta Chlanin in New York. From the letters, it appears that Geishin loved Chlanin and she him, but for some reason they could not marry each other. Thwarted love may have contributed to his decision to kill himself.

The first letter in the series is from Chlanin, who was responding to Geishin's earlier communication. (That initial letter is not in the file.) The fact that this reply survives indicates that it was part of Geishin's personal effects, which the police presumably turned over to Jacob Furth, the IRO's contact in Cleveland and the man who had received Geishin. Furth likely sent the letter, along with Geishin's belongings, to New York.

The second letter—the suicide note—is Geishin's response to Chlanin. When Chlanin received the letter, she apparently took it to the IRO and asked for help, which is probably why the letter appears in the files. In any case, she came too late. The last item in the file is an excerpt from a letter printed in Cleveland's *Jewish Daily News,* which someone forwarded to the IRO. The clipping reports the suicide of two removals, one of them Nachum Geishin. It also criticizes the IRO and the Cleveland agent. From the wording, the writer seems to be referring to Furth's assistant, Richter, who was disliked by many members of the Cleveland community.

All the items are undated but appear in the Cleveland folder, which is marked 1905. Chlanin's and Geishin's letters are translated from Yiddish.

My Dear Nachum:

I wish you much enjoyment and happiness. I received your dear letter. I thank you for it. First, I want to explain to you how I became aware that you were gone.

Friday I came to your aunt. I told Milke [a friend or relative], tomorrow we will visit Geishin. And he says, all right. You can imagine how I felt when I came and you were gone. Later your aunt says, I forgot all about it, and I've got a letter for you. And she gave me your letter, and I enjoyed it very much.

Please write to me about how you are and at what trade you are working. When the idea came to you to go away, why did you not come to see me? I think that you could have done it if you had wanted to. I was hurt and upset, and I was sick for two weeks. But now I'm beginning to feel better.

I only pray to God that he may give me strength to overcome my grudge and my longing for you. I don't know what will become of me. I ask you not to leave me without letters. Write as often as possible and write to me about everything.

Whenever I had any leisure I used to come to you, and that was my whole life. And now I am walking around numb and lost.

I have nothing more to write to you about. You yourself know the rest.

Best regards from me, your uncle and aunt, and Milke. I am sending you my address because your uncle will be moving. He bought a grocery. Send me your answer quickly because every day that passes is like a year to me.

Leta

*   *   *

To my dear Leta Chlanin:

I received your letter.

Pardon, pardon, pardon me. I am not your fate. I have decided to write to you to prevent your pain. I am tired of life in this world, and so I have taken a trip to the other world. I am commiting this by my own hand.

I wish you with all my heart to marry your destined one. From me, your deceased Nachum Geishin, [I tell you that] I die and my love for you dies with me.

If any letter comes from my parents, please write to them to say that I am indisposed.

I don't accuse anybody. I am my own murderer! Oy vey.[15] I remain your good friend forever. You have done everything possible for me.

My best and dearest friends, I take leave of you. I don't accuse you. I suffered for many years. I couldn't stand any more. The cup of fear and pain was too full. I decided two months ago to commit suicide. And now I have carried it out!

I wish you, my good friends, a good living and a joyous life in this world. And I wish rest to myself.

From,
Nachum Geishin

I ask you to send this to my bride.

*   *   *

In the past week something terrible has happened here. Two men sent here by the Removal Office committed suicide out of despair. One took poison and the other hanged himself. And these two tragedies happened in one week. That shows the deplorable condition of those who are sent here by the Removal Office. The Cleveland Removal Office is managed by an inexperienced young man who maintains his position merely through favoritism. And for his deplorable inability, he gets a salary of $75 per month.

It was told to me [the reporter] that the one who hanged himself came to this agent and implored him with tears in his eyes to provide some kind of employment for him, but the only answer he obtained was: "For my part, go and hang yourself," which advice he resorted to.

I trust you will let the Cleveland Jews understand that they are responsible for this spilt blood and some precautions must be taken to prevent the recurrence of such tragedies.

Respectfully yours,
S. Klein[16]
209 Woodland

CHAPTER 7

Immigrant Perceptions of America

T he final portion of the immigrant correspondence presents impressions of America expressed by three removals in their letters to the IRO. All the views are optimistic, even ecstatic.

LETTERS TO AND FROM ABRAHAM COHEN

The first selection is a letter from Abraham Cohen, whom the IRO sent to St. Louis in 1910.[1] Written in English, the letter may have been composed for Cohen or translated by someone from Yiddish. Although the notation "Original letter in Exhibition Cabinet" appears above Bressler's reply, the only letter in the IRO file is the one that appears here.

St Louis, Mo, Apr 3, 1910

To the Rem Office, of NY.

Dear Friends,

In my own name, and in the name of my wife & children, I come to thank you for your good work in sending me to St Louis.

Dear friends, to describe to you the impressions of the trip is a thing I am unable to do, for I lack words to convey my true feeling. Yet I shall endeavor to give you a slight picture of the trip and its effects upon me. You can believe me that throughout the entire journey my eyes did not close to get a few moments sleep, so absorbed was I in the picturesque landscape of the country. Think of the scenery in Jersey, the poetic mountains of West Virginia, the coal mines and the winding of the train along the magnificent river Ohio, the incomparable city of Washington. All these things have impressed me as a sweet dream. The greatest wonder of nature I observed at the junction, when we changed trains at Cinn. The distance from Cinn to St Louis is covered with the most beautiful & picturesque scenes, such as my eyes never beheld.

Excuse me for troubling you but I will only add a few lines expressing my views of your charitable institution, and hope it will interest you. Think of the large no. of hospitals that are being built, reformatories, that are unnecessary, all such institutions are increased yearly. And yet these people, philanthropists as they are called never for a moment stop to consider that the R.O. is the greatest institution of them all for by sending away people to the southwest, institutions such as hospitals etc, will not have to be increased. There will be no need for orphan asylums, as there shall not be any orphans. Another thing—I say down with those slanderers who try to injure such a noble inst.

I, on my side will always fight for the protection of the best institution existing among us.

About myself I can tell you that I shall begin to work (tomorrow the 4″) in a factory for 12.00 wk and I should like to ask you to send my family after Passover.

I wish to send my thanks to all, also to Mr. Bressler the Sup't for his honorable treatment, also special regards to the man who put us on the train. He is a gentleman. Please answer me by letter, if you do not feel insulted.

Wishing you a merry holiday I remain
Respectfully
Abraham Cohen
443 Biddle St
St Louis Mo

* * *

April 5, 1910

Mr. Abraham Cohen
443 Biddle St.,
St. Louis, Mo.

Dear Sir:—

It is with much pleasure that we received and read your letter of April 3rd, descriptive of your impressions of the country you traversed and your appreciation of the improved material condition in which you find yourself since you are in St. Louis. I sincerely hope that you will become more prosperous as time goes on, and that you will always have occasion to advise your friends and relatives that New York City is not the only place in America.

Regarding sending your wife and children, you had better call on Mr. Philip L. Seman, 901 Carr St., and make known to him your wishes. He will then write us. With renewed good wishes, I am,

> Yours very truly
> David Bressler

LETTER OF LEO STAMM

The following letter provides an interesting portrait of a small Jewish community in the deep south—in this instance, Meridian, Mississippi.[2] The removal, Leo Stamm, commented on the relations between Christians and Jews and hinted at the rivalry between the older, more established German Jewish community and the newcomers from eastern Europe. He also noted crimes committed by the immigrants, something the American Jewish community was always loath to publicize. An English translation of his letter is the only copy in the IRO file.

> February 6, 1906

Dear Sir:

With a feeling of thankfulness I am writing to you this letter, in which you will recognize one of the clients of the Removal Office by the name of Leo Stamm.

It is five months since I have arrived to Meridian, and with pleasure will describe to you the condition in which the Jewish immigrants are around this neighborhood. The city of Meridian, where I am living, consists of about 75 Jewish families which are here for the last 8–10 years, and are all well to do. The most part of them are rich, doing business in millions. Three quarters of them are German Jews and the rest of them are Russian Jews, but every one of them is trying to get the title of a German Jew. The most business of the town is in the hands of the Jews and they are growing very rapidly in both power and riches.

The Christian population is very friendly to the Jews and the antisemitism is very low, because the Jews in this town are very honest and doing business on a business principle. But here is a little exception with the Russian Jews in this matter, being there was some crimes committed by them to a few natives of this city, because some misfortune happened with a peddler, who stole from a farmer a gold watch and chain. And the other one was a clerk who escaped with a hundred dollars from his employer. And that what is done here in New York every day is unexpected in a small town like this. And the natives of this city recollected very often that this crime was done by a Russian Jew.

For a honest working man, the South is a very good place to live in. And here I send my advise to the enslaved Jews of New York, to leave the town as quick as they can, and come to get the benefit of the good climate and to conduct a good living. To you I send my gratefulness, for your kindness to the people whom are applying to the Removal Office for help. I will never forget that the immigrants on their difficult way are meeting such people like you.

My wife is in New York yet. she would be here long ago if not for the arrival of my friends, whom we are awaiting every day. I think that also they will be obliged to apply for the help of the office and that their impression will be the same as mine. The family of Davidson send their intimate regards to you, whom you rejected hither a few months ago. They settled themselves very well, as I expected. They remembered you as one who helped their leaving New York. Especially they are very thankful for sending them by way of Washington. It saved them, the way, almost from 35–55 hours. I hope you are all well as upon your own wishes.

Yours very respectfully,
Leo Stamm

LETTERS TO AND FROM SIMON SACHS

Simon Sachs came to the United States from Russia in 1892, apparently assisted by the Baron de Hirsch Fund. When he wrote this letter, he had been in the United States for fifteen years and had prospered. He now wished to share his good fortune with others. The letter that follows was written in English for him.[3]

The Jewish community of Dubuque, Iowa, numbered 250 persons out of a general population of 40,000 in 1907. The community supported one Orthodox synagogue, one Hebrew school, and one charitable organization. There were no Jewish social, fraternal, or cultural organizations in Dubuque at that time.[4]

Dubuque, Iowa. 6/7/07

Mr. David M. Bressler,
c/o Industrial Removal Office,
174 Second Ave.,
North East Corner 11th St.,
New York, N.Y.

Dear Sir:

In 1892 you helped me to come from Russia to America. I landed at New York; you then sent me to Chicago and from Chicago to Dubuque. I worked for the city a couple of days on the street and I then got work with the A. Y. McDonald & Morrison Mfg. Co. for whom I have worked ever since.

Not being good at writing letters and, as I am not able to write in English, I have asked Mr. Morrison to have this letter written for me. I am so comfortable and have prospered so well here that I would like to have some of my people here with me and I will try to do the best I can for them.

When I came to this shop, there were ten Jews here; the others have found different or better places, but there still remains, besides myself, my son, Jacob, and Isaac Greenfield. There are about 40,000 people in this city and there is no feeling against us.

There is a synagogue here, which we have built, and which is within two or three blocks of this shop. The Jews and people of other religions live together quietly and comfortably. I, and those of my race, are on the same footing as anyone else in the shop or anyone else in the city. Both men and women can get work in this factory—probably, fifty could get work in this shop, and, perhaps, a couple of hundred in the city.

What brought this to my attention was an agent's coming here before Easter and who was trying to send out some people every month—he said about ten, but I did not understand the matter properly then.

I can take care of a couple of people in my own house and I know that five or ten could get work at once in this shop and perhaps five or ten every month afterwards. Before you send anyone out, write me a letter.

What is wanted here are people who can work here the same as I, not business people. My address is Simon Sachs, 1398 Maple St., Dubuque, Ia. Our rabbi's name is Mr. Algase; his address, 14th & Maple Sts., this city.

As my son has had some of the advantages of the public schools of this city, I have asked him to sign my name—he lives with me at 1398 Maple St.

Yours truly,
Mr. S. Sachs
per J. Sachs

* * *

June 10th, 1907

Mr. S. Sachs
1398 Maple Street
Dubuque, Iowa

Dear Sir:

We are very glad to receive your letter of the 7th. inst. apprising us of the success with which you have met in Dubuque, Iowa. We have also received a letter from Rabbi Algase, telling us of the opportunities for our people with the firm of A. Y. McDonald & Morrison Mfg. Co. We have written him fully. We will always be glad to hear good news of you.

Yours very truly,
David Bressler

Epilogue
Motivations and Misconceptions

When American Jewish leaders created the Industrial Removal Office, their motives combined traditional Jewish ideas of communal responsibility with a desire to safeguard their status as established American citizens. The IRO records document their concerns as well as other issues that troubled the American and Jewish communities in the years up to World War I.[1]

One of the central themes in American Jewish history concerns the tensions that existed between the religiously liberal, assimilated German Jewish Americans and the more traditional Russian Jewish immigrants. The IRO files offer innumerable illustrations of this antagonism. The leaders of the IRO and its communal agents were all German-speaking Jews who had successfully integrated into American life. They generally lived in prosperous neighborhoods some distance—geographically as well as socially—from the poor districts inhabited by the immigrants. Although they had little in common with the eastern European Jews, they created a variety of institutions, such as settlement houses, to assist and "uplift" the immigrants intending both to mold the newcomers according to a German Jewish notion of what a good American should be and to fulfill a sense of obligation born of a common religious heritage.

The letters of the traveling and local agents reveal a paternalistic and condescending attitude toward the immigrants. These opinions mirrored the cultural and class arrogance endemic to German Jews in the United States at the turn of the century. Nothing the immigrants did seemed to meet with the Germans' approval. The Germans disparaged Yiddish as "anachronistic jargon" and called the Yiddish press socialistic or anarchistic. They ridiculed the immigrants' appearance, ceremonies, and behavior, calling them Asiatic, Oriental, or primitive. And they considered the religious Orthodoxy of the immigrants to be irrational and superstitious. The immigrants' so-called radical political proclivities proved especially unnerving. Establishment Jews lived in terror that the mad act of some lunatic Jewish anarchist would destroy everything they had built.

These hysterical reactions resulted in great measure from the rising public clamor of the xenophobes, the restrictionists, and the antisemites. After the turn of the century, the continuing wave of southern and eastern European immigrants to the United States generated fears about the consequences. Those who favored limiting and even halting immigration issued dire forecasts of race pollution and race suicide and blamed the immigrants for the growth of crime, delinquency, and prostitution in the cities on the East Coast.

German Jewish leaders believed that removing the immigrants from the evil influences of New York would help speed their Americanization, modify their foreign life-style, and diminish the chance of their becoming radicalized. This, the Germans hoped, would mitigate anti-immigrant and antisemitic sentiments and thwart restrictionist actions. Jewish leaders also presumed that the resettlement of Jews would not only relieve the congestion of the New York ghetto but also create a kind of chain migration in which resettled immigrants would attract friends and relatives from the old country to their new communities.

David Bressler promulgated these attitudes. As his letters make clear, he sympathized with the immigrants and genuinely desired to serve their needs. Despite any misgivings or ambivalence he may have held toward his charges, he went to extraordinary lengths to improve their situation and cater to their requests. His letters, and those he received from the traveling agents, show that the accusations of insensitivity and callousness often leveled against the entire Jewish leadership need modification.

The letters of the immigrant beneficiaries demonstrate that, while they appreciated the help they received, they strongly resented the attitude of their sponsors and the manner in which the assistance was sometimes tendered. The sensitivity and humiliation that so many of them displayed at having to accept the IRO's charity, and their prompt repayment of loans, refute the often-voiced allegation that eastern Europeans were all beggars.

Another factor that hindered better understanding between the two groups involved their differing conceptions of ethnicity. Often referring to themselves as "Americans of the Mosaic persuasion," German Jews advocated assimilation. The immigrants viewed the world differently. Decades of living as a restricted and tormented minority in tsarist Russia had fortified their communal and ethnic allegiance. They came to the United

States knowing exactly who and what they were. They worried less about their Jewish identity and what the gentiles thought and more about earning a living and getting established. The immigrants certainly desired to acculturate, but at their own pace. They may have been novices to American ways, but they were far from being naïve or submissive. The dignity and assertive manner displayed in their letters, and the fact that so many of them left the places where they had been sent, are examples of their recalcitrance. The immigrants' conspicuous and overt ethnicity distressed and agitated the German Jews, who continually fretted about their blatant Jewishness. The anger that many removals felt toward the IRO was never totally eradicated, tainting relations between them and the IRO's directors throughout the organization's existence.

The IRO's numerous circulars, bulletins, and public pronouncements created the impression that the organization enjoyed unlimited success. Nevertheless, the private correspondence between the central office in New York and the local agents throughout the country reveals a different state of affairs. These letters disclose the troublesome problems and disagreements that arose from day-to-day efforts to assist the immigrants. In part, these problems stemmed from the long-range goals of the New York office and the short-term goals and concerns of the local agents. The letters written by the local agents present a realistic picture of the difficulties they encountered in receiving and placing men who were unqualified for the jobs they sought, had misrepresented themselves to the New York office, or were simply unwilling to accept the jobs offered to them. Communications between communities and the New York office sometimes became contentious, revealing the discrepancy between the ideals and aspirations of the IRO and the daily problems of dealing with immigrants facing variable conditions of employment. Dissension also arose from ego clashes and misplaced pride. Local agents often felt that the New York office took them for granted, failed to consult them, or disregarded their wishes. For its part, the New York office felt that a number of local agents failed adequately to promote the program or help the immigrants and behaved tactlessly.

The correspondence and reports from the traveling and local agents are also valuable because they shed light on Jewish communities in small towns. As the greatest diaspora in Jewish history, the American Jewish community has received considerable attention from historians, sociologists, and anthropologists. Not surprisingly, these scholars have focused on the places where American Jews tend to cluster, namely the large cities. Nevertheless, fully one-quarter of the eastern European Jews who came to the United States during the Great Immigration settled in towns with fewer than 100,000 residents. Despite this fact, their adaptation has not merited much scholarly attention, although the IRO archives contain a wealth of material on the subject.

While sometimes subjective and biased, the reports and surveys that the IRO's traveling and local agents sent back to the main office provide data on the ethnic composition and character of small Jewish enclaves throughout the midwest, south, and west during the first two decades of the twentieth century. We learn about leading business and communal leaders; factions and conflicts; religious, social, and cultural situations; and economic conditions. We also discover details about the town itself, its current population, industrial conditions, and the relations between its Jewish and non-Jewish residents. Because the traveling agents visited these places over a period of time, we acquire some perspective on community changes. Since many of these towns had no histories written about them or their Jewish communities, the information provided by the agents is a valuable primary source on small-town America in the early twentieth century. In addition, this material allows us to compare the experiences and adjustment of these Jews with that of their brethren in the larger cities.

The immigrant correspondence from these places gives us a close look at the process of a second uprooting. The trauma of moving from Europe to the United States has been well documented, the shock of migrating a second time less so. Through the letters, we can sense the immigrants' apprehension, anguish, melancholy, and terror. We also acquire some sense of what it must have been like to be a greenhorn Jewish immigrant, such as Raphael Gershoni, forced to compete with African American laborers in the south. We learn about the consternation the newcomers felt at encountering new climates and environments and about the immigrants' opinions of the local Jewish community, its leadership, and the non-Jews with whom they came into contact.

Finally, the IRO material provides a window into the inner workings of a national Jewish organization intimately involved with eastern European Jewish immigrants. The material shows the kinds of pressures the IRO's leaders—especially the managing director—worked under and how and why they made the decisions they did. David Bressler had to walk a fine line between the goals of the Jewish leadership, the requirements and desires of the local communities, and the needs and wants of the immigrants, while not alienating any of his constituencies. The correspondence allows us to see the techniques he used to gain the confidence and cooperation of almost everyone.

Bressler ran an extremely efficient operation. From the dates on the correspondence, we can see that letters were answered almost immediately after they were received and read. The dates also confirm that the postal service delivered the mail everywhere in the country within two or three days. This says something about the post office's proficiency before World War I.

The creation and operation of the Industrial Removal Office offers a prime example of how American Jews worked to assist new immigrants once they perceived that their own fate was inexorably linked to the new-comers'. But despite the efforts of the IRO's administrators and the American Jewish establishment, the immigration restrictionists won. In 1921, the U.S. government passed the first quota law limiting immigration from southern and eastern Europe. The era of the Great Immigration had ended, and shortly thereafter the IRO ceased operation.

Notes

1. In 1897 the total population of the Pale numbered 42,352,039, of whom 4,874,636, or 11.4 percent, were Jews. They constituted more than 90 percent of Russia's Jews. After the February Revolution (1917) the provisional government abolished the Pale of Settlement. See Paul R. Mendes Flohr and Jehuda Reinharz, eds., *The Jew in the Modern World: A Documentary History* (New York, 1995), p. 379. For a history of the Jews in Russia, see Simon N. Dubnow, *History of the Jews in Russia and Poland*, 3 vols. (Philadelphia, 1916); Salo Baron, *The Russian Jew under Tsars and Soviets* (New York, 1987); and Louis Greenberg, *The Jews in Russia*, 2 vols. (New Haven, 1944; 1951).

2. For the role of Jews in the Russian revolutionary movement, see Erich Haberer, *Jews and Revolution in Nineteenth-Century Russia* (Cambridge, 1995).

3. For descriptions and analyses of the assassination and the events that followed, see Stephen M. Berk, *Year of Crises, Year of Hope: Russian Jewry and the Pogroms of 1881–1882* (Westport, Conn., 1985); Irwin Michael Aaronson, *Troubled Waters: The Origins of the 1881 Anti-Jewish Pogroms in Russia* (Pittsburgh, 1990); and John D. Klier and Shlomo Lambroza, eds., *Pogroms: Anti-Jewish Violence in Modern Russian History* (Cambridge, 1992).

4. For the role of economics in the emigration of Jews from eastern Europe, see Bernard Weinryb, "Eastern European Immigration to the United States," *Jewish Quarterly Review* 45 (April 1955), and Lloyd P. Gartner, "Jewish Migrants en Route from Europe to North America: Tradition and Realities," in *The Jews of North America*, ed. Moses Rischin (Detroit, 1987), pp. 26–27. Bernard K. Johnpoll, "Why They Left: Russian-Jewish Mass Migration and Repressive Laws, 1881–1917," *American Jewish Archives* 67 (Spring–Summer 1995), 17–54, enumerates the numerous restrictions enacted against Jews during the reign of Alexander III.

5. Quoted in Dubnow, *History of the Jews,* vol. 2, pp. 322–23.

6. Ronald Sanders, *Shores of Refuge: A Hundred Years of Jewish Emigration* (New York, 1988), pp. 41–64, describes the chaos in Brody and the process of emigration from there.

7. Elias Tcherikower, "Jewish Immigrants to the United States, 1891–1900," *Yivo Annual of Jewish Social Studies* 6 (1951), 158. See also Zosa Szajkowski, "The European Attitude to East European Jewish Immigration (1881–1893)," *Publications of the American Jewish Historical Society* 41 (December 1951). For the negative attitude of German Jews toward the eastern Europeans, see Jack Wertheimer, *Unwelcome Strangers: East European Jews in Imperial Germany* (New York, 1987), and Steven E. Aschheim, *Brothers and Strangers: The East European Jew in German and German Jewish Consciousness, 1800–1923* (Madison, Wis., 1982).

8. In 1880, more than 5.7 million of Europe's 6.7 million Jews lived in eastern Europe. Between 1881 and 1924, approximately 2.5 million emigrated, more than 2 million to the United States. For Jewish population figures, see Mendes-Flohr and Reinharz, *The Jew in the Modern World*, p. 704; and Evyatar Friesel, *Atlas of Modern Jewish History* (New York, 1990), pp. 15, 32–35.

9. For detailed portrayals of nineteenth-century American Jewry, see John S. Billings, *Vital Statistics of the Jews in the United States*, United States Census Bulletin No. 19 (Washington, D.C., 1890); Naomi W. Cohen, *Encounter with Emancipation: The German Jew in the United States, 1830–1914* (Philadelphia, 1984); and Hasia Diner, *A Time for Gathering: The Second Migration, 1820–1880*, vol. 2 of *The Jewish People in America* (Baltimore, 1992).

10. Gilbert Osofsky, "The Hebrew Emigrant Aid Society of the United States (1881–1883)," *Publications of the American Jewish Historical Society* 49 (March 1960), 174.

11. Esther Panitz, "The Polarity of American Jewish Attitudes towards Immigration (1870–1891)," *American Jewish Historical Quarterly* 53 (December 1963), 109–10.

12. Quoted in Yehezkel Wyszkowski, "The *American Hebrew*: An Exercise in Ambivalence," *American Jewish History* 70 (March 1987), 345. For other reactions to the newcomers, see Gerald Sorin, "Mutual Contempt, Mutual Benefit: The Strained Encounter between German and East European Jews in America, 1880–1920," *American Jewish History* 81 (Autumn 1993), 56, and Selma Berrol, "Germans versus Russians: An Update," *American Jewish History* 73 (December 1983), 142–56.

13. Quoted in Howard M. Sachar, *A History of the Jews in America* (New York, 1992), p. 123.

14. *Jewish Messenger*, 20 May 1881. See Panitz, "The Polarity of American Jewish Attitudes towards Immigration," pp. 99–119; Zosa Szajkowski, "Attitude of America Jews to East European Jewish Immigration, 1881–1893," *Publications of the American Jewish Historical Society* (March 1951), 221–44; and Sorin, "Mutual Contempt, Mutual Benefit," p. 36, for examples of these strong negative reactions.

15. Zosa Szajkowski, "The *Yehudi* and the Immigrant: A Reappraisal," *American Jewish Historical Quarterly* 63 (September 1973), 14–15.

16. Simon Kuznets, "Immigration of Russian Jews to the United States: Background and Structure," *Perspectives in American History* 9 (1975), 39–43; Gerald Sorin, *A Time for Building: The Third Migration*, vol. 3 of *The Jewish People in America* (Baltimore, 1992), pp. 12–37.

17. Osofsky, "Hebrew Emigrant Aid Society," pp. 175–76.

18. Ibid., p. 185.

19. Quoted in Marc Lee Raphael, "Intra-Jewish Conflict in the United States, 1869–1915" (diss., UCLA, 1972), p. 37.

20. Myron Berman, "The Attitude of American Jewry towards East European Jewish Immigration, 1881–1914" (diss., Columbia University, 1963), pp. 317–55; Uri D. Herscher, *Jewish Agricultural Utopias in America, 1880–1910* (Detroit, 1981), pp. 111–13.

21. On the movement to the cities, see Raymond A. Mohl, *The New City: Urban*

America in the Industrial Age, 1860–1920 (Arlington Heights, Illinois, 1985), pp. 7–26, 53–66. An excellent study of immigrant arrival and dispersal throughout the United States is David Ward, *Cities and Immigrants: A Geography of Change in Nineteenth Century America* (New York, 1971). Despite the trend toward the city, agricultural colonization continued to be discussed in the Progressive era as a method of ameliorating urban and immigrant problems. Progressives added an idealistic flavor by associating colonization with the agrarian myth. This doctrine taught that social virtue and a nation's moral fiber derived from the work of the yeoman farmer.

22. Baron, *The Russian Jew under Tsars and Soviets,* pp. 52–62; Sanders, *Shores of Refuge,* pp. 141–48, 193–226, 267–73.

23. Abraham J. Karp, *Haven and Home: A History of the Jews in America* (New York, 1985), p. 374; Zosa Szajkowski, "Jewish Emigration Policy in the Period of the Rumanian 'Exodus,' 1899–1903," *Jewish Social Studies* 13 (January 1951), 47–70; Raphael Mahler, "The Economic Background of Jewish Emigration from Galicia to the United States," *YIVO Annual of Jewish Social Science* 7 (1952), 255–67; Sorin, *A Time for Building,* p. 58.

24. Szajkowski, "The *Yahudi* and the Immigrant," p. 15; *Jewish American* (Detroit), 22 November 1901.

25. Quoted in Raphael, "Intra-Jewish Conflict," p. 84.

26. *American Hebrew,* 13 February 1891.

27. Esther Panitz, "In Defense of the Jewish Immigrant (1891–1924)," *American Jewish Historical Quarterly* 55 (September 1965), 57–95.

28. Quoted in Cohen, *Encounter with Emancipation,* p. 306.

29. Robert H. Bremner, *From the Depths: The Discovery of Poverty in the United States* (New York, 1969), pp. 46–66; Roy Lubove, *The Professional Altruist: The Emergence of Social Work As a Career, 1880–1930* (New York, 1969), pp. 1–21.

30. Robert A. Rockaway, "Ethnic Conflict in an Urban Environment: The German and Russian Jew in Detroit, 1881–1914," *American Jewish Historical Quarterly* 60 (December 1970), 137; Graenum Berger, "American Jewish Communal Service, 1776–1976: From Traditional Self-Help to Increasing Dependence on Governmental Support," *Jewish Social Studies* (Spring–Fall 1976), 233.

31. Sorin, "Mutual Contempt, Mutual Benefit," p. 56; Herman D. Stein, "Jewish Social Work in the United States (1654–1954)," *American Jewish Year Book* 57 (1956), 18–23.

32. Sorin, "Mutual Contempt, Mutual Benefit," p. 58.

33. Cohen, *Encounter with Emancipation,* p. 305; Ira Rosenwaike, *Population History of New York City* (Syracuse, 1972), p. 111. Detroit contained 285,000 people in 1900. By 1910, the two-square-mile area of the Lower East Side held 542,000 Jews. This made it one of the most densely settled regions on Earth (Moses Rischin, *The Promised City: New York's Jews, 1870–1914* [New York, 1970], pp. 93–94). At the outbreak of World War I, New York contained about 1,400,000 Jews—40 percent of the Jewish population of the United States.

34. Peter Romanofsky, "'. . . To rid Ourselves of the Burden . . .': New York Jewish Charities and the Origins of the Industrial Removal Office, 1890–1901," *American Jewish Historical Quarterly* 64 (Sept. 1974), 331–343.

35. In the United States, the Jewish Colonization Association was renamed the Jewish Agricultural and Industrial Aid Society. Its major goal was to create a class of American Jewish farmers. The society helped finance more than 160 agricultural settlements (Sorin, "Mutual Contempt, Mutual Benefit," pp. 41–42). On Baron de Hirsch and his philanthropy, see Samuel Joseph, *History of the Baron de Hirsch Fund* (Philadelphia, 1935).

36. In 1900, the de Hirsch Fund and the Jewish Colonization Association estab-

lished the Jewish Agricultural and Industrial Aid Society to promote "agriculture among Jews in America and the removal of those working in crowded metropolitan sections to agricultural and industrial districts" (Joseph, *Baron de Hirsch Fund,* p. 129).

37. The National Conference of Jewish Charities (NCJC) was an organization of lay workers and professionals. It was established in 1899 and modeled after the non-Jewish National Conference of Charities and Correction. Twenty-four states were represented at the first NCJC convention held in Chicago in 1900. By 1918 the NCJC had 177 constituent members in thirty-five states and Canada.

38. On the B'nai B'rith, see Edward E. Grusd, *B'nai B'rith: The Story of a Covenant* (New York, 1966), and Deborah Dash Moore, *B'nai B'rith and the Challange of Ethnic Leadership* (Albany, 1982).

39. Sachar, *Jews in America,* p. 138; Cohen, *Encounter with Emancipation,* p. 320.

40. Joseph, *Baron de Hirsch Fund,* p. 185. At first, the IRO lay under the aegis of the Jewish Agricultural and Industrial Aid Society. The IRO became an independent organization in 1903 (ibid., p. 189).

41. For biographies of Bressler, Waldman, and Seman, see the *Encyclopaedia Judaica* (Jerusalem, 1972).

42. David Bressler, "The Removal Work, Including Galveston" (paper presented before the National Conference of Jewish Charities, 17 May 1910), Industrial Removal Office papers, American Jewish Historical Society, Waltham, Massachusetts (hereafter cited as IRO papers); Joseph, *Baron de Hirsch Fund,* pp. 184–205. Bressler's approach to running the IRO coincided with the attitude of professional social workers of his generation. On this see Lubove, *The Professional Altruist,* pp. 1–21, 157–82.

43. *American Hebrew,* 24 July 1903.

44. "Removal Work and the Industrial Removal Office," p. 4, typescript, IRO papers; Joseph, *Baron de Hirsch Fund,* p. 188; Cohen, *Encounter with Emancipation,* pp. 321–22.

45. David Bressler, "Removal work—Further Efforts," in *Proceedings of the National Conference of Jewish Charities,* (1904), pp. 141–48; Cohen, *Encounter with Emancipation,* p. 321.

46. Sam Rostoff to IRO, 18 March 1907, Indiana file, Lafayette; Abraham Solomon to David Bressler, 1 October 1912, IRO papers.

47. Morris Waldman to David Bressler, 12 October 1906, Georgia file, IRO papers.

48. David Bressler to Abraham Solomon, 24 February 1913, IRO papers.

49. David Bressler to Max Senior, 29 March 1912, IRO papers; Joseph, *Baron de Hirsch Fund,* p. 187.

50. David Bressler to Max Senior, 29 March 1912, IRO papers.

51. Morris D. Waldman to David Bressler, 15 October 1906, IRO papers; Bernard Marinbach, *Galveston: Ellis Island of the West* (Albany, 1983), p. 50.

52. David Bressler to IRO, 27 July 1905, IRO papers.

53. Elias Margolis to David Bressler, 25 June 1908, IRO papers.

54. David Bressler to Abraham Solomon, 24 February 1913; David Bressler to IRO, 1 February 1914, IRO papers.

55. David Bressler to Morris Waldman, 22 July 1905; David Bressler to IRO, 27 July 1905; Morris Waldman to David Bressler, 7 August 1905, IRO papers.

56. Bressler, "The Removal Work, Including Galveston," p. 6.

57. Bressler, "The Removal Work, Including Galveston," pp. 6–9.

58. E. D. Freund to IRO, 11 June 1912, Alabama file, Birmingham; Rabbi M. Friedlander to IRO, 3 January 1913, California file, Fresno, IRO papers.

59. Bressler, "The Removal Work, Including Galveston," p. 11.

60. IRO to Miriam Hart, 31 March 1911, Michigan file, Detroit, IRO papers.

Miriam Hart was a young social worker employed by Detroit's United Jewish Charities. She served as the IRO agent in Detroit.

61. Robert A. Rockaway, "The Industrial Removal Office in Detroit," *Detroit in Perspective* 6 (Spring 1982), 41–42.

62. Miriam H. Hart to David Bressler, 14 June 1912; Alice K. Goldsmith to David Bressler, 6 October 1910, Michigan file, Detroit, IRO papers. Alice Goldsmith was a young volunteer who assisted in the Detroit office when the regular agent went on vacation.

63. J. Schwartz to IRO, 17 March 1912, Michigan file, Detroit; Elias Margolis to David Bressler, 27 April 1908; Harry B. Clark to IRO, 13 March 1910, Michigan file, Detroit, IRO papers.

64. Abraham Cahan to David Bressler, 14 December 1909, IRO papers. In addition to editing the *Forward,* the Russian-born Cahan (1860–1951) authored *Yekl: A Tale of the New York Ghetto* (1896), *The Rise of David Levinsky* (1917), and his memoirs (in five volumes) titled *Bleter fun mein Leben* (leaves from my life), published between 1926 and 1931.

65. Mrs. Samuel Friedman to David Bressler, 15 September 1912; David Bressler to Mrs. Samuel Friedman, 19 September 1912, Minnesota file, Minneapolis, IRO papers.

66. Joseph, *Baron de Hirsch Fund,* p. 197.

67. Elias Margolis to David Bressler, 21 December 1908, IRO papers.

68. Chaim Zadek Lubin to IRO, 16 March 1906, Kansas file, Wichita, IRO papers; Sorin, "Mutual Contempt, Mutual Benefit," p. 42; Joe Wolf to IRO, 29 July 1909, Alabama file, Birmingham, IRO papers.

69. W. Levitt to IRO, 29 April 1906, Michigan file, Detroit, IRO papers.

70. IRO memo to David Bressler, 2 August 1905; Assistant Manager to David Bressler, 7 August 1905, IRO papers.

71. Alter Battler to David Bressler, 28 January 1910, Washington file, Seattle, IRO papers.

72. Bressler, "The Removal Work, Including Galveston," pp. 12, 9.

73. Quoted in Sorin, "Mutual Contempt, Mutual Benefit," p. 43.

74. For a biography of Schiff, see Cyrus Adler, *Jacob H. Schiff: His Life and Letters,* 2 vols. (New York, 1928).

75. Marinbach, *Galveston,* pp. 1–20.

76. The Jewish Territorial Organization was a non-Zionist body that sought to locate a territory suitable for Jewish colonization on an autonomous basis. The Hilfsverein der Deutschen Juden was the central charitable society of German Jewry to assist Jews in eastern Europe and Asian countries.

77. Marinbach, *Galveston,* pp. 1–20; Gary Dean Best, "Jacob H. Schiff's Galveston Movement: An Experiment in Immigrant Deflection, 1907–1914," *American Jewish Archives* 30 (1978), 47. Waldman left Galveston in 1908 to become managing director of the United Hebrew Charities of New York.

78. Marinbach, *Galveston,* p. 34.

79. Ibid., p. 184.

80. Ibid., p. 113.

81. Ibid., pp. 113–14. In New York, Kaluzny worked as a night watchman, but he was unemployed more often than not. He spent many nights sleeping in Central Park, covering his face with a newspaper. After two years of this life, Kaluzny received a letter from a cousin in Detroit telling him about the growing opportunities in that city. Kaluzny arrived in Detroit in 1913. He brought over his wife and children and remained in Detroit till his death in 1971.

82. Joseph, *Baron de Hirsch Fund,* pp. 289–90.

83. John Livingston, "The Industrial Rmoval Office, the Galveston Project, and the

Denver Jewish Community," *American Jewish History* 68 (June 1979), 443–44; Romanofsky, " 'To rid Ourselves,' " p. 342; Joseph, *Baron de Hirsch Fund,* pp. 204–05.

84. Marinbach, *Galveston,* pp. 187–90.

85. Elias Margolis to David Bressler, 23 June 1908, IRO papers.

86. Rockaway, "The Industrial Removal Office in Detroit," p. 48, note 17; Marc Lee Raphael, *Jews and Judaism in a Midwestern Community: Columbus, Ohio, 1840–1975* (Columbus, 1979), p. 154, note 20; Judith Endelman, *The Jewish Community of Indianapolis, 1849 to the Present* (Bloomington, 1984), pp. 105–09.

87. Elias Margolis to David Bressler, 7 August 1908, IRO papers.

88. Isaac Max Rubinow, "The Jewish Question in New York City (1902–1903)," trans. Leo Shpall, *Publications of the American Jewish Historical Society* 49 (December 1959), 96, 129.

89. Quoted in Cohen, *Encounter with Emancipation,* p. 322.

90. The distribution figures are broken down by year, the total number of persons sent to each state, and the total number of cities in each state. See Joseph, *The Baron de Hirsch Fund,* pp. 289–90.

91. An excellent compilation of letters to the editor from the *Jewish Daily Forward* can be found in Isaac Metzger, *A Bintel Brief: Sixty Years of Letters from the Lower East Side to the Jewish Daily Forward* (New York, 1971).

PART ONE: THE IRO AS AN INSTITUTION

1. Letters from Traveling Agents

1. David Bressler, correspondence file, IRO papers.

2. Jacob Furth (1844–1918), a local businessman and communal leader, acted as the IRO's main representative in Cleveland. Furth was an important figure in the national B'nai B'rith and served as a representative on the national IRO committee. This committee oversaw the IRO's operations and provided its funding. Ulrich Richter served as Furth's assistant and managed the day-to-day operation of the Cleveland IRO office.

3. The IRO stationed a representative at Ellis Island, who received lists of the incoming immigrants from the immigration authorities. The agent then forwarded this information to the New York office.

4. In 1905, the Buffalo Jewish community numbered about 10,000 and supported one Reform and four Orthodox synagogues. *The Jewish Encyclopedia* (New York, 1906), vol. 3, pp. 423–24; Selig Adler, *From Ararat to Suburbia: The History of the Jewish Community of Buffalo* (Philadelphia, 1960), chap. 7.

5. Julius Saperston (1865–1909) manufactured men's clothing and owned a large department store. Active in numerous local charities, he became the first president of Buffalo's Jewish Federation (Adler, *From Ararat to Suburbia,* p. 229).

6. Sadie Strauss Altman (1860–1930) was a prominent Buffalo civic activist and women's rights advocate. She presided over the City Federation of Women's Clubs, helped to bring about the installation of nurses and public health centers in Buffalo's public schools, and influenced the city's government to appoint its first policewoman and first female probation officer (ibid., p. 203).

7. Theodore Hoffeler was a wealthy Buffalo merchant and civic leader.

8. In 1905, Milwaukee's Jewish community numbered approximately 9,000 out of a city population of 290,000. Louis J. Swichkow and Lloyd P. Gartner, *The History of the Jews of Milwaukee* (Philadelphia, 1963), p. 156.

9. Bressler referred to IRO removals as "pioneers" because they were the first such immigrants sent into the community.

10. Jacob Billikopf (1883–1950) was born in Lithuania and came to the United States at age fourteen. In a career that spanned more than forty years, he became one of America's most outstanding Jewish social workers. He headed Jewish philanthropies in Cincinnati, Milwaukee, and Kansas City; served as president of Missouri's state conference of charities (1911–12); and became a leader in employer-labor relations and overseas relief work. On Billikopf's career, see Jacob R. Marcus, *United States Jewry, 1776-1985* (Detroit, 1993), vol. 4, pp. 89, 304, 476, 498, 621–22, 627–29.

11. Hungarian-born Adolphus W. Rich (1843–1917) was a merchant, shoe manufacturer, and Milwaukee civic and communal leader. He founded a Jewish agricultural settlement in Arpin, Wisconsin, and headed the Milwaukee branch of the Industrial Removal Office. In this capacity, he supervised the work of the local IRO agent. Jacob R. Marcus, *The Concise Dictionary of American Jewish Biography* (Brooklyn, 1994), vol. 2, p. 514.

12. Morris Waldman to David Bressler, 27 July 1907, Waldman file, IRO papers.

13. The Jewish Emigration Society was created to recruit Russian Jews for Galveston. The society was based in Kiev and operated many committees throughout Russia. Bernard Marinbach, *Galveston: Ellis Island of the West* (Albany, 1983), pp. 13–14.

14. Cedar Rapids survey, Iowa file, IRO papers.

15. Margolis file, IRO papers.

16. *American Jewish Year Book* 49 (1948), 614–615.

17. This bomb-throwing incident involved a Russian Jewish immigrant.

18. *Temple* was the generic term for the Reform Jewish synagogue.

19. Margolis here refers to the method of contacting local employers directly without using an agent as an intermediary. This mode of working was used in smaller towns.

20. *Shul* is the Yiddish term for synagogue. *Chevra* is the Hebrew and Yiddish term for an immigrant society or club.

21. The Knights of Zion were an early Zionist organization established in Chicago in 1898.

22. This refers to the Panic of 1907, which resulted from a drop in the stock market compounded by a series of business failures.

23. Solomon file, IRO papers.

24. Judith Endelman, *The Jewish Community of Indianapolis, 1849 to the Present* (Bloomington, Ind., 1984), p. 60.

25. The agent referred to is Samuel B. Kaufman, an attorney and rabbi of the United Hebrew Congregation, Indianapolis's Conservative synagogue. Kaufman resigned both positions to assume the superintendency of the Indianapolis Jewish Federation. He held this post from 1908 to 1921. At the same time, he served as the local IRO agent. As in other communities, the Indianapolis Jewish Federation had been organized to consolidate fund raising efforts within the city. On Kaufman, see ibid., pp. 99, 105–6.

26. Edward A. Kahn (1875–1943) was a wealthy local merchant who served on the boards of a variety of civic and charitable enterprises. Sol Kiser (1858–1935) was a clothier who became a banker. He was a founder of the Indianapolis Jewish Federation and active in the city's civic and communal life. Gustav Efroymson (1870–1946) was a hosiery manufacturer who served as president of the Jewish Federation from its inception in 1905 to 1928. For information about these men, ibid., pp. 48, 38–40, 36–37.

27. The Indianapolis Jewish Federation and the local IRO cooperated closely from 1905 to the end of World War I. The same Jewish leaders often served in both groups (ibid., pp. 104–5).

28. Kaufman continually disparaged the removals and the local immigrant Jewish community in general. In a letter to Bressler in February 1910, Kaufman wrote that "the immigrant Jew, as a rule, belongs to the stiff-necked people more than any other

Jew. He is hard to please and often, the more you try to do for him, the less he will appreciate" (ibid., p. 107).

29. Max Senior (1962–1939) was a Cincinnati businessman, philanthropist, and civic and communal worker. He was a pioneer in the charity federation movement and the first president of the National Conference of Jewish Charities (Marcus, *American Jewish Biography* vol. 2, p. 514). Cyrus L. Sulzberger (1859–1932) was a textile executive, merchant, philanthropist, and national communal and civic leader (ibid., p. 520).

30. Here Solomon refers to critics who warned him of the obstacles he would encounter in trying to get Danville's Jewish leaders to cooperate with one another.

31. In 1913, the Birmingham Jewish community numbered about 1,800 Jews in a total population of 125,000. Most of the city's Jews were Russian immigrants. The community supported three Orthodox and one Reform synagogue and a variety of benevolent and fraternal organizations (Birmingham survey 1912–13, Alabama file, IRO papers).

32. The Young Men's Hebrew Association (YMHA) was patterned after the YMCA. But whereas the Christian YMCAs were church-oriented, the YMHAs were secular and interested in philanthropy and Jewish culture. The basic goal of the YMHA was intra-Jewish fraternization. See Marcus, *United States Jewry,* vol. 3, pp. 412–15.

33. Dr. Morris Newfield was rabbi of Birmingham's Reform congregation (ibid., pp. 387, 711).

34. Esther Finkelstein, a social worker and head of the local Jewish settlement house, was the IRO agent in Nashville, Tennessee. In an earlier letter to Bressler, Solomon described her as "Russian-Jewish, typical ghetto-ish; square-jawed, assertive, domineering" (Abraham Solomon to David Bressler, 15 February 1913, Solomon file, IRO papers).

2. Letters from Communities

1. Isaac Springer was a prominent Atlanta businessman who owned a large men's and women's clothing store and maintained purchasing offices in New York and Paris (Georgia file, IRO papers).

2. Steven Hertzberg, *Strangers within the Gate City: The Jews of Atlanta, 1845–1915* (Philadelphia, 1978), pp. 152, 216–17; Mark K. Bauman, "The Emergence of Jewish Social Service Agencies in Atlanta," *Georgia Historical Quarterly* 69 (Winter 1985), 488–508.

3. Georgia file, Atlanta, IRO papers.

4. Springer refers to the Leo Frank case. Frank, president of the local B'nai B'rith chapter, was accused, tried and convicted of murdering Mary Phagan, a thirteen-year-old girl who worked in the Atlanta pencil factory Frank co-owned and managed. Although the victim of a miscarriage of justice, Frank was sentenced to death. Georgia's governor, John M. Slaton commuted Frank's sentence to life imprisonment. Taking the law into their own hands, a band of men kidnapped Frank from the prison farm and lynched him. The case stands as America's most horrifying example of antisemitism. See Leonard Dinnerstein, *The Leo Frank Case* (New York, 1968).

5. Indiana file, Lafayette, IRO papers.

6. Lafayette, Indiana survey, Indiana file, IRO papers.

7. Gershuny was a local rabbi.

8. Los Angeles Workman's Circle file, IRO papers.

9. M. Hurwitz, *The Workman's Circle* (New York, 1936).

10. *The Jewish Encyclopedia* (1912), vol. 8, p. 185; Max Vorspan and Lloyd P. Gartner, *History of the Jews of Los Angeles* (Philadelphia, 1970), pp. 156–64.

11. The Los Angeles IRO committee consisted of six of the city's most prominent Jews: Rabbi Sigmund Hecht, spiritual leader of the city's Reform Temple; Albert M. Norton and George N. Block, businessmen active in local politics; Victor Harris, editor of the *B'nai B'rith Messenger;* and E. F. Gerecht and Henry L. Klein, wealthy merchants. All these men were volunteers (Vorspan and Gartner, *Jews of Los Angeles,* pp. 112–13).

12. *Forwarts* [forward], *Frei Arbeiter Shtimme* [free worker's voice], *Arbeiter* [worker], and the *Chicago Jewish Workingmen's World* were Socialist- or labor-oriented Yiddish newspapers.

3. Letters from Local Agents

1. Local agents, Illinois file, Bloomington, IRO papers.

2. Local agents, Ohio file, Cleveland, IRO papers.

3. Jacob R. Marcus, *American Jewish Biography* (Brooklyn, 1994), vol. 1, pp. 186–87.

4. The Removal Committee consisted of representatives of the Baron de Hirsch Fund, the Jewish Agricultural and Industrial Aid Society, and the B'nai B'rith.

5. Lloyd P. Gartner, *History of the Jews of Cleveland* (Cleveland, 1978), pp. 65–141.

6. Local agents, Illinois file, Champaign, IRO papers.

7. Marcus, *American Jewish Biography,* vol. 1, p. 147.

8. Selma Berrol, "Education and Economic Mobility: The Jewish Experience in New York City, 1898–1920," *American Jewish Historical Quarterly* (March 1976): 257–71.

9. The Jewish youngsters who managed to finish high school in the years before 1914 commonly were children of the more established German Jewish families. Only when the eastern European Jews improved their economic status did their children begin going to secondary schools and college (Howard M. Sachar, *A History of the Jews in America* (New York, 1992), p. 160).

10. This letter is addressed to the recording secretary of the Chicago B'nai B'rith regarding a B'nai B'rith circular asking local chapters to cooperate with the IRO.

11. Grand Prairie Lodge No. 281 was the B'nai B'rith chapter in Champaign.

12. *Yehuda* is the Yiddish and Hebrew equivalent of "Judah." The word was sometimes used as a nickname for a Jew.

13. During the first quarter of the twentieth century, 25,000 to 30,000 Sephardim (Jews of Spanish or Portuguese descent) arrived in the United States, settling on the Lower East Side of New York City. The largest group was composed of Judeo-Spanish–speaking Jews from Turkey and the Balkan countries. Most of the Sephardic arrivals were poor and had received only limited formal education in their countries of origin. See *Jewish-American History and Culture: An Encyclopedia,* ed. Jack Fischel and Sanford Pinsker (New York, 1992), p. 570, and Jacob R. Marcus, *United States Jewry* (Detroit, 1993), vol. 4, pp. 183–87.

14. Yom Kippur, the Day of Atonement, is the holiest day on the Jewish calendar.

PART TWO: THE IMMIGRANTS

4. Interactions with the IRO

1. For an explanation of this tradition, see Philip Birnbaum, *A Book of Jewish Concepts* (New York, 1964), pp. 520–22, and Simon Glustrom, *The Language of Judaism* (New York, 1966), pp. 12–13.

2. Chaim Zadik Lubin to IRO, 16 March 1906, Kansas file, Wichita, IRO papers.

3. Wichita survey, 1906, Kansas file, IRO papers.

4. Wherever they settled, the eastern European Jewish immigrants established their own network of social and charitable organizations.

5. Charles Zwirn to Mr. Seman, 13 May 1913, Wisconsin file, La Crosse, IRO papers.

6. La Crosse survey, 1912, Wisconsin file, IRO papers.

7. Louis Friedman to IRO, 5 April 1907, Michigan file, Detroit, IRO papers.

8. Robert A. Rockaway, "The Industrial Removal Office in Detroit," *Detroit in Perspective* 6 (Spring 1982), 40–49.

9. Robert A. Rockaway, *The Jews of Detroit: From the Beginning, 1762–1914* (Detroit, 1986), p. 52.

10. Birdie Pick was a young social worker and one of the early directors of the IRO operation in Detroit.

11. Moses Rischin, *The Promised City* (New York, 1970), p. 94.

12. Morris Goldstein to IRO, 13 October 1907, Ohio file, Columbus, IRO papers.

13. Marc Lee Raphael, *Jews and Judaism in a Midwestern Community: Columbus, Ohio, 1840–1975* (Columbus, 1979).

14. Orthodox Judaism strictly prohibits working on the Sabbath. Goldstein's willingness to work on the Jewish day of rest, shows that he was not an observant Jew. By 1906, an estimated 91 percent of eastern European Jewish immigrants had ceased to be strictly Orthodox in their religious practices. See Gerald Sorin, *A Time for Building: The Third Migration, 1880–1920,* vol. 3 of *The Jewish People in America* (Baltimore, 1994), p. 180.

15. Jacob Finkelstein to IRO, 5 August 1912, Ohio file, Cincinnati, IRO papers.

16. Cincinnati survey, Ohio file, IRO papers.

17. Jacob Schiffman to David Bressler, 11 November 1909, Michigan file, Detroit, IRO papers.

18. The feast of Purim commemorates the rescue of the Jews of Persia from the evil designs of Haman, an advisor to the Persian king Xerxes (about 450 B.C.). Many Jewish communities hold parades, carnival-like celebrations, and parties on Purim.

19. Joseph Lipetz to IRO, 4 May 1907, Oklahoma file, Oklahoma City, IRO papers.

20. Oaklahoma City survey, Oklahoma file, IRO papers.

21. Benny Finkelkraut to IRO, 30 April 1913, Minnesota file, Minneapolis, IRO papers.

22. Jenna Weissman Joselit, *Our Gang: Jewish Crime and the New York Jewish Community, 1900–1940* (Bloomington, Ind., 1983), pp. 45–53; Edward J. Bristow, *Prostitution and Prejudice: The Jewish Fight against White Slavery, 1870–1939* (New York, 1982), pp. 146–80.

23. A huge Jewish international traffic in prostitution existed at the turn of the twentieth century. Eastern European Jewry served as the major source of supply for Jewish white slavers. See Bristow, *Prostitution and Prejudice,* and Lloyd Gartner, "Anglo-Jewry and the Jewish International Traffic in Prostitution, 1885–1914," *Association for Jewish Studies Review* 8 (1982–83), 129–78.

24. Minneapolis survey, Minnesota file, IRO papers.

25. Anna Fox was a young social worker who acted as the IRO representative in Minneapolis.

26. H. Schreiber to IRO, 20 October 1916, Illinois file, Chicago, IRO papers.

27. Chicago survey, Illinois file, IRO papers; Simon Radowicz, *The Chicago Pinkas* (Chicago, 1952), p. 119.

28. Mrs. Samuel Friedman to IRO, 15 September 1912, Minnesota file, Minneapolis, IRO papers.

29. The Miss Foxe referred to was Anna Fox, the Minneapolis IRO agent.

30. Moses Goldstein to IRO, 2 April 1913, Tennessee file, Chattanooga, IRO papers.

31. Bakers and dressmakers earned $12 to $14 per week, machinists $14 to $18, carpenters $12 to $15, and ironworkers $9 to $15, while day laborers earned 75 cents to $1.50 per day (communal surveys for Chattanooga, Nashville, and Memphis, Tennessee folder, IRO collection).

32. Chattanooga survey, Tennessee folder, IRO papers.

33. Mary Rubin to IRO, 21 February 1905, Tennessee file, Chattanooga, IRO papers.

34. New Orleans survey, Louisiana file, IRO papers.

35. Israel Ginsburg to IRO, 19 July 1905, Illinois file, Chicago, IRO papers.

36. Charles Bernheimer, *The Russian Jew in the United States* (Philadelphia, 1905), p. 58; *American Jewish Year Book, 1916–1917* (Philadelphia, 1916), p. 278. For a portrait of Chicago's eastern European Jewish community, see Irving Cutler, *The Jews of Chicago: From Shtetl to Suburb* (Chicago, 1996), pp. 40–102.

37. Judith Endelman, *The Jewish Community of Indianapolis, 1849 to the Present* (Bloomington, Ind., 1984), p. 108.

38. Wolf was the IRO agent in Indianapolis. Ibid., pp. 36, 96.

39. The Yiddish newspaper *Tageblatt* published articles favorable to the IRO.

40. According to the Code of Jewish Law, "there is none so wicked as the one who commits suicide." Traditionally, the Jewish community treats suicides as pariahs. They are buried in a separate section of the cemetery, no one is to mourn for them, nor is the deceased entitled to a eulogy. Solomon Ganzfried, *Code of Jewish Law* (New York, 1961), p. 108. Nevertheless, rabbis have found all manner of reasons to treat suicides as accidents and thus natural deaths.

41. Memphis survey, 1906, Tennessee file, IRO papers; *The Jewish Encyclopedia*, vol. 8 (1906), pp. 463–64.

42. Joseph Davidowitz to IRO, undated, Tennessee file, Memphis, IRO papers.

43. Froim Kravitz to IRO, 27 April 1906, Tennessee file, Memphis, IRO papers.

44. Harry Liss to IRO, 28 December 1909, Washington file, Spokane, IRO papers.

45. Spokane survey, Washington file, IRO papers.

46. Kussner and Feuchtwanger were Spokane businessmen and members of the local IRO committee.

47. Jake Liboff to IRO, 20 July 1913, Indiana file, Gary, IRO papers.

48. Gary survey, Indiana file, IRO papers.

49. This charge seems dubious. Even if the agent had a strong aversion to the men, it is highly unlikely he would have allowed them to be given pork to eat. If it were true and had become known, it would have created a scandal in the Jewish community. No Jewish agent of the IRO would jeopardize his position and standing by committing this sacrilegious act.

5. Economic Adjustment

1. Robert A. Rockaway, *The Jews of Detroit: From the Beginning, 1762–1914* (Detroit, 1986), pp. 52, 70–89, 113.

2. Nathan Toplitky to IRO, 30 March 1908, Michigan file, Detroit, IRO papers.

3. Miriam Hart to IRO, 20 October 1913, Michigan file, Detroit, IRO papers.

4. Morris Weinkrantz to IRO, 16 May 1912, Iowa file, Des Moines, IRO papers.

5. Des Moines survey, Iowa file, IRO papers.

6. Wichita survey, Kansas file, IRO papers.

7. Alex Grubman to IRO, 24 November 1905, Oregon file, Portland, IRO papers.

8. Portland survey, Oregon file, IRO papers; William Toll, *The Making of an Ethnic Middle Class: Portland Jewry over Four Generations* (Albany, 1982).

9. Bavarian-born Sigmund Sichel (1857–1917) was a member of Portland's German Jewish elite. He owned a large cigar emporium, held posts in numerous Jewish organizations, and was an important local civic leader and politician. He took over when Portland's IRO representative, Benjamin Selling, was out of town (Jacob R. Marcus, *American Jewish Biography* (Brooklyn, 1994), vol. 2, p. 593; Toll, *Portland Jewry*, pp. 40, 90, 126).

10. Five years later, in 1910, Grubman wrote to Bressler about IRO removals who relocated to Portland from Spokane, Washington. These men solicited charity and complained about the failure of the IRO to find them work (Alex Grubman to David Bressler, 22 November 1910, IRO papers).

11. Stanley Bero was an IRO traveling agent.

12. Grubman refers to the San Francisco earthquake of 1905.

13. Barnet Marlin to IRO, 2 March 1906, Georgia file, Atlanta, IRO papers.

14. Leon Harris, *Merchant Princes: An Intimate History of Jewish Families Who Built Great Department Stores* (New York, 1979).

15. Steven Hertzberg, *Strangers within the City Gates: The Jews of Atlanta, 1845–1915* (Philadelphia, 1978), p. 149.

16. Ibid., pp. 91–92, 232.

17. It is interesting to note that Dr. Wildauer had been a policeman as well. This indicates that Jews had served as policemen in cities other than New York.

18. Atlanta's German Jewish community created a Central Immigration Committee to deal with the Russian Jewish immigrants coming into the city. This committee became the local IRO affiliate (Herztberg, *Strangers*, p. 134).

19. Max Fruchtman to IRO, 29 September 1909, Florida file, Pensacola, IRO papers.

20. Pensacola survey, Florida file, IRO papers.

6. Social/Cultural Adjustment

1. Raphael Gershoni to IRO, undated [probably early September 1906], Georgia file, Atlanta, IRO papers.

2. Steven Hertzberg, *Strangers within the City Gates: The Jews of Atlanta, 1845–1915* (Philadelphia, 1978), pp. 134–37.

3. David Selechanok to IRO, 1 June 1906, Ohio file, Columbus, IRO papers.

4. Sarah Goldenberg to IRO, 22 March 1906, Missouri file, St. Louis, IRO papers.

5. In 1905, of the 10,000 applicants for relief at New York's United Hebrew Charities, 2,000 were women whose husbands had abandoned them (Jacob R. Marcus, *United States Jewry* (Detroit, 1993), vol. 4, p. 553).

6. St. Louis survey, Missouri file, IRO papers.

7. Sol Bienstock was the IRO representative in St. Louis.

8. The National Desertion Bureau deliberately omitted the adjective "Jewish" from its name for the sake of communal honor.

9. Ari Lloyd Fridkis, "Desertion in the American Jewish Immigrant Family: The Work of the National Desertion Bureau in Cooperation with the Industrial Removal Office," *American Jewish History* 71 (December 1981), 285–99.

10. The letters are found in the National Desertion Bureau file, IRO papers.

11. Ohio file, Cleveland, IRO papers.

12. Charles Bernheimer, *The Russian Jew in the United States* (Philadelphia, 1905), p. 298. Maurice Fishberg (1872–1934) was a professor of medicine at New York University and author of the popular standard text *Pulmonary Tuberculosis*.

13. Gerald Sorin, *A Time for Building: The Third Migration,* vol. 3, *The Jewish People in America* (Baltimore, 1992), p. 81. A rise in suicide rates was not unique to Jewish immigrants. Studies have shown that suicide among immigrants in America far exceeded those of the native-born population. Like the eastern European Jews, European immigrants to the United States had higher incidences of suicide than those who remained in their native countries. See Howard I. Kushner, *American Suicide: A Psychocultural Exploration* (New Brunswick, 1991), p. 152, and Ruth S. Caven, *Suicide* (Chicago, 1928), pp. 3, 33–36.

14. These letters are located in the Cleveland folder of the Ohio file and dated 1905.

15. "Oy vey" is a Yiddish exclamation that can be translated in a myriad of ways. Depending on how it is used or inflected, it can express grief, surprise, pain, or worry.

16. S. Klein signed the letter in the *Jewish Daily News*.

7. Immigrant Perceptions of America

1. Abraham Cohen to IRO, 3 April 1910, Missouri file, St. Louis, IRO papers.
2. Leo Stamm to IRO, 6 February 1906, Mississippi file, Meridian, IRO papers.
3. Simon Sachs to IRO, 7 June 1907, Iowa file, Dubuque, IRO papers.
4. Dubuque survey, Iowa file, IRO papers.

Epilogue: Motivations and Misconceptions

1. For an excellent interpretation of German Jewish motives for creating the IRO, see Jack Glazier, "Secondary Migration and the Industrial Removal Office: The Politics of Jewish Immigrant Dispersion in the United States," in *Social Change and Applied Anthropology: Essays in Honor of David W. Brokensha,* ed. Miriam S. Chaiken and Anne K. Fleuret (Boulder, 1990), pp. 118–31.

Index

Adams, Henry, 11
Alder, R. L., 24, 47
Alexander II (Tsar), 3–4
Algase (rabbi), 202–3
Altabe, Albert
  family sent to, 102–4, 107, 111–12
  housing for, 109–10
  placement for, 95–96, 101
Altman, Sadie Strauss, 41, 216n6
Arnesti, Joseph, 102, 104
Atlanta (Ga.)
  economic conditions in, 176–78
  Jewish charities in, 10
  letters to and from, 71–77
  placements in, 34
  population of, 70, 177, 222n18
  promotional visit to, 19
  social/cultural conditions in, 183–86
August, Abraham, 129–32
Austria, immigrants from, 23
Austro-Hungary, refugees in, 4

Bagusin, Alexis, 57
Bagusin, Matush, 57
Balamut, Ben, 86, 89, 90
Basch, N. J., 62–63
Beinstock (St. Louis agent), 26
Belarus, immigrants from, 3
Berman, Harry, 105–6, 108, 111, 112
Bero, Stanley, 174, 222n11
Bienstock, Sol, 189–90, 222n7
Bijur, Nathan, 13
Billikopf, Jacob, 43, 217n10
Binstock, Ignatz, 23

Birmingham (Ala.)
  economy of, 23
  inspection tour of, 57–58, 64–69
  per capita expenditure in, 87
  population of, 218n31
  thank-you letters from, 26
Block, George N., 219n11
Bloomington (Ill.)
  inspection tour of, 53
  placement negotiations in, 21
  placement problems in, 81–85
Blumberg, Louis, 64
Boik, Baruch, 161
Braverman, 46
Bressler, David
  background and beliefs of, 15, 206
  Champaign concerns of, 93–113
  Cleveland concerns of, 86–92
  complaints to, 142–43, 146–49, 154–
    60, 179, 183
  goals of, 22, 27, 30, 33
  Indianapolis concerns of, 57–58, 61–62
  inspection tours and, 39–44, 68–69
  photograph of, 14
  placement process and, 19–22, 24–25,
    208–9
  promotional trips of, 19
  requests to, 27, 128–32
  salary issues and, 67–68
  thank-you letters for, 26
Brody (Galicia province), refugees in, 4
Buffalo (N.Y.), inspection tour of, 40–41
Burde, Meyer, 23
Buzik (agent), 156, 157

Cahan, Abraham, 24, 34
California, placements in, 30, 34. *See also*
    specific cities
Cedar Rapids (Iowa)
    dispute in, 54
    report on, 44–46, 55–56
Chajukin (immigrant), 45–46
Champaign (Ill.)
    inspection tour of, 53
    placement negotiations in, 21
    placements in, 93–113
Chattanooga (Tenn.), complaints from,
    143–46
Chicago (Ill.)
    complaints from, 149–53
    population of, 139, 149
    requests from, 139–41
Chlanin, Leta, 194–96
Chmelzitski, Shayeh, 123
Cincinnati (Ohio)
    per capita expenditure in, 87
    population of, 126
    thank-you letter from, 126–28
Clark, Harry B., 24
Cleveland (Ohio)
    inspection tour of, 40, 42–43
    IRO agent in, 21
    per capita expenditure in, 87
    placement problems in, 86–92
    placements in, 34
    population of, 85–86
    social/cultural conditions in, 194–97
Cohen (agent), 147
Cohen (immigrant), 97–99
Cohen, Abraham, 198–200
Cohen, Joe, 159
Cohen, Leo, 51
Colorado, placements in, 30. *See also* Den-
    ver (Colo.)
Columbus (Ohio)
    immigrants moved from, 30
    Jewish charities in, 10
    opportunities in, 1
    population of, 124
    social/cultural conditions in, 186–88
    thank-you letter from, 124–26
Cooper, A., 133–34
Corogin (Chicago resident), 152
Covnat, A., 57

Daneman (agent), 144–45
Danville (Ill.)
    committee established in, 62
    inspection tour of, 57–58, 63–64,
    218n30
Davenport (Iowa), placements in, 56

David, George, 81–85
Davidgorodok (Minsk), immigrant from,
    29
Davidowitz, David, 153–57
Davidson family, 201
Denver (Colo.)
    immigrants' impact on, 30
    thank-you letters from, 26
Des Moines (Iowa), economic conditions
    in, 167–72
Detroit (Mich.)
    economic conditions in, 165–67
    immigrants moved from, 30
    Jewish charities in, 10
    per capita expenditure in, 87
    placements in, 34
    population of, 8–9, 122–23, 165,
    213n33
    requests from, 128–32
    résumés sent to, 23–24
    thank-you letter from, 122–24
Dorf, Solomon (or Samuel), 71–73, 74–75
Dubuque (Iowa), attitudes toward America
    in, 201–3
Duncan, W. H., 48

Eastern Europe, Jewish immigrants from,
    5–11, 13, 18, 35
Edelstein, Abe, 172–73
Efroymson, Gustave, 58, 61, 217n26
Ellis Island
    alternative to, 28
    IRO representative at, 18, 216n3
Elwood (Ind.), inspection tour of, 49–50
Eplan, Leon, 72, 74
Epstein, Harry, 161–62
Europe, Jewish population in, 6, 212n8.
    See also Eastern Europe; *specific coun-
    tries*
Evansville (Ind.), placements in, 56, 57

Feffer (or Pfeffer) (agent), 169
Feuchtwanger (committeeman), 159–60
Fine (immigrant), 145
Finkelkraut, Benny, 136–38
Finkelstein, Esther, 66, 218n34
Finkelstein, Jacob, 126–28
Fishberg, Maurice, 195–96, 222n12
Fort Wayne (Ind.), placements in, 25–26,
    56
Fox, Anna L., 138, 143, 220n25
France
    Jews in, 4–5
    relief committee in, 6
Frank, Leo, 218n4
Franklin, Rabbi Leo, 8–9

Frank & Son (Terre Haute), 48
Freeman, Sadie, 138
Fresno (Calif.), wages in, 23
Freund, E. D., 23
Friedman, A., 179–82
Friedman, Louis, 122–24
Friedman, Mrs. Samuel, 25, 142–43
Fruchtman, Max, 178–82
Furth, Jacob
    background of, 85, 216n2
    letters to and from, 86–92
    role of, 40, 42–43, 195

Galicia province (Austro-Hungary)
    immigrants from, 43
    poverty in, 8
    refugees in, 4
Galveston (Tex.), as immigrant station,
    28–29, 44
Ganapol, Michael, 129, 132
Gary (Ind.), complaints from, 160–64
Geishen, Nachum, 194–97
Gerecht, E. F., 219n11
Germany
    immigrants from, 5–6, 35, 205–7
    Jews in, 4–5
Gershoni, Raphael, 183–86, 208
Gershorn, Sam, 72–73
Gershuny (rabbi), 77–78
Gingold, I., 65–67
Ginsburg, Israel, 149–53
Glickstein, Charley, 82–83
Glowatzky, Sam, 161–62
Gold, Morris, 105–6, 108
Goldberg, David, 103–4, 106
Goldberg, Ignatz, 161–62
Goldberg, Sam, 64
Goldenberg, Sam, 188–89
Goldenberg, Sarah, 188–91
Goldfish, A. M., 120–22
Goldman, Julius, 8
Goldman, Louis, 64
Goldsmith, Alice K., 215n62
Goldstein, Monroe, 191–94
Goldstein, Morris, 124–26, 186
Goldstein, Moses, 143–46
Goldstein family, 86–90
Goldstine, L. J., 49
Goodman, Augustus, 49
Gordon, Dora, 191–94
Gordon, Sam, 191–94
Gould, Leon, 160–61, 163–64
Great Britain, Jews in, 4–5
Greenbaum (agent), 51
Greenebaum, James, 64
Greenfield, Isaac, 202

Greenman, M., 65–67
Greifer, Isidore, 161–62
Gross, E. A., 160, 163–64
Grubman, Alex, 173–76
Grynberg (immigrant), 45–46

Haas, Leonard, 72
Hamburg, David, 107, 109, 111, 112
Hamburg, Max, 107
Hamburg, Rubin, 107
Harris, Victor, 219n11
Hart, Miriam H., 165, 167
Hecht, Rabbi Sigmund, 219n11
Henry, Henry S., 6
Herz, Milton, 49
Hirsch (agent), 194
Hirsch, Baron Maurice de
    fund established by, 11, 47, 157, 201
    portrait of, 12
    role of, 11
Hoffeler, Theodore, 41, 216n7
Houston (Tex.), relief committees in, 5
Huntington (Ind.), placements in, 56–57
Hutchinson (Kans.), placement in, 24

Illinois
    inspection tour in, 54–57
    placements in, 30, 34
    See also specific cities
Indiana, inspection tour in, 54–57. *See
    also specific cities*
Indianapolis
    complaints about immigrants in, 18
    immigrants moved from, 30, 149–52
    inspection tour of, 57–62
    Jewish charities in, 10
    per capita expenditure in, 87
Industrial Removal Office (IRO)
    approach of, 15, 18, 207
    archives of, 33–35, 207–9
    criticism of, 33, 206–7
    German vs. Russian Jews and, 205–7
    goals of, 1, 3, 13, 27, 30, 33, 205
    paid agents for, 21–22, 207–8
    process of placement by, 19–26
    success of, 26–27, 29–30
    traveling agents from, 19–21, 207–8
    women's travel and, 136–37
Iowa, inspection tour in, 54–57. *See also
    specific cities*
Isaacs, Myer S., 7

Jacob (farmer), 121
Jacobs, Bertman, 66–68
Jacobson, Jacob, 161
Judowitz, Betzel, 29

Kahn, Edward A., 58–59, 61, 62, 217n26
Kaluzny, Nathan, 29
Kansas City (Mo.)
    immigrant success in, 28
    IRO agent in, 21–22
Kaplan (immigrant), 174
Katz (immigrant), 59
Katz, Max, 161
Kaufman, Samuel B., 58–61, 217–18n28
Kessler, David, 49–50
Kiev, immigration committee in, 217n13
Kiser, Sol, 58, 60–62, 217n26
Klein, Henry L., 219n11
Klein, S., 197
Klimovitzky family, 77–78
Koblenz (immigrant), 145
Koff (immigrant), 161
Kopowitz (immigrant), 145
Koppel, L., 45–46
Kravitz, Froim, 153–54, 157–58
Kuhn, Isaac
    background of, 93
    letters to and from, 93–113
Kussner (committeeman), 159

La Crosse (Wis.), thank-you letters from,
    119–22
Lafayette (Ind.), letters to and from, 18,
    77–78
Lapper, Morris, 57
Latvia, immigrants from, 3
Leader, Benjamin, 66–67
Lee, Abraham, 135
Lee, Anna, 135
Lee, Joe, 132–36
Lefkovitz, Mrs., 89
Leipziger, Rabbi Emil, 49, 63
Leon (agent), 168–69
Levi, Leo, 11, 13, 19
Levin, Samuel, 62–63
Levitan, Mrs. D., 153
Levy, Samuel, 81–85
Liboff, Jake, 160–64
Lipetz, Abraham, 135
Lipetz, Anna, 133–35
Lipetz, Joseph, 132–36
Liss, Harry, 158–60
Lithuania, immigrants from, 3
Livingston, Abe, 82
Livingston, S., 82
Livingston, Sig, 53
London (England), relief committees in,
    4–5
Long & Morgan (painters), 50
Los Angeles (Calif.)
    letters to and from, 79–80

placements in, 30
population of, 78–79
Lottman (immigrant), 45–46
Louis, I. H., 64
Louisville (Ky.), placement negotiations
    in, 20
Lubin, Chaim Zadik, 117–19
Lubin, Chaye, 119
Lubin, Jake, 162
Lubin, Zvi Hersh, 119
Lvov (or Lvovsky) (immigrant), 174

Malowitz, Mr. and Mrs., 120
Mandel, Oscar, 53
Mann, B. L., 118
Margolis, Elias
    background of, 47
    on immigrants' move from placement, 30
    inspection tour reports from, 47–57
    letters of, 34
    on placement negotiations, 21
    on placement problems, 25–26
Marks, Max, 23–24
Marks, R., 168–73
Marlin, Barnet, 176–78, 183
Marshall, Louis, 10–11
McDonald, A. Y., 202–3
Mellinkopff, Joe, 81–83
Meltzer, I., 161
Memphis (Tenn.)
    complaints from, 153–58
    population of, 154
    wages in, 143
Meridian (Miss.), attitudes toward Amer-
    ica in, 200–201
Michigan, placements in, 30, 34. *See also*
    specific cities
Mies, Alphonse, 64
Milwaukee (Wis.)
    inspection tour of, 43–44
    IRO agent in, 21
    Jewish charities in, 10
    per capita expenditure in, 87
    placements in, 34
    population of, 216n8
    relief committees in, 5
Minneapolis (Minn.)
    complaints from, 142–43
    population of, 137
    requests from, 136–38
Missouri, placements in, 30, 34. *See also*
    specific cities
Moline (Ill.), placements in, 56
Morgan, Long & (painters), 50
Morganstern (doctor), 77–78
Morrison (employer), 202–3

Moshkowitz, Yechiel, 24
Muller, Isidore, 160

Nashville (Tenn.)
   agent in, 66, 218n34
   placement negotiations in, 20
   wages in, 143
Nathan, Emil, 156, 157
Nauterman, Louis, 159
Ness, Max, 77
Newfield, B., 66
Newfield, Morris, 66–68
Newman, Maurice, 192–94
Newman, Otto, 64
New Orleans (La.)
   complaints from, 146–49
   immigrant problems in, 28
   population of, 146
   relief committees in, 5
New York City
   attachments to, 18, 27, 29
   charities in, 10–11, 13
   conditions in, 1, 3, 13, 99–100
   immigrants' return to, 30
   population in, 11, 213n33
   relief committee in, 6–7
Nicholas II (Tsar), 8
Norton, Albert M., 219n11

Oberdorfer, A. Leo, 65
Ohio, placements in, 30, 34. *See also*
   specific cities
Oklahoma City (Okla.), requests from,
   132–36

Pale of Settlement, immigrants from, 3–4
Paris (France), relief committees in, 4–5
Pensacola (Fla.), economic conditions in,
   178–82
Peoria (Ill.), placements in, 56
Phagan, Mary, 218n4
Philadelphia (Pa.), relief committees in, 5
Pick, Birdie, 123, 220n10
Polansky, Lieb, 46
Polner, Israel, 161
Portland (Ore.), economic conditions in,
   173–76
Potashnik, Charles, 109
Prellman, Jacob, 78
Pross (agent), 158–59
Prox, Herman, 48

Quincy (Ill.), placements in, 57

Rabiner, Mendel, 77–78
Rich, Adolphus W., 44, 217n11

Richter, Ulrich
   Goldstein family and, 87–90
   reputation of, 195
   resignation of, 92
   responsibilities of, 86
   role of, 40, 42–43, 216n2
Rientsky (or Runetsky), Nathan, 103–4,
   106
Rimson, David, 108
Ringold Bros., 50
Rishes, Jonah, 161–62
Rochester (N.Y.)
   Jewish charities in, 10
   per capita expenditure in, 87
Rock Island (Ill.), placements in, 56
Romania
   conditions in, 8
   immigrants from, 11, 13, 43
Roseman, M., 65–67
Rosenberg, M., 180
Rosenthal, Abe, 157
Rosenthal (agent), 44
Rosenthal family, 146–47
Rosenthal (immigrant), 155
Rostoff, Sam, 18, 77–78
Rubin (immigrant), 147
Rubin, Mary, 146–49
Rubinow, Isaac Max, 33
Runetsky (or Rientsky), Nathan, 103–4,
   106
Rushevsky, I., 161
Russia
   conditions in, 4, 8, 99
   immigrants from, 3–9, 11, 27–29, 43,
   205–7
   immigration committee in, 217n13

Sachs, Jacob, 202
Sachs, Simon, 201–3
St. Louis (Mo.)
   attitudes toward America in, 198–200
   inspection tour of, 43–44
   per capita expenditure in, 87
   placements in, 26, 34, 57, 86, 132–33
   population of, 189
   social/cultural conditions in, 188–91
St. Paul (Minn.), immigrant success in, 28
Saltzman (expressman), 147
Sanders (judge), 75
Saperston, Julius, 40–41, 216n5
Saul, J. J., 183, 186
Schiff, Jacob Henry, 10–11, 27–28
Schiffman, Isaac, 129–32
Schiffman, Jacob, 128–32
Schiffman, Leo, 129–32
Schloss, Harry, 49

Schloss, Thorman & (tailors), 48–49
Schoen, Isaac, 72, 74
Schreiber, H., 139–41
Schwartz (agent), 40–41
Schwartz, J., 24
Schwartz, Rabbi Jacob, 179, 181–82
Seattle (Wash.), placements in, 26–27
Seelenfreund, A. B., 93–94
Selechanok, David, 1, 186–88
Seligman, Sam, 159
Selling, Benjamin, 222n9
Seman, Philip
    background of, 15
    complaints to, 160, 164
    family desertion concerns of, 192–94
    photograph of, 17
    requests to, 137–38, 200
    salary issues and, 68
    thank-you letter to, 119–22
Senior, Max, 60, 218n29
Shapiro, Anna, 65–67
Shapiro, Isidore, 65–66
Shapiro (immigrant), 78
Shlingbaum, Sam, 161
Sichel, Sigmund, 174–75, 222n9
Siegel, Nathan, 174
Siglin, Sam, 161
Silber, Rabbi Saul, 124–25
Silberman (immigrant), 157
Silver, Mr., 76
Silver, Mrs., 71, 73
Sincere, Sam, 64
Singer, H., 138
Singer, Morris, 108–9
Sinowitz (immigrant), 156
Sioux City (Iowa), placements in, 30
Slaton, John M., 218n4
Sobel, H., 141
Solomon, Abraham
    background of, 57
    inspection tour reports from, 57–69, 144
    letters to and from, 34, 145–46, 165, 167
South Bend (Ind.)
    inspection tour of, 51, 56
    per capita expenditure in, 87
Spokane (Wash.), complaints from, 158–60
Springer, Isaac, 70–77, 218n1
Stamm, Leo, 200–201
Stenbock, Hyman, 159
Straus, Oscar, 28
Strauss, Jules, 64
Streator (Ill.), placements in, 57
Sulzberger, Cyrus L.
    on agency activities, 9

background of, 218n29
    on immigrant conditions, 13
    promotional trips of, 19
    role of, 60

Tellon, Clara, 193
Terre Haute (Ind.), inspection tour of, 47–49
Texarkana (Tex.), placement negotiations in, 20
Thorman & Schloss (tailors), 48–49
Toledo (Ohio), placements in, 191–94
Toplitzky, Nathan, 165–66

Ukraine, immigrants from, 3–4
United States
    immigration to, 5–7, 8, 212n8
    IRO placements mapped, 31–32
    Jewish population in, 8–9
    See also specific cities and states
Urbana (Ill.), 93. See also Champaign (Ill.)

Varon (professor), 95–96
Vienna (Austria), relief committees in, 4–5
Voorsanger, Rabbi Jacob, 6

Waldman, Morris D.
    on agent, 21–22
    background of, 15
    on Cedar Rapids, 44–46
    Galveston plan and, 28, 44
    letters to Bressler, 41–42
    mention of, 174
    photograph of, 16
    promotional trips of, 19
    role of, 40
Weinberg, John, 81, 84–85
Weiner, Idshize, 123
Weinkrantz, Morris, 167–73
Wichita (Kans.)
    economic conditions in, 168, 172–73
    population of, 118, 168
    thank-you letters from, 26, 117–19
Wildauer, Benjamin, 72–74, 176–78, 184–86, 222n17
Wisconsin, placements in, 30. See also specific cities
Wise, Rabbi Isaac Mayer, 6, 9
Wold, Morris, 23
Wolf (agent), 150, 152, 221n38

Zaik, Aaron, 174
Zavinstein (immigrant), 157
Zeppin, Sam, 64
Zin, Max, 56–57
Zwirn, Charles, 119–22

DOCUMENTS IN AMERICAN SOCIAL HISTORY

A series edited by
Nick Salvatore

---

*Their Lives and Numbers: The Condition of Working People in Massachusetts,
1870–1900*
edited by Henry F. Bedford

*We Will Rise in Our Might: Workingwomen's Voices from Nineteenth-Century
New England*
by Mary H. Blewett

Dutch American Voices: Letters from the United States, 1850–1930
edited by Herbert J. Brinks

Peter Porcupine in America: Pamphlets on Republicanism and Revolution
by William Cobbett, edited by David A. Wilson

Out of the Shadow: A Russian Jewish Girlhood on the Lower East Side
by Rose Cohen (with an introduction by Thomas Dublin)

*Invisible Immigrants: The Adaptation of English and Scottish Immigrants
in Nineteenth-Century America*
by Charlotte Erickson

Keepers of the Revolution: New Yorkers at Work in the Early Republic
edited by Paul A. Gilje and Howard B. Rock

News from the Land of Freedom: German Immigrants Write Home
edited by Walter Kamphoefner, Wolfgang Helbich, and Ulrike Sommer,
translated by Susan Carter Vogel

*History of My Own Times; or, the Life and Adventures of William Otter, Sen.,
Comprising a Series of Events, and Musical Incidents Altogether Original*
by William Otter, edited with an Introduction and Commentary by
Richard B. Stott

Words of the Uprooted: Jewish Immigrants in Early 20th-Century America
by Robert A. Rockaway

The Six Nations of New York: The 1892 United States Extra Census Bulletin
with an Introduction by Robert W. Venables